Encountering New Tentacles of Terrorism

Encountering New Tentacles of Terrorism

Dr. Sudhir Hindwan

GLOBAL VISION PUBLISHING HOUSE
20, Ansari Road, Daryaganj, New Delhi-110002 (INDIA)

GLOBAL VISION PUBLISHING HOUSE
F-4, 1st Floor, 'Hari Sadan' 20, Ansari Road,
Daryaganj, New Delhi-110002 (INDIA)
Tel.: 23261581, 23276291, 43037885 Mob: 9810644769
Email: nsingh_2004@vsnl.net, info@globalvisionpub.com
Website: www.globalvisionpub.com

Encountering New Tentacles of Terrorism

First Edition 2012

ISBN: 978-81-8220-464-5

PRINTED IN INDIA

Published by Dr. N.K. Singh for Global Vision Publishing House, New Delhi-2 and *Printed at* G.S. Offset, Naveen Shahdara, Delhi-32.

Preface

Present world order is in the midst of a major transformation, largely on account of rapidly changing value system across the globe. Transformation is seemingly ubiquitous concept. Whilst some view it as a source of aggrandizement, others treat it as a disruptive process.

Despite years of concerted efforts to eliminate major threats, terrorism, caste violence and class violence have managed to taunt us time and again. It will certainly be naive if we blame others for the problems we face. To a great extent we are equally responsible for the mess. It is good to preserve one's identity for maintaining our diaspora. But at times such efforts of preservation of identity, whether cultural, linguistic, regional or religious damage the deep layers of our socio-political system. It is apparent from the kind of threat we are encountering so often. The world is also gradually witnessing the over expansion of a parochial version of faith and the desperate attempts of promoting it as the only pious one, but history bears testimony to the fact this has happened due to hegemony of the majoritarian identities and resentment of multiculturalism particularly on account of migration, the problem of refugees and search for survival in the competitive world order.

The latest serial blasts in Delhi, Mumbai, Jaipur, Lucknow, Faizabada, Ludhiana, Ajmer and Hyderabad and the incidents of terrorist violence in Norway, Islamabad, Karachi, Afghanistan, China, Russia and a number of other countries have not only exposed the pitfalls of the security and intelligence network but also robbed the confidence of nations in controlling the menace of terrorism.

Over the years terrorism has found its niche in the political scene across the globe. International terrorism, though comparatively less in volume than the domestic variety, has crossed all limitations despite increased government efforts to combat it. Much blood if not ink has flowed since terrorists struck a shocking sequence of plane attacks and bombing at the World Trade Centre and Pentagon in the U.S. This followed by tremendous upsurge in terrorist activities across the globe. Nowadays the ongoing quagmire in Arabian world has created the possibility of an outbreak of devastating terrorist onslaught. Early indications of this has come from Yemen. It's capital Sanaa was recently used by terrorists to plant PETN explosive devices at Dubai and Midlands airports. The young unemployed youth is easy target of Al Qaeda. Whether terrorism is unleashed at local, regional national or international level it cannot survive for long without international support and collaboration. There are many terrorist groups operating across the globe and creating an atmosphere of fear and anxiety. In past there were many revolutionary groups. The Irish Republican movement traces the cause of Ireland's woes in British occupation of the six counties. Although many Irish Republican groups have stepped up cooperation with the British in an effort to control terrorism, the violence continued for a long time (until Good Friday Agreement was signed) due to many factions among the negotiating parties. During the later half of twentieth century terrorist groups such as the Direct Action of France, the Japanese Red Army, the Baader Meinholf of West Germany created havoc due to their mission of destruction.

In India political violence has been the chief feature of terrorist activities as evident in the violence in Nagaland, Mizoram, Punjab and Jammu & Kashmir. Examination of terrorist incidents in various parts of India reveals a four-fold threat. First, the threat from Kashmiri militants who are demanding a separate state on the basis of historical, geographical and religious differences. Secondly, militant threat launched by the Khalistan supporters in Punjab during 1980's. Thirdly, terrorism has assumed a nightmarish proportion in the northeast. The proclaimed goal of over last three decades of secessionist campaign in the North-East has been to get more autonomy. Militant outfits like, the United Liberation Front of Assam (ULFA), the Bodo Ultras, the Nationalist Socialist Council of Nagaland (NSCN), etc. are posing serous threat to the entire security apparatus. Lastly, the recent upsurge in serial bomb blasts has marked the beginning of the pernicious era of terrorism. The conflict between Tamils and Sinhalas dominated the affairs of Sri Lanka. It caused enormous loss of life and posed serous threat to national security. The liberation Tigers of Tamil Eelam (LTTE) led by Velupillai Prabhakaran, emerged as the strongest Tamil militant organization demanding a Tamil homeland in the northern and the eastern districts of Jaffna. Although Sri Lankan Government has been successful in eliminating LTTE recently but past experience shows that the Government still needs to be cautious about the resurgence in terrorist violence. Sometime, terrorism can be revolutionary. Revolutionary terrorists may also take over and replace existing structures of governance. Hitler was a revolutionary before he came to power and on the strength of the organisation he mobilised and manipulated the masses to form a strong base. Publicity plays an important role in the process and without it they cannot expand the field of influence. Targets are significant for revolutionary terrorists and are mainly selected as a means to spread messages to change or shape public attitudes and behaviour. There is a growing nexus between terrorists and internationally organized crime networks. Mr. Alison Jamieson, a British analyst on organized crime and political violence commented that a distinction between terrorism and organized crime has become very blurred recently. Italian organised crime expert Professor Ernesto says "the goal is different. The terrorist's goal is an ideological one, while organized crime's goal is financial, but the instrument is same. They both need money and arms". In Sri Lanka, the Tamil Tigers engage in drug trafficking to finance their struggle, in north-eastern India guerrillas kidnap tea planters and hold them to ransom to help fund their fight for independence. In Chechnaya, the secessionists were heavily involved in drug distribution.

The rapid international transportation and use of sophisticated weapons like AK 47 assault rifles and plastic explosives (RDX) have helped to facilitate the expansion of terrorist networks around the world. Besides, the new suicide squards of terrorist have left the entire security apparatus of the affected states in a state of shock. A leading anti terrorism expert Mr. Brian Jenkins believes that though more articulate and multiplied effort by police and intelligence can tell us about a possible terrorist attack, there is still confusion over whether such a mechanism is successful in dealing with terrorists driven by fundamentalism. The world is also gradually witnessing the over expansion of a parochial version of faith and the desperate attempts of promoting it as the only pious one, but history bears testimony to the fact that such faith has hardly survived the nemesis of time. The bigotry perpetuated by glorification of self claimed cultural discourses as the sole receptacles of genuine faith has in past ripped off the civilizations one after another. During the mid 90s in the nerve gas attack on Tokyo subway, police suspected the hand of apocalyptic sect Aum Shinrikyo. Few Years earlier, Moscow intensified its efforts to set up "Troika" alliance to drive away the spectre of Islamic militants. The problem of Refugees who have fled due to disturbances in Afghanistan, Kyrghizstan and Uzbekistan has added a new dimension to the existing problem.

For effective administrative measures, various sources of terrorism must be found first. There is a need for truly effective preparedness programme at the government level. First of all we must know about the people involved in terrorist activities and their motivation. The relationship dealing with terrorist incident and mitigating its consequences need to be carefully thought out. Sufficient data about the area within which the event is unfolding could be of immense use. This is simple work of good intelligence and police. The intelligence should be able to provide the information about terrorist's targets, timings and sites in advance. But government alone cannot do much to stop it. Individuals and groups can make a significant contribution towards improving the general security environment.

On the other hand, there is a need for the sophisticated security procedures which can go all the way from airport screening to the border area. Some kind of positive programmes which can replace the frustration of terrorists can prove effective. There is also a need to promote open institutions, including political institution to absorb the ethnic, religious and political pressure and allow them (the terrorists) to vent their feelings in a proper way. This will change their mind and thus encourage them to settle their differences in some peaceful way.

There is an apprehension that with the availability of biological and chemical weapons the terrorists will start their campaign with renewed vigour and pursue their mission of destruction which will be virtually unstoppable.

There is a smooth international network of collaboration among the various terrorist groups supported by a few countries throughout the world. For example, Pakistan's involvement in orchestrating terrorism in Kashmir and the Japanese Red Army's collaboration with Italy's Red Brigade. It is sometimes the wide converge by the media which provides the rationale for terrorism and increases the problem by stimulating it. This is a classic example of how astute media management can reduce the level of moral opposition to counter terrorism.

European nations alone have witnessed more than 10000 terrorist incidents since 1970, representing about 31 per cent of the total incidents. The rise of modern terrorism with frightening ramifications has resulted in a demand for strengthening the national law and order machinery. Of late, the pressure on the police and security agencies has been mounting. But the existing laws still pose many problems. The use of police and paramilitary forces for combating terrorism has created an apprehension that it might lead to the oppression of the general populace. Surprisingly, a proper legal definition of terrorism is yet to be found.

The widening gap between the various governments regarding evolving common strategy for suppression of terrorism needs to be viewed in the context of the potential for threat that it holds. Even the European convention on suppression of terrorism is restricted by Article 5 and Article 13, which refuse the extradition of a terrorist on many grounds. In an environment where terrorist violence is endemic and the world stands hopelessly divided on various laws, all countries should shun their national prerogatives for dealing with terrorism. Many efforts have been made by a number of nations to control state-sponsored terrorism, such as through economic sanctions, but so far they have not reached a consensus either at the national or international level. The continuing uncertainties with regard to terrorism have encouraged various countries to launch psychological warfare against terrorism. In 1984, an international conference was organised in Washington by the Jonathan Institute. Some consensus began to emerge among the various scholars, politicians and decision-makers the world over. Some of the important suggestions were: the concept that one man's terrorist can be another man's freedom fighter must be done away with; local populace should cooperate with law enforcement machinery even at the cost of personal misery; prompt and strict decisions should be undertaken by various nations for controlling terrorist psychologically.

The London Economic Summit Conference organised by NATO States and Japan provided certain measures for the eradication of terrorism. It was deliberated in the conference that unless we attack the roots of terrorism, only superficial relief could be seen but terrorism would increase in the total quantum of its impact. Creation of general awareness and organisation of public support against terrorist acts could be of immense use. While it is desirable to allow police and the armed forces to employ better informed judgment about the local problems, there is of course a danger that this attempt of the government could dilute the benefits to those deemed deserving and, thus, any possibility of peace and negotiation.

Many governments across the world have formulated reform measures to improve the situation. But terrorists interpret these steps as a surrender by the state to international criticism. In such a situation, the role of the military and the security forces has become crucial because most of their operations in terrorist-affected areas require a multi-layered approach. Although military actions have normally been accorded the highest priority for the maintenance of security, sometimes such action damages the deep layers of social and individual interests. For example, the role of the security forces in tackling the problem of terrorism in Punjab, Kashmir and the North-East has opened a controversial debate. This leads to a dilemma. Is this merely a work of simple Police and Paramilitary network or that of a special force trained for counter-terrorist activities? The deployment of special forces in countering terrorist activities has become a reality in many countries. In this regard, the experience of different countries can help. For Example the way the West German Police defeated terrorist faction, the way the French Army took measures to improve their anti-terrorist capabilities. The Italian Police too had to combat large-scale terrorist violence from new-fascist groups and the left wing challenges of the Red Brigades.

On the other hand, there is a need for the sophisticated security procedures which can go all the way from airport screening to the border area. We have to learn certain anti terrorist strategies from the western world for example the United States Patriot Act 2001 empowered the security agencies to get the information about the communication network and properties of the suspects in terrorist related incidents. Besides, the immigration officials in the US got sanction to either detain or deport the illegal immigrants. The British Prevention of Terrorism Act 1984 authorised the security agencies to deal with terrorists firmly. Under this Act suspects of any terrorist act can be detained and imprisoned for even one and a half month without having charges framed. In India many attempts were made to ensure serious implementation of laws against terrorism. But due opposition in one account or other these Acts were allowed to lapse. Terrorism And Disruptive Activities Act 1987 (TADA) was not given any extension beyond 1995. Similarly, The Prevention of Terrorism (POTA)2002 was not given any further extension beyond 2004. On the other hand, various states such as Maharashtra and Gujarat have made attempts to enact separate criminal acts. But there is still lack of a federal agency that can come down heavily on terrorists.

To combat 26/11 like situation the Indian Parliament passed the bill related to the National Investigating Agency and the Unlawful Activities Prevention Act (UAPA) in December 2008. The NIA appears to be slightly milder than Prevention of Terrorism Act (POTA) in the sense that while in POTA the confession made before a Police Officer was treated as an evidence but in case of NIA the accused is to be produced before magistrate to record confession. Probably this is done to avoid any chances of the misuse of authority by the police. The NIA authorizes the security agencies to seize the funds and prevent the entry of any suspect of terrorist activities. Besides, the NIA has made attempts for providing quicker trials with a provision of setting up special courts. In case of POTA there was too much emphasis on the available evidences before the courts to try an accused but in case of Unlawful Activities Prevention Act (UAPA) an accused will be presumed as guilty in terrorist related cases if otherwise proved innocent. In addition, the NIA can investigate a case either on a request from state government or on direction from central government. The recent attempts from government will certainly work as deterrent.

During the last two decades, the increasing drug smuggling and the obnoxious nexus between drug smugglers and terrorists have posed a serious problem to the internal state-security networks and compelled various nations to organise themselves and wage a relentless war against such a nexus. But mere implementation of vigorous drug laws cannot become effective unless the judicial procedure is modified for ensuring speedy trials.

The concept that one man's terrorist can be another man's freedom fighter must be done away with; local populace should cooperate with law enforcement machinery even at the cost of personal misery; prompt and strict decisions should be undertaken by various nations for controlling terrorist psychologically.

In changing environment the security apparatus and police need to diversify its activities by bringing together technical and professional expertise based on many decades of experience in maintaining internal security. In this regard the most crucial thing is to develop capability to anticipate security needs. This is possible by conducting specialized courses for monitoring security situations.

Policy makers need to acknowledge that questions related to terrorism can in fact have a direct impact on the nation's life. The anti terrorist policies should have the ability to adapt in response to the challenging environment and efficiency that can potentially be used for implementation of various recommendations. Since the present day terrorists are very well organised and sometimes more professional than their counterparts a decade ago, new conceptions of safety and security should be followed. A vigilant and assertive intelligence, police and paramilitary network should replace the old one. Many of the important suggestions and recommendations of the various committees are not in tune with the existing circumstances.

The need of the hour is the political will to solve the problems that generate terrorism. The states affected by terrorism should open the avenues for negotiated settlement of disputes and exhibit genuine willingness to resolve long festering problems. The efforts of the state to maintain security on the face of terrorist threats should go hand in hand with increased devolution of power to the people and greater democratisation of the system of power and administration. This threat can be encountered by training and development of a new mechanism bolstered up of a multidimensional and multilayered approach based on checks and balances.

Although the structural adjustment and condition of society are responsible for growth of terrorism, the psychological postulates provide a vivid and deeper insight into the problem of terrorism and its causes. The book is an attempt to examine and analyse the genesis and changing nature of the problem of terrorism and its causes. Besides, it analyses and suggest:

- some preventive methods for the removal of the grievances of the people, thus striking at the roots of the problem.
- The strategic methods which the security forces and the intelligence agencies ought to be preparing for,

- after carefully examining the widening gap between the various governments to formulate a common strategy for the suppression of terrorism some strategic measures are suggested for formulating international strategy to counter this menace,
- How Indian government dealt with the problem and what policies are available to deal with terrorism and insurgency.
- What are the security constraints in dealing with the problem of terrorism? In this regard a comparative analysis of terrorism is done to search new areas of coordination and cooperation.

Areas of Concern the Book

The First Unit of the book deals with general introduction to the phenomenon of terrorism. It views terrorism both theoretically and empirically and examines various causes of terrorism.

The Second Area: There is an attempt to find the sources of international terrorism. This includes funding of terrorism, nexus between arms dealer, drug traffickers, smugglers and terrorists.

The Third area New Trends: Book attempts to analyse the role of new technology and weapons including the possibility of grabbing the biological and nuclear weapons. Besides, an attempts are made to study the role of religion and ideology in motivating terrorists for their cause.

Terrorists Threat: In order to understand the inner dynamics of violence case studies of Jammu and Kashmir and Assam are conducted. Besides, this chapter also examines terrorist violence as an instrument of geo-political instrument.

Measures: Attempts are made to suggest various measures (both at the national and international levels) for eradication of the problem of terrorism. Overall it is going to be a modest attempt to generate new insights relevant for policy makers across the globe.

All efforts were made in collection and analysis of data available in primary and secondary sources. In addition to the authoritative reports, numerous manuscripts containing the problem of terrorism and security management have been analysed. Constant interaction with experts in strategic areas have only enriched me further. An accurate inquiry of the existing literature on this area revealed certain inadequacies. Very few comprehensive and up-to-date studies were available. Since the phenomenon itself is so ambiguous. Some important studies on the problem of international terrorism and combating strategies in last few years which enthralled me include the work of eminent authors like Prof. Paul Wilkinson, Prof. Yonah Alexander, Brian Jenkins, David Fromkin, Seymour Maxwell, Williams Cutteridges, louis Rene Beres, R S Eliotm, W H Dundas, T A Jackson, W D Hussey, John Magee, David Watt, Ronald Jacquard, Prof Gunaratne, K.P.S Gill, B. Raman, Maj. Gen Afsir Karim, Ved Marwah, Prof Brahma Challeny, Prof Jake Lynch, Parveen Swamey and most importantly remarkable work done by Professor Bruce Hoffman. Recently many new changes have taken place in the strategy of terrorism. The most notable of this is the increasing role played by sophisticated arms and weaponry system. The emerging new challenges of modern terrorism has put a lot of pressure on the security forces. Thus, all attempts are made to present a proper understanding of the role of intelligence, police and paramilitary forces in dealing with the menace of terrorism. It goes without saying that a solid intellectual framework always prepares required rationale strategies. The book draws attention to the issues which deserve immense attention on part of international community. I owe a deep sense of gratitude towards the Centre for Policy Research (a leading Think tank) where I worked as Fellow (Research) from 1994 to 1998 for sharpening my research skills and the University Grants Commission awarding me two research projects (2005-07 & 2008-11) which helped me further in comprehending complex issues such as naxalism, caste violence and terrorism.I am grateful to my wife Shuchi for bearing with my odd schedule and my daughter Manvi with whom I could not spend enough time for Tennis. I wish to also thank my diligent research assistant Shagun for her relentless efforts in helping me complete the work. Many thanks to Dr. N. K Singh, the proprietor of Global Vision Press for publishing the manuscript from such an internationally renowned publishing house.

Contents

1

Genesis of Terrorism

INTENSITY OF TERRORISM

The recent terrorist attack on the naval base in Karachi that left more than 10 people dead and many injured sent out a common message about the ability of modern terrorists to attack with accuracy at a time and place of their choice. The fact that the attack was so meticulously executed just three weeks after the death of Osama Bin Laden makes it clear that terrorists were only down for sometimes but not wiped out, certainly not withstanding the claims of security agencies. Pakistan needs to realise that to a great extent it is gradually becoming victim of its own game. Pakistan's involvement in aiding and abetting training camps in PoK has been exposed many times. On 7th June, 2011 at a Federal court trial in Chicago Pakistani-Canadian militant Tahawwur Rana admitted that he conspired with David Headley in carrying out 26/11 Mumbai attacks. He also admitted having clandestine links with Pakistan's Inter Services Intelligence and Lashkar-e-Toiba. The recorded statements of David Headley and Tahawwur Hussain Rana by the Chicago Court, USA clearly reveal ISI links to Mumbai attack. Rana who once served as a Doctor with the Pakistan army, later declared as deserter and finally utilized by ISI for terrorist plots. The recent Guantanamo Bay (US prison in Cuba) disclosure by WikiLeaks made it amply clear that presently operating terrorist groups in India such as

Harkat-Ul-Mujahideen (HuM), Harkat-ul-Jihad al Islami (Huji), Lashkar-e-Taiba (LeT) and Jaish-e-Mohammed have been constantly receiving patronage from ISI. The linkages of Let, JeM, HuJI and HuM with Al Qaeda in one way or another makes it all the more alarming for India to devise multi-layered strategy to encounter such threats. It is demoralizing that despite committing heinous crime Dawood Ibrahim and Hafiz Saeed are still operating from Pakistan. Open threats by Hafiz Saeed from Pakistani soil such as an all-out Jihad and the possible use of nuclear weapons against India only underlines the deep rooted level of hatred. American drone attack in South Waziristan on 3rd June, 2011 killing Ilyas Kashmiri, a leader of Harkat-ul-Jihad-al-Islami and its mission 'Geronimo' carried out by naval commando unit SEALS in Abbottabad near Islamabad killing 'Osama Bin Laden' bring forward a major strategic question: Is combating terrorism a merely work of simple Police and Paramilitary network or that of a special force trained for counter-terrorist activities. It goes without saying that recent success may provide only temporary relief from the threat of terror. History bears testimony to the fact that it has tremendous potential for resurfacing with gusto.

Terrorism has become nightmarish phenomenon which has led to the civilized world towards complete decay. Although terrorism is not a new concept but it acquired enormous dimension after 9/11 attack on World Trade Centre in New York killing more than 3800 people. Since then the most destructive nature of terrorist violence was acknowledged by many countries across the globe. Earlier terror used to more of domestic variety and confined to the geographical limitations but now a completely new era of trans-national terrorism has emerged on world stage. The advent of globalization has also contributed in this direction to a great extent. The manner in which recent terrorist strikes were carried out speaks volume about the dare devil audacity of modern terrorists. Terrorism for a long cannot survive for a long unless it has external support base both in terms of money and ideological backing. It is no longer confined to an individual or a single nation but it has spread its tentacles throughout the world as with each passing day the dimension and gravity of its deadly striking capabilities change manifolds. During initial years of insurgency, in Punjab militants used to normally kill about five people in an open fire but gradually the nature of attack has undergone a sea change. With the help of sophisticated weapons like AK 47 and AK 56 assault rifles modern terrorists kill more than two dozen people in a few seconds. With the recent increase in postal and Anthrax attacks terrorists have created havoc. The possibility of potent nuclear and biological weapons falling into the hands of these new breed of terrorists could lead the world to a state of extreme fear and anxiety. In past only a few countries were witnessing terrorist incidents but gradually it has increased manifold. Even communist countries like Russia and China are grappling with the problem of Chechen rebels and Xinxiang's uprising. The West Asian zone has been witnessing four fold rise in militants violence. It is worst in case of Pakistan. The fighting between militants and security forces appears to have become order of the day. The tribal areas of Pakistan such as Kamra, Muhamand tribal region and Peshawar faced severe problem of terrorist violence. Every one in these areas is in a state of shock. News about suicide bombers detonating their explosives in different areas of the region are quite common. In recent years bombs were detonated in Islamic University in Islamabad. The suicidal car bomb attacks on NATO Head Quarters at Kabul, deadly attack by terrorists on Abu Gharib prison which killed two journalists and 33 civilians, only justify their plan of destruction. The recent advances of the Tehrik-e-Taliban (a militant organization has been operating from Pakistan) in Swat Valley and near Afghan border area are matter of serious concern. The purpose of this group is to attack any authority backed by America. According to the intelligence inputs Tehrik-e-Taliban is planning to attack Europe. It has already claimed the responsibility of May 2010's bombing at New York Times Square. The army and the intelligence will have to gear up to encounter any threat from this group particularly after its recent threat of avenging the death of Osama. Differences between Shia majority and the Sunni minority further deteriorated already vulnerable situation. Examples of ruthless killings are numerous. In one such attack approximately more than 245 people were massacred in a Mosque in Peshawar. This was followed by yet another strike of terrorists in North West Pakistan within a span of less than two months of the previous mosque attack. Consequently, these attacks have undermined the authority of state and central government and brought forward the issue of civilian security in public places. A few months ago terrorist attack on Sri Lankan players led to the death of six policemen and left six players injured. In order to drive people out of rebel dominated Jaffna, one female LTTE suicide bomber detonated her explosives in a crowd of soldiers and refugees in northern Sri Lanka. In Peshawar a Taliban suicide bomber even targeted school bus.

A week after this incident four militants opened fire and killed twenty people.

The increasing influence of Taliban and its supporters can be seen by their hold on area of Swat Valley which rose from fifteen per cent to about seventy five per cent. This only demonstrates the volatile state of affairs. Merciless agenda during 2007 had virtually turned entire Swat Valley into a bloodbath. Their suicide bombers killed 41 people and left many more injured. During the last one decade there has been increasing transportation of arms from Afghanistan to North West Frontier Province. According to an estimate, more than six million automatic assault rifles were found in the tribal areas of NWFP. Gradually, the entire Swat Valley came under Taliban's control.[1]. Taliban used state broadcasting machinery and whole media network in building public opinion against state machinery and American influence[2]. The recent wave of parcel bomb attacks in Athens, Greece has already sent alarming signals of the rising tide of international terrorism. In another part of world Yemen, the increasing tentacles of Al Qaeda in Arabian Peninsula (AQAP) Franchise confirms the fact that Al Qaeda still remains deadly force.

Terrorism also spread its tentacles in Iran. In one such terrorist incident, Forty Shiaite people were killed in a suicide bomb attack, which was followed by the blowing up of Moussa-al-Kadhim shrine in the Khadimiya neighborhood. This led to death of many pilgrims. Soon after this, in an another terrorist attack, a toy bomb exploded in front of a girls school and killed more than 11 students. The incidents of a Jordanian militant attempted to bomb a skyscraper in Dallas and acid spray in a popular market filled with shoppers on a busy street of Hong Kong injuring 30 people are disturbing reminder of an array of issues which the civilized nations have yet to come to grips with.

On the other hand, at the domestic front India has been grappling with worst form of terrorism, naxalism and insurgency in different parts of country. The simmering rural unrest has continued to find its outlet in the form of naxal violence throughout Andhra Pradesh, Bihar, Orissa, Chhattisgarh, and Jharkhand. The brutal murder of CRPF personnel in the Bijapur district in a powerful land mine blast and attack on Gadchiroli district that killed four policemen are recent incidents which portray the level of barbarism permeated by the modern breed of naxalites. The Maoists were found involved in unlawful activities. They launched consecutives strikes at Bastar in M.P. and Belpahari district of West Bengal. Dissatisfied with government policies, Maoists attacked with explosive devices in Medinipur district of West Bengal. The series of violent activities by the banned People's War Group in Andhra Pradesh and the Maoist Communist Centre in Bihar suggest that naxalism has entered a new phase, and security agencies are in a state of shock. Attacks on important government buildings, telephone exchange, railway stations, villages and police pickets have become quite common. In some areas where there was a lull for a long, a recurrence of naxalite activities have disturbed peaceful ambience.

During last few decades or so, the government of Andhra Pradesh has suffered a heavy loss of public and private property because of the upsurge in naxalite activities. The main purpose behind these activities is to induce fear in the minds of police and administration. On the other hand, in Bihar, there are various such extremist organizations operating, including the Indian People's Front, the MKSS (Mazdoor Kisan Sangram Samiti) and the Maoist

Communist Centre. There have been a number of attacks on police pickets by them. In some areas of Central Bihar their underground operations are on the rise. These organisations raise funds by means of extortion from contractor, securing small contacts, subscription from corrupt officials and powerful landlords. Although it is difficult to know the actual strength of these groups, the Maoist Communist Centre is considered to be the most organised with sophisticated weapons. A few years ago, the massacre of 11 people near Dodadih Hills in Bihar by the MCC almost turned basic issue into caste-war like situation. There have been numerous instances of such gruesome acts by the MCC. The group is very active in Central Bihar districts such as Patna, Jehanabad, Gaya, Nalanda and Navada. In Jehanabad areas, the mobilisation of weaker section by the IPF and the MKSS has been mainly on the basis of a common concern for equitable distribution of land and payment of minimum wages, among other things. The MCC has been responsible for the Darmiam, Dalelchak Baghora, Bakridh and Bara incidents. After the Dalelchak Baghora (Aurangabad) massacre, the state government declared a ban on the activities of the MCC. But it has emerged quite a powerful organisation by bringing about changes in its tactics since 1990's. The MCC has organised an armed outfit called the Lal Raksha Dal and captured sophisticated weapons like AK-47 rifles. The MCC considers the land owning caste exploiters of the rural poor. In mid 1970s, it was very active in Aurangabad district, particularly in the Gurva, Guraru and Amar Paraiya regions. Its ideology are based on the assumption that the Government, the rich and upper castes have acquired maximum benefits and are denying justice to the rural poor. The MCC is in favour of adopting violent means to sustain its struggle. It was reported that the MCC organised a parallel judiciary system (Kangaroo courts) in certain districts. In Chatra, Khagaria, Jehanabad and Ranchi the MCC has been successful in building a strong base at the rural level. The naxalites have also killed members belonging to rival factions. In past the PWG killed two persons belonging to the rival Janashakti faction and a former PWG member in Nizamabad districts of Andhra Pradesh.

The situation has become worse than before because of the migration of population under economic pressure. This has led to the problems in housing, employment, law and order and other areas. The presence of labour force in the cities and towns has brought about a link between rural and urban areas. The rural and far-flung areas thus provide a base for the naxalites to carry out their clandestine activities. The existing inequalities in urban areas have added a new dimension to the problem. As a result, some sections without sufficient means to propel their cause, found themselves in the lurch. Thus, violence is gradually becoming a common strategy. Gangs which initially confined themselves to committing murders and theft are now involved in full-scale naxal violence against those whom they consider responsible for their miserable life.

In the last two decades the People's War Group has made several attempts to emphasise its rights. Dissatisfied with government policies, it has lashed out violently and continues its activities which include bank robberies, murder of policemen, kidnapping of businessmen and officials and political assassination attempts.

North-East still remains vulnerable area. The terrorist attacks have demonstrated the audacity and level of coordination among the present-day insurgents. The use of grenades and low-intensity bombs showed the well thought out plan which was so meticulously executed. Bombing by the insurgents preceding the visits of important dignitaries have sent out message loud and clear that they can resurface with new vigour. The latest blasts are just new addition to the long saga of insurgency in the North-East. A few years ago, bomb explosion in the Delhi-bound Rajdhani Express killed five persons and left many injured. Similarly, serial blasts near railway tracks in Guwahati by ULFA militants killed two innocent people and left scores injured. Conflicts between the tribal population and sundry separatists groups in different parts of the North-East have added another deadly dimension to the already vulnerable situation. The proclaimed goal of these insurgent groups has been either independence or autonomy. In the past a number of attempts were made by them to pressurise the Government to meet their demands.

In the process of deployment of paramilitary forces the government incurred heavy losses both in terms of public property and lives. Militant outfits like the United Liberation Front of Assam (ULFA), the Bodo ultras have been posing a serious threat to the entire security apparatus. Secessionism in North-East is basically a sequel a variety of factors such as economic underdevelopment, lack of industrialisation, local incompetence and outside support, which over the years generated acute unemployment. The international linkage of the area has added deadly dimension to the ongoing problem of insurgency in North-East. The Bodo militants have used Bhutan, and ULFA have crossed over to Bangladesh for procuring arms and training. Similarly, in past Naga insurgents made full use their border with Myanmar. The news of Chinese involvement in backing insurgents during 1970 is not news anymore. Besides, to a great extent militancy has become a new avenue for providing a means of livelihood to most rebels. Operation Bajrang and Operation Rhino were successful in driving the rebels underground but could not destroy the potency of insurgents. Although the Central government has made various efforts to find solution in the past by initiating the Tripura accord, the Assam accord and the Mizo accord but the grievances of various emerging factions within the militant organizations still remain live. Consequently, insurgent activities against the government and clashes between the factions have continued unabated. We should be extremely cautious in handling the present crisis, particularly after witnessing the deadly performance of rebels under changed conditions . Since the entire region is a hilly area with thick forest it provides excellent base for carrying out clandestine guerrilla activities that has been responsible for the death of numerous people over the years. For example, several security officials have died on the National Highways No-53 and 39 which connect Manipur to the rest of country. These days, rebels seem to be reasonably confident of their access to vantage points. Moreover, the strategies and methods have become more sophisticated and they are successful in acquiring more lethal weapons from across the border. This is clearly visible in the recent attacks wherein terrorists planted explosive.

The criticism of the government's policies by the insurgents and their supporters created tremendous support in local population to rebels. Moreover, their preconceived notions of "we versus they" have helped in keeping the morale of insurgents high. Lack of sufficient resources has also created a serious problem of force deployment over the years. Consequently, training and ground force exercise have been affected. In addition to this, the geographical location of north east has made it difficult for army to gain reliable intelligence. Fresh difficulties are presented by the mobile members of the rebel organizations who are trained in guerrilla warfare and get logistical help from border areas of Myanmar and Bangladesh. The disturbing issue is that neither withdrawal of entire army from the North-East nor the occupation of the entire region seems tenable anymore. The military operations will gradually get unsustainable.

The rising tide of continuing insurgency in Jammu & Kashmir has further worsened the situation. The cross border terrorism supported by Pakistan has disturbed the life of the valley. Various militant outfits such as Lashkar-e-Toiba, Jaishe-Mohammad, Hizbullah, etc., have been engaged in the process of elimination of innocent bystanders.

There has been mushrooming of non-state actors in India. Explosive devise strike closely on the heels of Allahabad High Court's verdict has not only demonstrated the deadly striking capabilities of the distraught minds but has also confirmed that militants have openly declared war against Indian State. Although it was the first attack by Indian Mujahideen since June 2010 when the Government banned it yet its background is more than sufficient for sending out dangerous signals. The IM was involved in more than 9 blasts in different parts of the country murdering more than five hundred people. Founded by Amir Reza Khan and headed by Karnataka based Iqbal Bhatkal is a sister outfit of the banned SIMI and Pakistani-based Lashkar-e-Taiba. It's specialization lies in coordinating and executing low intensity attacks. According to recent military intelligence sources, the IM is planning to strike throughout country. The recent incident cannot be viewed in isolation.

Rise in the incidents of sporadic attacks at crowded places with steep increase in death tolls is a new dynamic of domestic terrorism. The magnitude of the lethality can very well be understood from the recent serial blasts in the cities of Delhi, Bangalore and Ahmedabad. Well thought out plan, coordinated attacks and incredible execution of terrorists could be seen in 26/11 when eight different sites in Mumbai were simultaneously attacked by Pakistani-backed terrorists. These attacks did not even spare the elites of the society as it resulted in the death toll rising up to 183 including 22 foreigners. This attack was the worst terrorist attack in India during recent years.

The entire incident has left the global community reeling from the magnitude of the terror. It has given a clear message that the terrorism in the subcontinent is set to become even more lethal. The terrorist strike in Mumbai attack is normally compared with the 2002 terrorist attacks on Bali, Indonesia. It is astonishing that in both the incidents of terrorist attacks European and American citizens were singled out. Some strategic analysts described the Mumbai attack as the second deadliest after September 11, 2001.[3]

Over the years there has been a number of changes both in the nature and magnitude of terrorist strategies, capabilities and nature. Earlier terrorist used to have a well-defined ideological, economical, social and political motive. It used to be more formal in approach with ideological orientation. In the past, terrorist groups such as the LTTE of Sri Lanka, the IRA of Northern Ireland, Red Army of Japan, Red Brigades of Italy, ETA of Spain, Abu Nidal Organization and the Basque separatists had a separate command and security apparatus with a well-defined ideological leaning. These groups took full responsibility of their actions in eliminating whom they considered responsible for their miseries. These groups have highly choose in selecting their victims. In order to arouse psychological state of fear among general public, they mainly utilize tactics such as bombing railway stations, tubes, parks, embassies, banks, national airline, courier centers, etc. Kidnapping and specific assassination are few other methods of their operation.[4] Last few years have seen emergence of a different set of terrorists who are less formal, more diffused and more closely inclined towards cultural and religious sentiments.

In the past, Bin Laden's open declaration of Islamic war on America shows how religion has been misused by terrorist against a democratic nation.[5] These religiously motivated groups have only misled people by misinterpreting religious teachings. These days terrorists have developed better following with a tremendous commitment base from core group members who are ready to give away their lives for a justified cause. whereas in the past terrorists groups such ETA of Spain, the Red Army faction of Japan and the Italian Red Brigade did not have more than hundred inner circle members ready with arms all the time on the other hand, the Abu-Nidal group has always being ready with more than four hundred and eighty men-at-arms at any given time.[6]

In order to grab more public attention modern terrorists always want to remain in news. This could only become possible by causing more destruction of public and government property and killing innumerous number of people. By way of ruthless tactics they want to convey their message about the inability of security and intelligence agencies to provide protection. The increasing use of sophisticated weaponry and new sources of funding have caused serious concern about the outbreak of a different warfare. The support of the so-called rogue nations for settling their personal scores against a state has further created breeding grounds of trans-national militancy. It is a known fact that Pakistan, Iraq, Saudi Arabia are sponsoring many religious terrorist organisations. These days, new types of religious terrorists are slowly overshadowing the separatist and ideologically motivated militants. Religion has therefore worked as a wonderful drug for motivating the young generation towards separatism and terrorism. There were hardly 5 per cent terrorist organizations during the period between 1960s and 1980s which were religiously motivated. But the period between 1990 and 2000 saw an upward rise in the religiously motivated terrorist organizations. By mid 1990, there were more than fifty per cent religiously motivated international terrorist organizations[7]. The recent violent incidents in the Xin Xiang province of China are indicators of religious and cultural concern among ethnic minorities. Recently the Uighur Muslims lynched more than one hundred Hans neighbours. This led to retaliations from Hans Chinese who targeted some Uighurs. These skirmishes were immediately exploited by Turkestan Islamic Party which planned a series of bomb attacks on many places throughout China and mainly attacked Shanghai and Kunming.[8]

Religiously motivated terrorist always carve for clerical sanctions to provide theoretical, sentimental and legitimate base for carrying out even the worst crime against humanity. The growing unemployment and increasing desires among the present generation is delicate ground. The tinge of religious opium brings forward a toxic compound for modern terrorist as they do not hesitate in massacring general masses. The serial killings of innocent people at Taj Hotel in Mumbai on 26/11 is the tip of an iceberg. There have been a number of such examples when thousands of people were killed on the name of religion.

With the rapid increase in information technology the traditional set up of terrorist organization is no longer as important as it used to be a few years ago. The level of comprehension, courage, determination, right training, skill of operation and focused execution strategy what is required to make a hardcore terrorist. These terrorists are more professional, innovative, computer savvy, more educated and more financially sound then their counterparts a decade ago. The emergence of new class of high-tech terrorists has broken a well founded belief that terrorism is mainly an outcome of poverty. Their strategy and method of operation have become more discrete then terrorists during 1970s and 1980s. The old class of militants used to publicly take responsibility of the attacks but modern terrorists are not so keen in publicizing their actions. The form of terrorism has also undergone major change as it has become spectator sport with multiplied harmful impact. Nations and intelligence agencies are gradually employing these non state actors for fulfillment of their strategic and military aims. These days there is no scarcity of funding for terrorists. Their operations are mostly funded. Cold War and post-Cold War politics has created peculiar tendencies and base for the rise of such state sponsored terrorism. But gradually, the whole strategy is proving pernicious. Modern terrorists have acquired the most sophisticated weapons of mass destruction and states have merely remained spectators.[9]

The rise in suicidal terrorists has made terrorists threat more lethal. The suicide bombing has increased casualty to manifold. There has been seventy eight per cent rise in the number of suicidal attacks by terrorists during the last two decades.

Suicidal attacks show the level of motivation and fearlessness among terrorist who are willing to sacrifice their lives for a cause according to their own perception of justice. The 9/11 suicidal attacks by terrorists on World Trade Centre, USA, proved that it is just impossible to stop such terrorist attacks. These terrorist attacks caused twenty times more damage than previous attacks. The level of potentiality and lethality of causing damage by such terrorist attacks make the suicidal method more popular among modern terrorists.[10] Moreover, the rapid increase in the means of modern transportation system has rather helped terrorists in their mission.

To sustain their struggle sources of finances are very vital and for this terrorists connive with drug traffickers. Tremendous amount of revenue generated by illegal drug trafficking provide a continuous flow of support to terrorist groups. Therefore, there have been continuous efforts to eliminate drug trafficking and reduce drug abuse. Rohan Gunartna sees an obnoxious nexus between terrorism and organized crime. The increasing proximity has helped terrorists groups to be more independent and less dependent on the state sponsors. There is no dearth of domestic and international supporters for modern terrorists. The increasing proximity between narcotic dealers, arms smugglers and militant groups transformed Afghanistan into a very dangerous place. It is believed that Al Qaeda and its supporters got support from Taliban, and drug producers of Afghanistan. Middle east militant organizations like Hezbollah or

Hamas carried on their struggle with the support of money generated through narcotic trade in other parts of the world.

With the growing influence of globalization there has been rapid increase in the use of dual technologies like GPS, satellite imagery, radar, computers, secure communications etc. There have been a many instances in the past when terrorists have misused these devices for expansion of their activities. As a result the level and intensity of fatalities and casualties per attack has increased more than hundred times. Latest in the series has been the desperate attempts by terrorists to obtain Chemical, Biological, Radiological and Nuclear material and expertise for easy target destruction. In the past, the LTTE and Al Qaeda have been found of having increasing access to cellular and satellite phones, internet and various instant messengers which have ultimately helped them communicate with other terrorist organizations. Easy availability of CRRN technology has made the world highly unsafe place. There has been a paradigm shift in the mode of operation, level of reliability, ideological commitment and international security scenario the world over. With modern terrorists turning tech-savvy their nature of threat has become more focused and qualitative in approach. There are various terrorists groups operating in different parts of world. Few organizations have left oriented ideological commitment and few others are right-wing terrorists. There are some ethno-separatist type and few others are religious in nature. The Left-wing terrorist organizations normally take recourse to revolutionary methods for justification of their idealist principles against an authority whom they consider authoritarian. These terrorists do not hesitate in applying most uncivilized and savage methods which include murder, kidnapping and bombing. The only thing which differentiates them with other kinds is that they mainly select elite targets whom they consider responsible for their miseries. The Red Brigade of Italy had lashed out violently and mainly focused on elite targets. On the other hand, there have been mainly terrorist organizations driven by other considerations such as race and ethnicity. The rise of Neo-Nazi organizations in Europe and Ku Klux Klan group in United States gave a strong foundation to the Right-wing terrorists. The

Right Wing organizations have also used ruthless techniques to send out their messages. The Separatist and the Ethno-Nationalist organizations are highly traditional in their approach. Mostly they carry forward clear political aims. Although in the beginning they were not very volatile, they turn out to be highly volatile if their demands are not met. There is enormous ambiguity between the aims related to ethnic identity and matter related to taking control over an area. The Separatists are often successful in generating tremendous mass base and popularity by virtue of their local connections. To carry forward their struggle most of these organizations often build strong paramilitary structures and units to expand their activities. Their ability to generate "We Vs They" Syndrome in past has helped them build a strong base. Gradually, they are becoming more confident than ever before because of their increasing access to the vulnerable points. They have acquired the skills to plan an attack in a demonstrating and heroic manner to justify their cause to the government and the people. Thus, they attempt, by their acts, to inspire and manipulate fear to achieve variety of purposes. Therefore, busy hotels, crowded trains, shopping malls, are increasingly becoming targets of terrorism.[11]

DEFINING THE INDEFINABLE

Defining terrorism is the most daunting task. There are numerous definitions provided by the individuals, groups and nations and international organizations. The parameters selected by different people vary as per their own perception of analyzing the phenomenon. Therefore, definition of terrorism becomes highly subjective. The only common thing is the indiscriminate killings of people in any act of violence. The persisting diversity in the views and lack of a satisfactory definition creates hurdles in the way of developing a comprehensive policy against terrorism. Although many countries in past have tried to generate a consensus on the definition of "terrorism".

Some countries have defined terrorism as pejorative type of violence which is completely contrary to the standards of legitimacy and morality. More often than not the attempts of defining terrorism has created more debates and generated argumentation. Certain definitions have included some groups and their actions in the definitional aspect of terrorism while excluded some others of the same kind. It depends upon how to legitimize the basis for employing violence for attaining their political, ideological and economic goals. In his book "Inside Terrorism" Bruce Hoffman argued, "On one point, at least, everyone agrees: terrorism is a pejorative term. It is a word with intrinsically negative connotations that is generally applied to one's enemies and opponents, or to those with whom one disagrees and would otherwise prefer to ignore".[12] Brian Jenkins, a leading author of anti-terrorism strategies wrote, "thus seems to depend on one's point of view. If one identifies with the victim of the violence, for example, then the act is terrorism. If, however, one identifies with the perpetrator, the violent act is regarded in a more sympathetic light, and it is not terrorism".

Walter Laqueur claims that it is just impossible to find any definition of terrorism without subjectivity. Many definitions have been rejected on their being prejudiced and lacking in neutrality. The disturbing issue has been the ongoing debate regarding "One man's terrorist being another man's freedom fighter." The question regarding personal perspective of looking at violent activities has caused further confusion about terrorism. Whereas few people and nations define certain acts of violence as terrorism few others consider these acts as legitimate strategy designed for self defense. There is a growing concern among some scholars from third world countries to treat certain category of violence as liberation struggle and fight against, colonialism, apartheid and racism. On the other hand, there is a prevalent perception among the scholars from United States and western Europe to treat all violent acts as terrorism irrespective of the background, ideological leaning and causes of grievances. Robert A. Friedlander observes that "terrorism exists in the mind of the beholder, depending upon one's political and national origins. For others, terrorism consists of criminal acts according to the laws any civilized society. Thus he argues that an exact legal definition of terrorism is unnecessary."[13] The dichotomy and ambiguity about the definitional aspects of terrorism has resulted in so many definitions of terrorism. A satisfactory definition is yet to be found. Walter Laqueur argues that terrorism can only be identified in terms of violence. An act of terror which either involves violence or the fear of violence is a part of terrorism. However, Walter does not understand that many violent acts such as war, riot, organized crime, cannot be included within the definitional framework of terrorism. What is more important is the purpose and motivational factors that created compelling condition for violence.

In order to undermine the legitimacy of political institution terrorists often target important symbols of national importance. This is done to arouse a sense of insecurity among people. At times repeated acts of terror create severe problem for the legitimacy of government. There is a common belief that the dynamics of terrorism can only be understood by the analyzing the selection criteria of terrorist targets. Often the victims are chosen for their symbolic importance "that tie into a specific view of the world that the terrorist possess. Their suffering accomplishes the terrorists' goals of instilling fear, getting a message out to an audience, or otherwise accomplishing their political end".[14]

Terrorism is also seen as an act of illegitimate political, violence. Use of violence is a common strategy applied in an act of terror either by an individual, organization or a country. The issue of violence applied by whom and against whom is the only criteria that separates terrorism from other forms of violence. Many times definitions provided by governments and supported organizations are accused of being biased. Thus, all forms of political violence cannot be included in terrorism. An important Report on International Terrorism by the United Nations' addressed the practical problems in providing proper definition of terrorism. The report took into account the largely held view and concern to include terror outcome, instrumental or immediate victims, primary targets, violence and political purpose while providing a satisfactory definition of terrorism.[15] Professor Paul Wilkinson in his famous book Political terrorism has classified terrorism in the following ways: Repressive terror {complete suppression}; Revolutionary terror; War terror (in which terrorists apply all kinds of arms and weapons to terrorise people.

Louis Rene Beres interpreted Thronton's definition which lays huge importance on symbolic charter of terrorist acts. Therefore, terrorism is a symbolic act intended to influence political behaviour of the country by extra normal means, entailing the use or threat of violence. The most important element in Thornton's definition is the claim that all acts of terror in an internal war are deliberately propagandist acts, which are always designed to convey a message, sign or warning to either their opponents, the 'neutral' population or to those who belong to or sympathises with the terrorist movement. (Louis Rene Beres in Terrorism and Global Security: the nuclear threat (West-view, Colorado, 1979, p. 18)

Although people have given different definitions of terrorism and in spite of immense inclination of the world community in the problem of terrorism, there has not been any agreement on its satisfactory definition. (John F. Murphy, "International Legal Controls of International Terrorism", Illinois Bar, Vol.63, (1975),p.444.) For example, the Government of France has given different arguments in term of defining terrorism. According to it, "any act of barbarism committed in the territory of third state by a foreigner against a person who has a nationality – other than of the offenders for the purpose of exerting a pressure on a conflict not strictly internal in nature is called an act of terrorism and that foreigner is a terrorist". On the other hand, government of Haiti defines terrorism as an act of violence committed by a person or a group under international jurisdiction against any one for political purpose. (U.N. General Assembly Official Records, Supplement No.28, (A/9028), 1973, p. 21)

Grant Wardlow defines political terrorism as "the use of violence by an individual or a group, whether acting for or in opposition to established authority, when such action is designed to create extreme anxiety or fear indicating effects in a target group larger than the immediate victims with the purpose of coercing that group into the acceding to the political demands of perpetrators. This definition gives an elaborate commentary on various aspects such as state terrorism, state-sponsored terrorism and terrorism by non-state actors, like the various factions of the Palestine Liberation Organization (PLO). The Baader Meinholf Gang of West Germany, the Sikh extremists, the Red Brigade of Italy, etc. ". (K. Subrahmanyam, "Terrorism; To the forefront of the stage; Strategic Analysis, Val X, No3, June 1986, pp. 338-99.)

An incident of violence can be judged to have an international terrorism dimension if it signifies that (1) the terrorist action is supported by one or more foreign pro-terrorist regime; (2) the act was aimed to influence international opinion and whether the attack is on foreign personnel or it is aimed at overthrowing a foreign government. (Saleem Qureshi, "Political Violence in the South Asian Sub Continent" in Yonah Alexander, ed., International Terrorism: National, Regional and Global Perspectives (praeger, New York, 1976, pp.151.2.)

Frantz Fanon observes that:

> "In the colonies it is the soldier a policeman who are the official instituted to go between the spokesman of settler and his rule of oppression; on the other hand, in colonial countries,the policeman and the soldier by their immediate presence and their frequent and direct actions maintain contact with native and advise him by means of rifle and napalm not to budge. It is quite obvious that the agents of the governments use pure force only. The intermediary does not lighten the oppression, nor seek to hide the domination, he shows them up and puts them into practice with the clear conscience of an upholder of peace, yet he is the bringer of violence into the home into the mind of native". (Frantz Fanon, The Wretched of the Earth (Penguin, Harmondsworth, 1967),p.29.)

Terrorism was firstly used at the Third Conference for the unification of Penal Law held at Brussels in 1931. In this conference terrorism was defined as

> "The deliberate use of means capable of producing a common danger' to commit 'an act of imperalling life, physical integrity or human health or threatening to destroy substantial property. Such acts included : "Arson; explosion; flooding or submersion; ignition

of asphyxiating or noxious substances: interruption of the normal operation of means of transport or communication: damage to or destruction of government property and public utilities: pollution: fouling, or deliberate poisoning of drinking water or staple foods, causing or propagating contagious or epidemic disease any willful act which endangers human lives and the community and so on." (Surya P. Sharma, "International Law; Consensus, Still Elusive"; World Focus, Vol. VII, No. 2, February 1986, p.7)

Terrorism is also defined on the basis of the target and nature of victims involved in any act of violence. The aim and level of interactions of the participants also play crucial role for determining the category of terrorism. Besides, strict parameters of legal jurisdictions play crucial role in explaining the nature of an act of violence. Therefore, a holistic approach concerning various elements and aspects of violence is a must for comprehension of the multidimensional facets of the phenomenon. This would help in differentiating and categorizing terrorism as a non-state actor or as an act sponsored by state. [16]

Due to lack of general consensus about the definitional aspects of terrorism at the international forum, world agencies preferred terms like "bombers," "militants," instead of terrorists. Analysis of the National Research Council (NRC) panel once again reconfirmed the fact that it is just impossible to find a proper definition of terrorism. [17]

Terrorism is not a recent phenomenon. Its origin goes back to the ancient history of Greece and Rome. Whereas some political analysts cite the example of the assassination of Julius Caesar in 44 BC as the earliest terrorist incident, few others consider Zealot struggle in Palestine; and the violent attacks by the Secret Islamic armed organizations in the twelfth and thirteenth centuries the oldest incidents of terrorist violence. The Jacobin reign of terror is another example of terrorist violence of early years.

According to Edmund Burke terrorists are normally devoid of any logic and reasons for justifying any act of violence. Therefore, he sees a close link between a terrorist and an oppressor or an assassin and a murderer.[18] Some political scientists have defined terror as an act of continuous and systematic violence and coercion.

The 1937 Convention on the Prevention and Punishment of Terrorism describes acts of criminal conspiracy motivated with a purpose of creating harm to authenticity and legitimacy of state apparatus as terrorists' acts. [19] The convention laid a lot of emphasis on the safety and security of the innocent civilians as they fall easy prey to terrorist violence. The recommendations of the convention were logical, yet not taken seriously due to lack of a consensus on the interpretation. A similar explanation was brought forward by the United Nations in 1990 which defined terrorism as an act of violence intended to create extreme state of fear and anxiety. There has been mushrooming of a new set of definitions on terrorism particularly after attacks on World Trade Center and Pentagon. The European Union included acts such as assassination, hostage taking and use of indiscriminate bombings violent strikes aimed at altering the socio-political and economic institutions of a country in the new definitional interpretations. [20]

Neil J. Smelser in his famous work "Terrorism: Perspective from behavioural and Social Sciences quoted the U.S. Department of State's new definition. According to this definition terrorism is a "Premeditated, politically motivated violence perpetrated against noncombatant targets by sub national groups or clandestine agents, usually intended to influence an audience." Although Smelser agrees with broader framework of the new definition but criticises for its overemphasis on the terms like 'politically motivated', 'non combatant' and 'sub national.[21] This definition separates terrorism from other forms of violence on the basis of its being directed towards influencing the policy of the establishment, thus being political motivated. It does not include many acts of violence committed for personal reasons in its new framework of definition. New definition includes violence acts directed against innocent civilians. Besides, the new definition of terrorism propounded by the State Department only includes violence acts committed by non-state actors. This definition does not take into account political violence committed by a State in its criteria. Going by the complex nature of terrorists operations it is difficult to anticipate such threat in advance. Their clandestine methods of attack make them even deadlier. The methods employed by terrorists fall outside legal and social norms of a society. [22] Thus, giving enough basis to states to employ legal actions against the perpetrators of these unlawful activities.

The planned tactics of modern terrorism is different from the earlier version of more spontaneous acts of terrors. This strategic shift has lately added new dimension to the definitional framework of terrorism.[23]

The United States has defined terrorism under the Federal criminal code, 18 U.S.C. as: "Activities that involve violent or life-threatening acts, that are a violation of the criminal laws of the United States or of any State and appear to be intended (i) to intimidate or coerce a civilian population; (ii) to influence the policy of a government by intimidation or coercion; or (iii) to affect the conduct of a government by mass destruction, assassination, or kidnapping...." According to the United States Department of Defense Terrorism is: the "calculated use of unlawful violence to inculcate fear; intended to coerce or intimidate governments or societies in pursuit of goals that are generally political, religious, or ideological." This definition appears to be more balanced as it includes a broader canvas about terrorist methods and their targets. Whereas the definition includes ideological and religious factors but it does not attempt to draw the lines of demarcation between attacks on combatant and noncombatant military personnel.[24]

Prof Bruce Hoffman, a well known authority on the study of terrorism and author of *Inside Terrorism* has analysed the various aspects of the definition provided by the U.S. National Counterterrorism Center (NCTC) which described an act of terror as: "premeditated; perpetrated by a sub national or clandestine agent; politically motivated, potentially including religious, philosophical, or culturally symbolic motivations; violent; and perpetrated against a noncombatant target."

Hoffman further states that FBI or Federal Bureau of Investigation of the United States of America terrorism provided a new definition of terrorism which concedes "the unlawful use of force and violence against persons or property to intimidate or coerce a government, the civilian population, or any segment thereof, in furtherance of political or social objectives." The additional tinge of coercion and level of intimidation sets it apart from the rest.[25] Identification of targets, causes for motivation and methods of employing violence therefore remain main components of terrorism. The level of outside support and international linkages both in terms of arms and economic aid remain important parameters in judging the nature of trans-national terrorism.

A special committee/panel constituted by the UN on 17th March 2005 described terrorism as a strategy of employing violence with a purpose of sending danger signals in the minds of noncombatants (unarmed military and other official not on duty and unarmed innocent civilians).

Former Secretary-General Kofi Annan calls for strict actions by the states against the perpetrators of unlawful activities and terrorist violence. He also addressed the issue of mindless bombing and international financing. These definitions only described only a certain kind of violence as terrorism but did not adequately address the issue of ideological, motivational and political aims. Some strategic analysts view these interpretations as biased and inadequate as the issue of state sponsored terrorism was also not addressed in the definitions provided by these conventions. Besides, all these conventions overemphasized the need for law and law enforcement agencies without addressing the basic causes of terrorism.

European Union

Article 1 of the *Framework Decision on Combating Terrorism* (2002) prepared by the European Union to address the issue of terrorism defines it as an act of criminal offences that can pose serious threat to security and safety of a nation as well as international organizations. Terrorism is normally committed with a purpose of terrorizing and intimidating civil society, political institutions and international politics. Terrorists do not recognize territorial limitations, human rights, duties and socio-political and economic institution within and outside the country. The ultimate aim is to create a state of extreme anxiety and fear in much larger group of masses than the immediate targets. Thereby, insulating a sense of persisting fear and dither among people.

The definition of Daniel D. Novotny (2007) is not free from blemishes. He defines terrorism in a limited framework. According to him, terrorism is an act of violence directed towards innocent people committed either by an individual or a group of individual against legal jurisdiction of a country and aimed at creating fear. His definition of terrorism is limited as far as it only defines it in terms of non state actor. Walter Laqueur defines terrorism as an illegitimate use of force against people to achieve a political purpose. This definition has been criticized of its unnecessarily laying a lot of emphasis as what is legitimate use of force and what is illegitimate.[26]

Boaz Ganor definition is very similar to the definition of Walter Laqueur. Ganor defines terrorism in terms of deliberate use of violence targeted against innocent bystanders for achieving political aims.

Alex Peter Schmid provides a new dimension in the definitional framework of terrorism. According to him, "Terrorism is an anxiety inspiring method of repeated violent action, employed by (semi) clandestine individual, group or state acters, for idiosyncratic criminal or political reasons whereby — in contrast to assassination — the direct target of violence are not the main targets. The immediate human victims of violence are generally chosen randomly (targets of opportunity) or selectively (representative or symbolic target) from a target population, and serve as message generators. Threat and violence based communication processes between terrorist organization imperiled victims, and main targets are used to manipulate the main target. (Audience is) turning it into a target of terrorism, a target of demands, or a target of a attention, depending on whether intimidation, coercion or propaganda is primarily sought." [27]

Schmid further says that "Terrorism is a method in which random or symbolic victim become targets of violence. Through the previous use of violence or the credible threat of violence, other members of a group are put in a state of chronic fear (terrorism). The victimizations of the target is considered as meant to terrorize observers, which in turn, creates an audience beyond the target of terrorism or the act of terrorism. The purpose of terrorism is either to immobilize disorientation or compliance, or to mobilize secondary targets of demands or targets of attention."[28]

James M Lutz says terrorism a strategy that threatens violence to create a sense of fear in a target audience that extends beyond the immediate victims of violence. Therefore, the purpose is more psychological. According to him, it is difficult to ascertain the clear picture of the perpetrator of merciless violence as it is sometimes sponsored by the non state actor or sometimes by state actors. Another important objective of terrorism is to enhance the ability to capture power. A terrorist therefore, makes all attempts to justify use of violence by acquiring power.[29] Terrorists often employ violence for attainment of political aims. The penchant of change in the cruel and dictatorial regime/political leadership is portrayed as the sole reason for justification of illegal acts. In such cases there is a difference between the immediate victim and the targeted people. [30] At times terrorist justify the illegitimate use of use of violence against a corrupt political establishment responsible for the miseries of the people at large. This is done to create mass base for their actions. The US Committee on Combating terrorism commissioned RAND Foundation, a leading think tank on strategic planning of the US based at Washington, DC. The RAND commission included politically motivated kidnapping and murder in the definition of terrorism. The Foundation appeared to be more concerned about the intensity of violence and the purpose of the violence thereby giving more importance to the psychological motives behind an act of terror. This perception did not pay much importance to the perpetrators of violence and identification of victims. The matter of concern here was the purpose behind creating alarming situation. The purpose of destruction was therefore given precedence over destruction and level of destruction. The capability to send out symbolic messages of a terrorist act therefore, became the talisman of comprehending and defining terrorism. [31]

According to Brian Jenkins terrorists want wide spread publicity. The number of people watching their act of terror is more important than the number of people left dead."[32] Terrorism is also defined as an action of causing harm to government, individual and group of individuals or it is designed to damage property public order. These days terrorists find maiming, lynching, bombing, kidnapping, hijacking, poisoning of substances and chemical and biological attacks as important components of their strategies. Terrorism is also intended to cause panic among general masses about the inability of political system to provide security.

RELIGIOUS TERRORISM

Former Harvard University Prof Samuel P. Huntington in his book on the Clash of Civilizations observed that future generation is bound to would witness increasing level of conflict on the bases of religious and cultural differences. He conceded that cultural and religious causes will lead to more violence than political and economic reasons. Nations and various organizations will gradually be at loggerhead with each other due to religious and cultural differences. This will ultimately lead to the emergence of violence-based religious movements and ultimately clashes of civilizations. Due to globalization there will be increasing mass mobilization on the bases of cultural and religious identities for achieving political ambitions. This is not a new phenomenon. History is full of instances where attempts to garner political support based on religious differences have led to the outbreak of tremendous violence.[33]

Since mid-eighties of twentieth century there has been unprecedented rise in the instances of religious based conflicts. Groups increasingly started identifying themselves with religion for justification of their illegitimate activities. The blunt declaration of religious sanctions by clergies provided boost to newly emerging militant groups. Their violent acts were justified on the bases of the misinterpretation of sacred texts. Terrorism based on religion led to the emergence of the worst form of terrorism both in its modus operandi and intensity. Barbaric and indiscriminate acts of violence were portrayed as the most desirable acts of their divine mission and an important part of executing almighty's will.[34] The rise of religious terrorism saw a smooth sailing as it helped people began identifying themselves with each other for justification of their grievances. Terrorists found religion as the most potent substances for achieving success as it helped them to convey their message to a larger audience. The skill of powerful oratory to deliver the religious sermons left an indelible impression on the minds of the people. Smart terrorists started linking religion with all heinous acts of killing for garnering larger support.[35] There has been a close relationship between terrorism and religion. During 68 A.D there have been numerous attempts of selective murder and large scale massacre by Zealot, a Jewish Sect which vehemently resisted the occupation campaign of Romans. A radical group of Shia Muslims from Iran and Syria lashed out a series of violent attempts against the occupation of their territory by Christian crusaders. A bunch of murderers and looters right from early sixth century onwards drove their motivation from the traditional Hindu custom of sacrificial offerings to Ma Kali. The portrayal of an act of Thug as sacrifice was a pretext of getting justification for illegal and immoral acts. The attempts to provide a linkage between religion and swindling activities remained an important strategy of the Thugs in India even during eighteenth and nineteenth centuries. The post Cold War period witnessed misuse of religion and ethnicity by the strategists. The forces of bigotry and hatred were used by blocks to pursue their strategic interests. The problem became worse after Soviet intervention of Afghanistan in 1979. The US and its allies Cold War strategy and appeasement policy towards fundamentalist forces worked as a base for organizing international terrorists organization the Al Qaeda.

It is ironical that now devastation of America has become the ultimate goal of Al Qaeda. The world is already witnessing sharp increase in the incidence of religiously motivated terrorist attacks. Media hype has further provided psychological strength and motivation to modern terrorists. There have been many instances where Muslims and the West Asia started getting linked with the increasing tentacles of terrorism. Islam started getting its distorted pictures portrayed by a few bands of mindless murderers. Similarly, a few other comparatively smaller groups and cults started committing crime by portraying distorted versions of Christianity, Judaism, Hinduism, etc.[36] The Sarin gas attack in Tokyo subway by the followers of the Aum Shinrikyo sect and the attempts of bombing and assassination in America by the American Christian White Supremacist Patriot movement are some important offshoots of the deeply rooted religious terrorism. The ethnic, nationalist, separatist and the leftist terrorists are gradually getting replaced by a new breed of religious terrorists. Because misinterpretation of religion has provided them most sought after legitimacy for carrying out the most heinous crime against innocent civilians and nations. Consequently, there has been a manifold rise in the number of religion-based terrorist groups and instances of such attacks. [37]

Anyone who is not a member of their religion or religious sect may be "evil". They consider non members to be infidels. Religious terrorists are not constrained by secular values or laws. Indeed the very target of the attacks may be the secular society which is endorsed by the modern states. They also give an impression of alienation from the existing social system. They are not trying to correct the system, rather they are trying to replace it.[38] Religious terrorism is especially much pondered over issue and troublesome because of its dispersed popular support prevalent in civil society. Groups such as Al Qaeda have found support from some Muslim foundations throughout the world, making it truly a worldwide network.

In his book *Inside Terrorism*, Bruce Hoffman writes that for the religious terrorist, violence is first and foremost a sacramental act or divine duty executed in direct response to some theological demand or imperative. Terrorism thus presumes an inspirational aspect, and its executors are unimpeded by the political, moral or practical restrictions that may affect other terrorists. [39]

Difference Between Religious and Secular Terrorist Organizations

Hoffman presents a detailed analysis of difference between secular and religious organizations and their motives. He also explains the tactics these organizations are resorting to. Secular terrorists generally try categorized killing because selective violence is consonant with their political aims and objectives, whereas religious terrorists often hunt for the eradication of categories of enemies. The large-scale violence is not only morally justified by them but it also acts as a necessary means for the accomplishment of their goals. The sacred texts and clerical authorities legitimize the mass violence. This explains that clerical consent is important to religious terrorists and religious figures are often required to 'bless' terrorist operations before they are executed. Article 7 of the covenant of the Hamas states, "The time (of redemption) will not come until the Muslims fight the Jews and kill them, and until the Jews hide behind rocks and trees when the call is raised, Oh, Muslim, here is a Jew hiding! Come and kill him."[40]

Religious and secular terrorists also differ in their constituencies. Secular terrorists attempt to plead to a constituency that is composed of actual sympathizers, members of the communities whom they 'defend' or the aggrieved people for whom they claim to speak for. But religious terrorists are occupied in the so called 'a total war.' They seek to plead to no other constituency than themselves. Therefore, the chains on violence that are forced on secular terrorists by the desire to appeal to a supportive or indifferent constituency are not significant to the religious terrorist. Moreover, this nonexistence of a constituency in the secular terrorist sense leads to a sanctioning of almost limitless violence. This gives the explanation regarding the 'oratory' common to 'holy terror' manifestos describing persons outside the terrorists' religious community as infidels. The determined use of such terminology to justify terrorism has become significant as it wears away control on violence by portraying the terrorists' victims unworthy of living.[41]

Religious and secular terrorists also have dissimilar opinion of themselves and their violent acts. Religious terrorists see themselves as 'outsiders' seeking changes in the existing order. The secular terrorists regard violence necessary for the rectification of a defect in a system. They regard violence good for the creation of a new system. This sense of marginalization enables the religious terrorist to be far more destructive and use deadly types of terrorist operations than secular terrorists, and indeed to embrace a far more open-ended category of 'enemies' for attack. [42] To the religious terrorists, the present world order is unjust and a challenge and insult to God's will on earth. It cannot be reformed through any progressive measures or through conciliation and compromise. The system, cannot be improved, it must be swept aside.[43]

The religious terrorists don't have to overcome the hurdle to mass murder that other secular terrorists do. The secularist terrorists all use violence for its symbolic or demonstrative value. The IRA's success against the British government in the 1990s was non lethal terrorism: they issued warnings, in some cases they disrupted mass transit, they had big bombs in downtown areas, they pulled in on Saturday morning that is opposed to religious terrorists that hit the World Trade Center exactly when everybody was arriving for work or explode a bomb outside of Oklahoma City Murrah building exactly when people were arriving for work, or attack at Luxor exactly when it was most filled with tourists. These are two very different mindsets. Once they have made the commitment to violence, religious terrorists have less compunction about inflicting mass violence compared to secular terrorists. It is because of the legitimization and justification of liturgy that creates a mentality out of religious order where anybody is fair target. Muslims were killed in Kenya and Tanzania; Muslims were killed in the World Trade Center, in the Pentagon attacks. Bin Laden has made a distinction between good and bad Muslims. With secular groups, there is still some hesitation in inflicting justification of religion, saying there are good or bad Muslims, the bad ones are therefore fair game.[44]

One of the biggest ideological differences between religious and secular terrorists is their definition of the enemy, while secular terrorists see their opponents as representatives of a certain socioeconomic order or regime; Islamist terrorists espouse a broader definition.[45]

Terrorism and Islam

The contemporary revival of religious terrorism is chiefly acknowledged with trends in the Muslim world. Today, the image of Islam as created by the Western media is that of a religion of violence. Many Muslims identify themselves as victims rather than assailants. It should also be kept in mind that the people of Islam had suffered from inequality and injustice imposed on them.[46] The terrorist forces are seeking justification for their cause by referring to unresolved conflicts like Arab-Israel and Kashmir conflict. An Islamic practice that is mainly responsible for the current violence and intolerance is Jehad. Fundamentalists argue that Jehad is an obligation on all Muslims of the world. Al Qaeda also urged all Muslims to join Jehad against the USA and to attack Washington's interests around the world. "From today onwards, the Islamic nation would not keep silent. Jehad today is a duty of every Muslim," Al Qaeda spokesman has been quoted by Al-Jazeera TV. [47] In Koran, violence is justified if it is carried out to fight injustice or against infidels. The faithful and so called 'true Muslims' are in permanent struggle against the non-Muslim world.

Islamic movements demanding independence are mainly sponsored by the hard core groups having blind faith in their religious ideology. International terrorism is the design of these Jehadi groups. Several terrorist organizations have emerged in the zones of conflict. There is rise in the number of fundamentalist organizations in Kashmir Valley also which are largely supported by Pakistan. Several Pan Islamic terrorist organizations are running a number of training camps. Organizations like Jamaat-i- Islami, Muslim United Front, Jaish-e- Mohammad etc. raised the slogan of Jihad against India. The Kashmiri version of Islam was very tolerant and believed in the indigenous culture. But the fundamentalist groups replaced the local Kashmiri Muslim Imams and inducted the rigid and extremist Imams. The wide network of mosques was taken over by the Islamic extremists and consequently used to spur Kashmiri Muslims for Jihad. During the first phase of militancy in Kashmir which started in 1989, the Islamist militant groups strived to 'bring structural changes at cultural levels, seeking to Islamicise the socio –political set up in the valley to bring in tune with the Islamic state of Pakistan and the Muslim Ummah. The Islamist orientation of insurgency in Kashmir became more pronounced after the terrorist organizations like Hizbul Mujahideen, Lashkar-e- Taiba etc. launched a religious crusade against the non- Muslims and have been taking pride for killing Hindus in the name of Jihad. These outfits have also been threatening the Hindu pilgrims against their participation in the annual pilgrimage to the holy Amar Nath cave. They have resorted to mine blast and firing upon the Hindu pilgrims on numerous occasions.[48]

Suicide terrorism, an instrument of Jehad, has emerged as the most powerful tactic in the hands of Islamist terrorists today. Historically, it has been extremely infrequent. Nonetheless, it has been increasing now at an alarming rate in Islamic terrorist organizations, it has also spread among and beyond entirely secular groups like the Tamil Tigers to others like the Kurdish PKK. Also, there is an intimate connection between terrorism's overall increasing levels of lethality and the growing incidence of suicide bombings.

The phenomenon of martyrdom terrorism can be traced back to the Assassins, an off-shoot of the Shia Ismaili movement, who some 700 years ago waged a protracted struggle against the European Crusaders' attempted conquest of the Holy Land. The Assassins embraced an ethos of self-sacrifice, where martyrdom was regarded as a sacramental act—a highly desirable aspiration and divine duty commanded by religious text and communicated by clerical authorities that are evident today. An important additional motivation was the promise that the martyr would feel no pain in the commission of the sacred act and would then ascend immediately to a glorious heaven.[49]

The major Islamist terror approach has been the suicide bombs. The role of suicide bombers have been increasing in the religious terrorist organizations especially in the name of Jihad. The Islamic terrorists largely adopted the suicide bombing strategy to target maximum number of civilians they could kill. The other groups generally threaten hostages against concrete demands, Islamists seek to kill first and address later. The 9-11 hijackers, for example, resisted U.S. air traffic control attempts to communicate because their goal was not a wish to transmit demands but rather the desire to kill as many people as possible. Suicide bombers insist that 'martyrdom operations' are necessary to fulfil one's commitment to God They are focused to engage in Jihad and the need to embrace martyrdom to achieve liberation and end justice.[50]

There is also another school which does not regard religion responsible for suicide bombing. Rather political objective and strategy are major reasons for it. Pape makes two major assumptions about suicide bombing: first, that it is motivated primarily by resistance to foreign occupation and, second, that religious ideology has only a minor role in suicide attacks perpetrated by Muslims. The suicide bombers kill themselves only as a means to an end, using suicide only "to outbid rival militias through the use of shocking tactics" and, in the Palestinian case, to "compete for leadership." According to Pape and Bloom, strategy and political objectives rather than religion are the primary incentive for suicide attacks.[51] Robert Pape argues that Islam has little to do with suicide bombing. Rather suicide bombers are motivated much more by tactical goals. He put besides the suicide terrorism of the Liberation Tigers of Tamil Eelam (LTTE) with Islamist suicide bombing to demonstrate that a desire to end occupation is the common factor rather than religion.[52]

The war against the enemies of Islam is not limited by time, territory, or a specific socioeconomic agenda, and it is being waged against an entire culture and civilization. The religious heads give orders in the name of religion against the infidels and the people largely follow them. Bin Laden himself did not have any theological credentials, yet he issued *fatwas* because he knew people will listen to them. The clerical figures in Islam, Judaism, in Christian Churches in the United States, use liturgy to justify violence. Ben Laden did it on September 11th. He was the first one to use and manipulate religion to justify higher levels of lethality and he achieved it. Osama Bin Laden established Al Qaeda during 1990. The organization helped finances, recruits, transports and trains sunni Islamic extremists for the Afghan resistance. Its current goal is to re establish the Muslim state throughout the world. The organization works with allied Islamic extremists groups to overthrow regimes it considers and deem non Islamic and to remove westerners from Muslim countries. The organization reminds the Muslim world about their sufferings because of aggression and injustice. Wahhabi Islam has also become unifying ideology for Islamist warriors as many young Muslims have responded to its message.

Sikh Terrorism

The bloodshed which occurred in Punjab, provides indication of the relationship between terror and religion. Bhindarwale, the Sikh leader, launched the terrorist movement in the state. He publically urged his followers to commit violent acts. A series of assassination of prominent Nirankari and Hindu leaders followed. The Sikhs aimed at gaining independence from India and establishing the state of Khalistan. Pakistan got actively involved in supporting terrorism in the state in 1983 when it began supplying AK-47 rifles to the groups. An estimated 20,000 persons have been killed as a result of Sikh violence during the past decade. The Sikh attacks were largely indiscriminate in character.[53] The 1984 Blue Star Operation by the army in the Golden Temple resulted in the death of more than 4000 innocent people. Large number of Sikhs became alienated from India. Gradually end of terrorism in the state came in 1995. The following table shows the rising number of casualties due to terrorist attack in Punjab.

Year	*Casualties*
1981	13
1982	13
1983	75

Contd....

Contd....

1984	359
1985	63
1986	520
1987	901
1988	1949
1989	1168
1990	2467
1991	2586
1992	1461

Christian and Jewish Terrorism

The bombing of Murrah federal building in Oklahoma by right wing extremist Americans in 1995 depicts their anti-state views. These organizations stand for the accomplishment of religious and racial cleansing of their countries. In fact, the removal of whole segment of society is a major objective of the White Christian groups as well as Jewish terrorist organizations. In 1984, a group of Israelis were convicted of plotting to blow up the Dome of Rock in Jerusalem, Islam's third holiest shrine. Similarly the Christian organizations of the U.S.A. aimed at the racial and religious purification of their country from the Jews. Violence is not only sanctioned but divinely decreed. Similarly the Jewish terrorism repeatedly made it clear to their leaders that they could not implement the group's battle plans without rabbinical blessings.[54]

CONCLUSION

The religious terrorism has steadily become more influential than the past. Religious terrorists are increasingly becoming dangerous to international community and there are many reasons attributed to it. Religious terrorists are engaged in a struggle of good against evil, us against them, implying random human targets. There are no ethical limits of the brutal acts when it acquires a religious nature. With morality, it gets a certificate for the merciless killings of the people other than their religion. Men never do sin so cheerfully as when they do it from religious conviction.

REFERENCES

1. Kamran Arif, "The establishment of a Taliban Emirate", *Himal*, Vol.22, 2009. pp. 29-33.
2. Manzoor Ali Shah , "Mullah Radio", *Himal,* Vol. 22, 2009. p. 34.
3. John Cherian , "Axis of terror", *Frontline,* Dec. 19, 2009. p. 127.
4. Bruce Hoffman, "Terrorism Trends and Prospects" in Ian O. Lesser..., ed., *Combating the New Terrorism,* RAND, Santa Monica, 1999. p. 8.
5. *Ibid.* 9
6. *Ibid.* 10
7. *Ibid.* pp. 13-18.
8. John Cherian, "Sparks of Seperatism", *Frontline,* July 31, 2009. pp. 132-133.
9. Jasjit Singh, 'Strategic Context of Terrorism', in Wilson John and Swati Parashar, eds., *Terrorism in Southeast Asia: Implications for South Asia,* Delhi, Pearson Longman, 2005. p. 20.
10. Tore Bjorgo, *Root Causes of Terrorism: Myths, reality and ways forward,* Routledge, Oxon, 2005. p. 70.
11. Sudhir Hindwan, "Challenges of Trans-National Terrorism", *Man & Development,* Vol.XXXV, No. 3, 2003. p.67.
12. Bruce Hoffman, *Inside Terrorism*, Columbia University Press, 2006, p.23.
13. Amrith Rohan Parera, *International Terrorism,* Vikas Pub. House, New Delhi, 1997. p.11.
14. 'The Definition of Terrorism, *A Guide for Delegates,* Cambridge International Model United Nations XIII, 2007. p.3.
15. Jordan J. Paust, "A Definitional Focus", in Yonah Alexander & Seymour Maxwell Finger eds., *Terrorism: Interdisciplinary Perspectives,* The John Jay Press, New York, 1977. p. 19.
16. *Ibid.,* pp. 19-20.
17. Joshua Sinai, "How to Define Terrorism", Perspectives on Terrorism, Volume II, Issue 4, 2008.
18. Joseph S. Tuman, *Communicating terror: The Rhetorical Dimensions of Terrorism*, Sage Publications, 2010. p.6.

19. Walter Laqueur, *No End to War,* Continuum International Publishing Group Inc, New York, 2004. p. 233.
20. *IBID.* p.234.
21. Neil J Smelser, *Terrorism: Perspectives from the Behavioral and Social Sciences,* The National Academies Press, Washington DC, 2000. p. 14.
22. *Ibid.*
23. Bruce Hoffman, *Inside Terrorism*, Columbia University Press, 2006. p. 32.
24. *Ibid.* p. 33.
25. *Ibid.* p. 32.
26. James M. Lutz, Brenda J. Lutz, *Global Terrorism,* Routledge, 2004. p. 9.
27. Alex P. Schmid, "The Response Problem as a Definition problem", in Alex P. Schmid and Ronald D. Crelinsten eds., *Western Responses to Terrorism,* Frank Cass Publishers, Oxon, 1993. p.8.
28. Farhad Mehdiyev, "Legal Policing Responses to Terrorist Operations" in Huseyin Durmaz edt. *Understanding and responding to Terrorism,* IOS Press, Amsterdam, 2007. p. 208.
29. James M. Lutz, Brenda J. Lutz, *Global Terrorism,* Routledge, 2004. p. 9.
30. *Ibid.* p.10.
31. Arnab Goswami, *Combating Terrorism: The Legal Challenge,* Har-Anand Publications, New Delhi, 2002. pp. 31-34.
32. Cited in Arnab Goswami, *Combating Terrorism: The Legal Challenge,* Har-Anand Publications, New Delhi, 2002. p. 31.
33. C.P. Bhambhari, "Globalization and Neo-Premordialism", in Mahavir Singh, eds., *International Terrorism and Religious Extremism,* Anamika Publishers, New Delhi, 2004. pp. 23-24.
34. Aref M. Al-Khattar, *Religion and Terrorism: An Interfaith Perspective,* Praeger, New York, 2003. p.5.
35. The interview with Dr. Bruce Hoffman by Religioscope that took place in Washington on 21 November 2001. He was interviewed by Jean-François Mayer.

36. Aref M. Al-Khattar, *Religion and Terrorism: An Interfaith Perspective,* Praeger, New York, 2003. pp. 6-7.
37. Bruce Hoffman, *Inside Terrorism,* Columbia University Press, New York, 2006. p. 88.
38. Audrey Kurth Cronin, "Behind the Curve: Globalization and International Terrorism", *International Security,* Vol. 27, No. 3,pp. 41-42. http://www.jstor.org/stable/3092113 Accessed: 29/09/2009
39. Bruce Hoffman, *Inside Terrorism,* Columbia University Press, New York, 2006. *p.*89.
40. *Ibid.*, p. 92.
41. *Ibid.*, p.89.
42. *Ibid.*
43. K.P.S. Gill, 'Introduction' in K.P.S. Gill and Ajai Sahni, eds., *The Global Threat of Terror,*New Delhi, 2002. p.190.
44. The interview with Dr. Bruce Hoffman by Religioscope that took place in Washington on 21 November 2001. He was interviewed by Jean-François Mayer.
45. Jonathan Fine, "Contrasting Secular and Religious Terrorism", *Middle East Quarterly,* 2008. pp. 59-69
46. Walter Laqueur, *The new terrorism: fanaticism and the arms of mass destruction, OUP,* New York, 1999. p.128.
47. M.G. Chitkara, *Combating Terrorism,* APH, New Delhi, 2003. p.131.
48. K. Warikoo, "Religious Extremism and Terrorism in Kashmir", in Mahavir Singh, eds., *International Terrorism and Religious Extremism,* Anamika Publishers, New Delhi, 2004. pp.251-259.
49. http://joe.sagepub.com
50. James William Jones, *Blood that cries out from the earth: the psychology of religious terrorism,* Oxford University Press, New York, 2008. p.8.
51. Jonathen Fine, "Contrasting Secular and Religious Terrorism", *Middle East Quarterly,* Winter 2008. http://www.meforum.org/1826/
52. *Ibid.*
53. Bruce Hoffman, "Holy Terror: The Implications of Terrorism motivated by a religious imperative", Rand, C.A., 1993. p. 10.
54. *Ibid.*, pp.8-9.

2

New Tools of Terrorism

NEXUS BETWEEN TERRORISTS AND DRUG MAFIA

The cultivation and distribution of narcotics is the biggest originator of political violence and crime in the world. Earnings from these sources are being used to fund and arm terrorists and insurgents. The revenue generated by organized crime offers a stable flow of money for terrorist groups and organizations. A peep in the world of narcotic trafficking reveals that many actors like local farmers, criminals, transnational networks and militant organizations are occupied in drug smuggling to generate resources to maintain their radical movements. These groups are not cut off from each other and operate at different stages. The link between different international criminal organizations is multifaceted. Many things are involved like linking funds, geography, politics, arms and tactics to craft a mutually beneficial relationship. It has been confirmed that a considerable portion of the incomes of different terrorist organizations come from selling drugs in different parts of the world. The relationship between crime and terrorism is particularly observed where three aspects unite which are poverty, a weak state and corruption. The nexus between crime and terrorism has received much attention today. After 9/11, the international community has found out more about the narco-terrorist links and terrorist financing angles in Columbia, Afghanistan, Morocco, Europe, South East Asia and other parts of the world.

The term 'Narco- Terrorism' was first used by former Peruvian President Belaunde Terry in 1983 to describe terrorist type attacks against his nation's anti-narcotics police by the Shining Path Marxist rebels. Later in 1986, former U.S. President Ronald Reagen also spoke of 'Narco-Terrorism' when referring to purported links between international drug trafficking and terrorism.[1]

Terrorism and Drug Traffickers have a symbolic connection. They are linked by money, strategy, geography and politics. Both of them use more or less same kind of methods to achieve their criminal ends. Many drug trafficking organizations are involved in various kinds of acts which are terror in nature such as killing, abduction, blasting etc. People often believe that religious revolutionaries do not involve themselves with drug traffickers, but it has been argued that Morality is situational and is applied when it best serves the need of the terrorists.[2]

Terrorist groups are mainly fascinated with the drug trade because of the prospective returns. The international drug trade generates large amount of revenue, making drugs the most profitable illegal activity. Not only funds are generated through selling the product, drugs also provide many different opportunities of making money like taxing farmers and local interest groups, and providing sanctuary for its secure production, trade, and distribution. Groups like the Afghan Taliban, the Columbian FARC, and the Lebanese Hezbollah generate significant resources from the extortion fees they collect from drug cartels and poppy or coca farmers operating in their territory.

Major Drug Producing Regions of the World

Golden Triangle

The major narco producing region are Myanmar, Laos and Thailand popularly known as the 'Golden Triangle'. The market of this triangle is in the North America, North Asia and Australia. The main producer country in the Golden Triangle is Burma, currently accounting for approximately 92 per cent of the heroin that is refined in the region. Over 60 per cent of the world's current poppy cultivation and opium production takes place in Burma. Laos remains the third largest producer of illicit opiates in the world after Burma and Afghanistan, accounting for approximately 7 per cent of the Triangle's total heroin output. Opium is mostly grown by small-scale farmers. Thailand currently accounts for less than 1 per cent of illicit opium in the region. But it remains important as a passage state for the trafficking of drugs and centre for illicit money laundering operations. Most refining of opium takes place in laboratories located in the Shan regions of eastern Burma that border China, Laos, and Thailand.[3] In smuggling heroin beyond the region, both India and Bangladesh are used as transit points, and this aggravates the problems related to narco terrorism in the region. In fact, a serious trouble arising out of the coming together of two major narco producing regions is the bolstering of an association between insurgent groups and narco terrorism. Such affiliation is visible in the Thai-Myanmar and Bangladesh-Myanmar borders. The insurgent groups of these areas do not themselves engage in narco production or narco trafficking, instead they tax and exhort money from the traffickers while providing them protection for drug trafficking.

Heroin from the Golden Triangle is consumed by the Asia-Pacific region which has major passage routes to Europe and North America. The increase in consumption within the region has also resulted in the regional insecurity because of terrorist criminal nexus. There is an increasing apprehension that Southeast Asia could soon collapse due to the "narco-terrorist" course already taken by a number of South American countries. The region has many ethnic and religious extremist organizations that are seeking new ways to finance their revolutionary activities. Although bank robberies and kidnappings can be lucrative, drug trafficking is a far more successful and reliable means of quickly generating cash for arms, foreign expertise, communications, and other logistical equipment.

Golden Crescent

The Golden Crescent is the name given to the Middle East's area of illicit opium production, covering three nations — Afghanistan, Iran, and Pakistan, whose mountainous fringes characterize the crescent shape. A broader geographic description describes the Golden Crescent area as extending from South West Asia to Turkey. At the region's core is Afghanistan (world's largest producer of opium poppy), with Pakistan and Iran lying in its borders. The real problem began in the 1980's when heroin traffickers started exporting heroin outside the region. The impact of Afghanistan's poppies is global, not just national.

Afghanistan is on the verge of turning into a narco-state as the government is unable to receive obedience in the southern Pashtun region. Heroin production got an advance because of the prospective opium farming by Central Asian countries like Uzbekistan and Tazakistan. The Taliban regime of Afghanistan had encouraged opium production and collected tax from opium dealers. The cultural bonds between the tribesmen on both sides of the Afghan border provide the trans-national link which safeguards the passage. Afghan politicians have also time and again indicated a direct linkage between drug traffickers and insurgents. They have referred to collaboration between drug trade and terrorism and observed that 'the question of drugs is one that will determine Afghanistan's future. If we fail to fight drugs, we will eventually fail as a state and we will fall back into the hands of terrorism'.[4] The narcotic traders get good hold up from militant groups in Afghanistan.

Pakistan is one of the world's principal drug transit countries. Smuggling, money laundering, *hawala*, remain common methods used to launder money and finance terrorism in Pakistan. Pakistan's porus borders are easy to infiltrate. The failed state is also responsible for drug trafficking. The uncontrolled charities in Pakistan provide a major source of illicit funds for international terrorist networks. Under the mask of madrassas, terrorist organizations get financial support in the name of Islamic education.[5] There are many small markets just outside the tribal belt in NWFP, where the Pakistan Government's law is not effective.

India lies stranded between the three largest opium producers in the world, Afghanistan, Pakistan and Myanmar. India shares a 2747 km border with Pakistan, 1634 km with Myanmar, 4127 km with Bangladesh and 1751 km with Nepal, thus making an appropriate passageway for narcotics trade. There exists a narco link between the drug smugglers from Pakistan and the Punjab terrorists in India. The Indian states of Madhya Pradesh, Rajasthan and Uttar Pradesh are known as poppy growing areas. New Delhi has been a centre for the heroin products brought from these neighbouring states and transported to the other countries. North east too, has emerged as a major link in the narco trade and consumption. The Naga-Kuki violence has its roots in the drug trade. The main reason for conflict is primarily to gain control over the drug smuggling route.

Drug smugglers are also being used by the ISI for smuggling arms and explosives into India. It is reported that ISI's major network is built around these drug smugglers and organized crime. "More than 25 per cent of the money spent on terrorist activities in India by the ISI comes from the narcotics drug trade," said M K Sharma, NCB Zonal Director, Jammu and Kashmir.[6] The Indo-Pak border is also used extensively for transporting narcotics first to India and then to other countries. Militancy in Jammu and Kashmir and smuggling of narcotic have mutually complimented each other's requirement *i.e.*, need for easy money. Terrorism has been largely funded in Jammu and Kashmir by the cultivation and sale of cannabis in South Kashmir and the pumping in of narcotics by Pakistan's Inter Services Intelligence (ISI). The sale of narcotics has been the main source of funding of terrorists by Pakistan in Jammu and Kashmir since 1989.[7] In south Kashmir districts of Pulwama and Anantnag, cannabis is cultivated and licenses have been issued to cultivators in the areas, but they "misuse" it. The geography of the region gives it ample scope to have a good crop of cannabis which grows wild in these areas. In January 2002, Phagwara police arrested five persons including two surrendered militants of Hizbul Mujahideen with 20 kgs of charas. In May 2003, the Narcotics Control Bureau, Delhi arrested Mohammed Amin Jaffer of Bijbehara, Ananatnag who is an active member of Al Jehad outfit with 25 kgs of charas. There is a strong nexus between terrorists and narcotics in J&K.

South America

The Tri border area in South America where Argentina, Brazil and Paraguay meet is known for drug trading. The region is popular among smugglers and is abode to the Arab drug trafficking gangs that move cocaine from South America to Europe and the Middle East. Some of their profits are reportedly ending up with radical groups such as Hamas and Hezbollah. The rewarding drug trade could become an unlimited source of cheap and easy revenue for terrorist groups. The major drug Andean groups are Columbia's FARC and Peruvian Shining Path (Sendero Luminoso). Columbian right wing terrorists also have strong bonds with drug traffickers and have been known by the name of their umbrella organization, the United Self Defense Forces of Columbia (AUC). The drug-related money of these rural-based terrorists comes primarily from the taxes which they levy on the traffickers in return for the protection they give to the illegal plantations. These organizations have produced and transported drugs, usually cocaine.[8]

The two major insurgent groups of Columbia, FARC and ELN, are connected to drug trafficking through an adhoc 'alliance of inconvenience' with drug trafficking organizations.[9] The relationship between drug traffickers and insurgents in Columbia is marked by both cooperation and conflict. Columbia's geographical location, diverse terrain and climate are important elements contributing to the country's illicit drug industry. Pacific and Caribbean drug smuggling routes are available to Columbian traffickers. Buenaventura is believed to be the most important Pacific coast port used by Columbian traffickers to export cocaine and to import the essential chemicals. These units operate in Sierra Nevada and Perija mountains which are the traditional cannabis growing areas. FARC units also operate in Columbia's north west border with Panama, Llanos and eastern low lands are known for coca cultivation and cocaine processing. The ELN operates along Columbia's north eastern border with Venezuela. Territory under ELN influence includes Columbia's traditional cannabis cultivation areas. FARC and ELN extort revolutionary taxes from drug traffickers operating in areas under their control.[10]

Other insurgent groups which have appeared or are prevalent in Columbia are M-19 (19th of April Movement), EPL (Popular Liberation Army), Simon Bolivar National Guerrilla coordinating Board.

Link between Terrorist Outfits and Drug Traffickers

Many terrorists groups control the territories where the narcotics are cultivated. Terrorist organizations are believed to have links with the drug traffickers and many are engaged in the financial and other forms of crime. Taliban regime controlled parts of Afghanistan where heroin was produced and taxed the cultivators and the transporters of opium. Al Qaeda is also deeply involved in drug trafficking. Many believe that business model for Al Qaeda's drug trafficking quest is FARC.[11] Hizbullah justified its participation in the drug trade as a means of not only funding terrorism, but also in putting forward the cause of Islam by weakening western societies through drug addiction. Drug trafficking is a major money maker for Hezbollah. It cooperates with the FARC or with the "Abadan drug ring", an Iranian drug network, allowing them to use the Hezbollah-controlled drug routes in Lebanon to transport heroin and opium from Iran and Afghanistan to Europe and North Africa. The Islamic Movement of Uzbekistan (IMU) also is very active in this drug trade to finance its activities.[12] Its leader, Juma Namangani was actively involved in drug smuggling and used his network of IMU militants in Central Asia and his links with the Chechen militants to increase his trade. Allegations were also levelled that 60 per cent of Afghan opium export passed through Central Asia and that IMU might be responsible for 70 per cent of the heroin and opium transiting the area. The armed ethnic groups in Myanmar controlled the flow of narcotics from Myanmar and the armed Islamic groups taxed and control organized crime networks regulating the flow of narcotics from Afghanistan. The Kosovo Liberation Army and Kurdish Workers Party play a significant role in the transportation of narcotics and protection of organized criminal networks in the European area. Two major West European Terrorist Groups, The Basque Fatherland and Liberty Organization (ETA) and the Irish Republican Army of

Northern Ireland have been involved in Arms and Narcotics trafficking in recent years. Both have been linked with narco terrorist organization in Los Angeles, particularly the FARC. Abu Sayyaf group exploits marijuana plantations in Philippines.

LTTE Tigers in Sri Lanka employed this method of drug business, to meet the costs of their struggle. The main drugs involved are mandrax and heroin. Initially, the drug business began as a small activity limited to Tamil Nadu but has today extended. The local agents made use of the Tamil Nadu fishermen to transport drugs. The LTTE also has links to the Golden Triangle and the Golden crescent. It is deeply involved in massive drug trafficking with the Burmese regime in making and distributing heroin. The Tigers are allowed to train at military bases in Southern Burma in return for supplying couriers for the worldwide smuggling of Burmese heroin.

It is also argued that the LTTE is directly involved with the Burmese regime in making and distributing heroin. The direct evidence of close collaboration between Burma and the Tamil Tigers has been revealed.

Today groups engaged in terrorism and organized crime operate together. These relationships have helped the terrorists groups to be less dependent on the state sponsors. They now depend on their domestic and international supporters. The nexus between terrorist organization and criminal networks has strengthened. The lines between organized crime, drug trafficking and terrorism are becoming blurred. Terrorist organizations are now looking forward towards organized crime and are also resorting to the tactics of Multi National Companies to generate huge amount of money. Contemporary Trans National Crime is on an increase and Narco terrorism is an instance of collaboration of organized crime with terrorism. Many terrorists group have generated huge amount of revenue from video and CD piracy, credit card scams and business in phone cards. These organizations are operating through different networks in major part of the globe. A large proportion of 'back money' is being used to breed smuggling networks and narcotic cartels. An examination of emerging trends in organized crime specify that most groups with the national reach are involved in illegitimate business like narcotics and alien smuggling, abduction etc. and on the other hand, a majority of the groups with a global reach are involved in semi-legitimate businesses; example, manufacturing, CD piracy etc. These groups have started acquiring new technologies and in not lacking in communication network. Smugglers and terrorists have also come together in the illegal international migration. The international migration has increased manifold. Terrorists and criminals use ships to smuggle humans. Organized crime groups that are often linked to terrorists groups control narcotic distribution. Narcotics trafficking is a major source of revenue for terrorists and organized crime networks, particularly groups with trans-state reach.

Terrorist organizations need money and resources not only to carry out operations but also to recruit, maintain safe havens, travel, take care of day-to-day expenses and to provide money to the families of the dead martyrs. The assets required to fund such extensive global operations come from a variety of resources. Heroin, cocaine and marijuana are cheap to produce but because they are illegal and therefore risky to supply, they can earn more than their weight in gold on the vast international black market.

ROLE OF TECHNOLOGY

Enhance in intensity and fatality of terrorist attacks can be attributed to our growing reliance on technology. The terror groups are resorting to various tools of technology to make weapons and increase their fatality and to communicate with the other like minded organisations, etc. The new computer-savvy generations of terrorists are harnessing these tools to increase the intensity of the attack. Every day technology used by hundreds of millions of people are now a new tool in the arsenal of terrorists and this form of terrorism is known as cyber terrorism. The threat of cyber terrorism and the misuse of internet is alarming because it is giving rise to more violence and chaos in the society. The intensity of the terror attacks has also increased due to the use of dual technologies like GPS, satellite imagery, radar, computers, secure communications etc. by the terrorists. The fatalities and casualties of an attack have increased now. Terrorists have also made efforts to obtain CBRN (Chemical, Biological, Radiological and Nuclear) material and expertise in production. Easy access to global communication network has enabled many organisations to conduct their terrorist operations. Through it, the organisations are able to associate with other groups that are compatible with their aims and objectives. Thus, the shrinking of geographical borders has assisted in transforming the ill-equipped groups into sophisticated entities. Proliferation of information technologies — satellite TV, fax, internet, mobile phone — enhanced terrorist command, control, communications and intelligence capabilities with their members and supporters, domestically and worldwide.

Role of Communication and Information Technology

Schmid & de Graaf have observed that, "without communication there can be no terrorism," Terrorist groups are taking help of widespread availability of communication tools. The global communication system enables a subversive entity like a terrorist organization to exploit various functions that the system supplies to its users, to preserve a 'low profile signature' inside the system and turn the system itself including all its branches into an arena for activity and a target for attacks.[13] This has made the groups more powerful and sophisticated. There is growing transfer of technology of land mines, mortars etc., between groups. With the increased use of technology and communication, tactics such as hijacking and blasting buildings to create mass casualties appear to be emulated by other groups. Many groups like LTTE, Al Qaeda have employed CBRN technologies. The arrival of the cellular and satellite phones, internet has assisted the terrorist in communicating through different means and mode. Moreover, the tools of mass disruption are easily available in various websites. Hackers are also flourishing and selling there services to terrorist groups.

Cyber Terrorism

The term 'cyber terrorism' was defined by Berry Collin to signify the convergence of cyber space and terrorism. Cyber space does not need any territorial base or the growth of a permanent and susceptible infrastructure. Cyber attacks come in two forms. One is against data and the other against controlled systems. Theft and corruption of data leads to services being damaged and this is the most common form of internet and computer attack. Attacks which focus on control systems are used to disable or control physical infrastructure. The computer 'virus' can destroy major data and control system. Such actions successfully disrupt the normal life in a country. Cyber terrorism, whether targeting the internet or conducted by means of the internet, represents a serious threat. This phenomenon can be classified into[14]:

1. Attacks via internet that could damage not only the essential electronic communication systems and the IT infrastructure but also the other infrastructure systems including human life.
2. Dissemination of illegal content including threatening with terrorist attacks, advertising, and glorifying terrorism, fundraising, recruiting for terrorism.
3. Other logistical uses of IT systems by terrorists, such as internal communication, information acquisition and target analysis.

Using the system to communicate with the public or with each other gives organization new possibilities in a 'war of ideas.' Many propaganda videos have shown up on video sharing platforms such as You Tube. These videos often depict terrorism in a glorious light. Young terrorists can gather such information from the Internet in order to prepare their assaults.[15]Websites are presented as a method of emphasizing injustices. Many sites assert that they have been forced to turn to violence. They describe themselves as being subjugated. Hammas published a written statement on its official website calling on Muslims all over the world to wage an economic jihad against the US. Hammas can now openly give technical classes in preparing bombs over the web. The cyber learner may even find voluminous WMD-related knowledge online.[16] Terrorist also present websites with information on how to build chemical and explosive weapons. Web destruction, hijackings of websites and automated e-mail bombings that may not kill anyone but do attract media attention, provide a means of operating anonymously and are easy to coordinate internationally. The use of FM radio has also proved beneficial for religious extremists to propagate their ideas among the population. By using illegal FM radio broadcasts, militants in Pakistan are gaining the structure of a parallel government. In Swat Valley, in Pakistan, a cleric called Fazlullah has set up an illegal radio FM station, known as Fazlullah FM. The technology to do so was quite affordable and completely portable. He used the radio to propagate hatred towards Americans and the then President Parvez Musharraf.[17]

The internet also serves as a tool that can be used for real world as well as for digital attacks. Information such as satellite maps that was only available to experts until recently is now a common good. These graphics are already being used by terrorists. They use encryption technology to obscure their communication. The infiltrating apparatus of globalization, such as media, internet are exploited. The significant changes in the terrorist methods are clear in the use of new technologies. The use of information technologies such as internet, mobile phone etc., have extended the global reach of many terrorist groups. Activists and terrorist groups have increasingly tuned to 'hactivism' attacks on internet sites including a specific conflict between western consumerism and religious fundamentalism.[18]

Terrorist groups are increasingly using the new Information Technology and the internet to formulate plans, raise funds, spread propaganda, and communicate securely. The terrorist organizations are using computerized files, e-mails, encryption to support their operations. Terrorist organizations also use the internet to target their audiences without depending on other mechanisms such as Radio, TV or the Public Relations. Many of the terrorists are recognizing that information warfare tools offer a low cost way to support their causes. These tools require minimal technical understanding.

In 1998, a terrorist organization flooded Sri Lankan embassies with 800 emails a day for two weeks. The messages read 'we are the internet black tigers and we are doing this to interrupt your communication.' This attack is the first-known attack by the terrorists against the country's computer system. In July 1997, the leader of a Chinese hacker group claimed to have temporarily disabled a Chinese satellite and announced that he was forming a new global cracker organization to protest and disrupt western investment in China.[19] Many of the Kashmiri Jihadi organizations and North eastern extremist groups have their own websites for propaganda against Government of India.[20] Terrorist organizations recognize the importance of computer training, and are actively recruiting people with the necessary skills. Information about hacking, cracking and attacking is freely available.

There has been a shift in the international threat environment. The new threats have changed the security environment transforming the nature of terrorist group and state response.[21]

The use of internet-based attacks now seems to be highly attractive for terrorist purposes for following reasons:

- Attacks can be launched from anywhere in the world
- Attacks are quick
- It is extremely difficult to trace evidence

Weapons of Mass Destruction

The continuing possibility of terrorist attacks using nuclear, biological, or chemical weapons is an ongoing concern. Terrorism using arms of mass destruction is now realistic, and it will be easier to achieve in the future. With the easy access to technology, it is now known that terrorists are capable of producing WMD or also obtaining them due to looser controls of stockpiles and technology in the former Soviet states. After the end of Cold War and collapse of Soviet Union, many of the terrorists gained access to automatic weapons like M-16, M-203, AK-47 including stand-off weapons like mortars, artillery and explosives like RDX and TNT. This lead to the misuse of technology by the violent groups as the secretive information about the making of the weapons passed into their hands. Thus, there was widespread proliferation of weapons which are now easily available in any rag-tag group.

The Central Intelligence Agency has reported that most terrorists will maintain preferring conventional explosives over WMD. However the Al Qaeda network badly wants to obtain WMD capability. This opinion came into being with the detection of documents in Afghanistan indicating the interest of both the Taliban and the Al Qaeda network in weapons of mass destruction. These terrorists are now experts in the use of improvised explosive devices (IEDs). They also have solar activated explosives. They also have hi-tech weapons and the era of AK-47 is over. These groups also comprise of machine guns, automatic grenade rocket launchers and heavy mortars.[22]

Weapons of mass destruction can be divided into three sub categories:

1. Nuclear Weapons
2. Biological Weapons
3. Chemical Weapons

Nuclear Weapons

Nuclear weapons can give terrorist groups considerable advantages as they can cause large number of casualties and attract worldwide attention. A nuclear terrorist attack is an incident in which a terrorist organization uses a nuclear device to cause mass murder and destruction. There are a number of ways through which the nuclear terrorist act can be committed. They include blasting a nuclear plant and stealing of nuclear weapons.[23] Terrorists also threaten the state authorities by using the nuclear device, targeting nuclear power stations and breeder reactors, and also dispersing the radioactive substances in what is called as 'Dirty bomb'.[24] While a nuclear weapon is the most destructive of all WMD, obtaining one poses the greatest difficulty for terrorist groups. The key obstacle to building such a weapon is the availability of a sufficient quantity of fissile material.[25] The technical barriers to construction of a nuclear weapon are not very high or complicated. It is difficult to imagine that a determined terrorist group could not acquire a nuclear weapon manufacturing capability once it had the required nuclear weapon materials.

There are many aspects to the threat of nuclear terrorism.

1. *Suitcase Bombs:* During the 1980s, the Soviet Union manufactured between 100 and 250 suitcase bombs. The technology to deliver this type of bomb is simple.
2. *Power Plant attack:* It requires no knowledge of nuclear technology at all. In this type of attack, the idea is to cause a meltdown at a power plant, releasing radioactive contaminants into the air. An attack on a power plant is perhaps the most likely method of nuclear terror.
3. *Dirty Bombs:* They are not strictly nuclear bombs. They are conventional explosive device containing radioactive material.[26]

In view of these threats, it can be argued that the prospect of nuclear destruction by terrorists is both probable and dangerous. The threat appears impending mainly as result of these developments:

1. The easy access of terrorist groups to nuclear weapons, nuclear power plants and nuclear waste.
2. Special nature of terrorist groups as actors in world politics.
3. The global trend towards tolerance of terrorist activities.

Taken together these technological, contextual and behavioural problems indicate a high probability of such terrorism taking place.[27]

Biological Weapons

There is an increasing amount of concern over the possibility of terrorist use of biological agents in post 9/11 world. Bio terrorism largely takes the form of introducing disease into enemy controlled area. Since the anthrax attack that followed the 9/11 event, the fear of bio terrorism has grown massively. It is much less expensive weapon than nuclear and chemical weapons. It is also very hard to protect against such attacks as biological arsenals can be airborne or waterborne and spreads at a very fast rate. They also have a long history. The easy availability of the ingredients of the biological weapons and access to the internet just a click away, has been proved beneficial for the new young terrorists.

The Aum became the first terrorist group to resort to a major biological attack. In the morning of March 20,1995, cult members placed 11sarin filled bags wrapped in newspapers on five Japanese subway trains causing 1038 injuries and 12 deaths. In another incident, five letters containing a highly lethal preparation of anthrax spores were sent through the US postal system shortly after the 9/11 attack, killing 5 persons, injuring 18 others and forcing tens of thousands of people to take antibiotics. Groups like Al Qaeda are also known to have shown interest in acquiring biological weapons as revealed by plans seized from its hideouts in Afghanistan.

The development of bio weapons is easy to cover up unlike nuclear weapons. These weapons can be distinguished by high efficiency. Access to them is not hard and their means to deliverance are uncomplicated. Small quantities can cause large number of casualties. Their effects are more pushy and likely to spread quickly over large areas.[28] The agents of biological weapons are difficult to detect. They are invisible, odourless, tasteless and their dispersal can be effected silently. The small quantity required to kill thousands of people in a densely populated area make the concealment, transportation and dissemination of biological agents relatively easy.

The prospect of terrorists using chemical or biological material may increase. The number of potential executors is increasing. Many terrorist groups have international networks and may not need state sponsors for financial and technical support. Small groups with humble finances too can develop effective biological weapons. Instructions for manufacturing biological weapons are available even on internet.[29]

A relatively new concern is agro terrorism which is the use of biological agents against agricultural targets. The outbreaks of foot-and-mouth and "mad cow" disease in Europe have done damage to agricultural markets. Agro terrorism also causes considerable economic and social trouble without actually causing human casualties.[30]

The risk of bio terrorism is getting bigger because of the geo political shift to asymmetric warfare, better access to knowledge, major limitations in medical intelligence and advances in biotechnology which increase threat diversity and complexity.

Chemical Weapons

Chemical warfare agents are 'chemical substance, whether gaseous, liquid, or solid, which might be employed because of their direct toxic effects on man, animals and plants.' They are highly toxic and may persist in the environment for long periods of time. There are a number of ways in which chemical warfare agents can affect humans, depending on the agent, and these are via the skin, inhalation, ingestion of contaminated water or food, or entry through other mucous-lined areas such as the eyes, nose, and open cuts.

Increasing use of explosives by the militants is causing huge casualties. Bombing is the most preferred terrorist act. The technology required to make a bomb is relatively simple. Toxic industrial chemicals are easily available and do not require great expertise to be adapted into chemical weapons. It is also not easy to detect the explosives or completely ban the ingredients which are used to make the explosives. Improvised explosives made out of completely available mixtures, consisting of fertilizer etc., are more difficult to ban and detect. The use of RDX is common in the terror explosions. Samtex explosives emit virtually no vapour. Therefore, plastic explosives, RDX can be detected neither by metal or vapour detectors.[31] Home made explosives are also very simple to manufacture. Terrorists also use 'Molotov cocktails' bottles filled with a mixture of gas and oil which are used as 'Incendiaries'. In agricultural areas, farm fertilizer can be processed to produce a powerful explosive.[32]

Dual purpose materials like nitrate fertilizers also do not normally attract suspicion. Thus the Al-Ummah of Tamil Nadu and the LTTE have mostly been using such dual purpose materials.[33]

The chemical industry has begun to pay greater attention to the possibility of terrorist damage of facilities housing toxic chemicals. This approach could provide the effects of a chemical weapons attack without requiring a terrorist group to either develop or obtain chemical agents on their own.[34]

CONCLUSION

The proliferation of nuclear weapons and the civilian nuclear programmes by the developed and developing nations of the world has given rise to the fear of nuclear terrorism as the terrorist groups are increasingly becoming tech-savvy entities. The new communication tools have altered the terrorists tradecraft and enabled them to plan and carry out operations, to network with other similar minded terrorist groups and expand there knowledge and expertise and to constantly interact with their state sponsors through cyber space while reducing drastically the need for trans border travel and for personal meetings. There is no question that technology has changed terrorism for better and for worse. As technology continues to advance, terrorists will continue to find new means of attacking. Technology has the power to change the future of terrorism. It has the power to advance it and it has the power to destroy it.

REFERENCES

1. Pierra A Chouvy, "Narco Terrorism in Afghanistan", *Terrorism Monitor*, Vol. 2, 2004.
2. Jennifer L. Hesterman, "Transnational Crime and Criminal Terrorist Nexus: Synergies and Corporate Trends", 2004, p. 36.
3. Peter Chalk, "Southeast Asia and the Golden Triangle's Heroin Trade: Threat and Response", *Studies in Conflict and Terrorism,* 23(2), 2001, p. 96.
4. Nalin Kumar Mohapatra, "Political and Security Changes in Central Asia: The Drug Trafficking Dimension", *International Studies* , Vol. 44, 2007, p. 166
5. Jonathan M. Winer, "Countering Terrorist Finance: A work, Mostly in Progress", *The ANNALS of the American Academy of Political and Social Science*, 2008, p.117.
6. Arjun Sharma, "Pak nurturing terrorism in J & K with drug money", *The Hindustan Times,* Sept. 12, 2008.
7. *Ibid.*

8. Mark S Steinitz, "The Terrorism and Drug Connection in Latin America's Andean Region", *Policy Papers on the Americas,* Vol. XIII, 2002, pp. 1-2.

9. Drug Intelligence Report, "Insurgent Involvement in the Columbian Drug Trade", Drug Enforcement Administration, 1994.

10. Drug Intelligence Report, "Insurgent Involvement in the Columbian Drug Trade", Drug Enforcement Administration, 1994.

11. JennifernL, Hesterman, "Transnational Crime and Criminal Terrorist Nexus: Synergies and Corporate Trends", 2004, p. 37.

12. Nalin Kumar Mohapatra, "Political and Security Changes in Central Asia: The Drug Trafficking Dimension", *International Studies,* Vol. 44, 2007, p. 164.

13. Yoram Schweitzer & Shaul Shay, *The Globalization of Terror,* Viva Books, 2004, p. 217.

14. Council of Europe, *Cyberterrorism: the use of the internet for terrorist purposes,* Council of Europe Publishing, 2007, pp. 17-18.

15. *Ibid.,* pp. 35- 37.

16 Gil Ariely, "Knowledge Management, Terrorism, and Cyber Terrorism" in Lech Janczewski, Andrew M. Colarik (edt), *Cyber Warfare and Cyber Terrorism,* IGI Global, 2008. p. 9.

17. Manzoor Ali Shah, "Mullah Radio", *Himal Southasian,* April 2009, p. 34.

18. Audrey Kurth Cronin, "Behind the Curve: Globalization and International terrorism", *International Security,* Vol. 27, No. 3, p. 46.

19. Kevin Curran, Kevin Concannon, Sean McKeever, "Cyber Terrorism Attacks" in Lech Janczewski, Andrew M. Colarik, eds., *Cyber Warfare and Cyber Terrorism,* IGI Global, 2008, p. 3.

20. M.L. Sodhi, *Terrorism and Political Violence: A Sourcebook,* Har-Anand Pub., 2000, p. 108-09.

21. Rohan Gunaratna, "Organised Crime and International Terrorist Networks" in K.P.S. Gill & Ajai Sahni (edt), *The Global Threat of Terror,* Bulwark Books, 2002, p. 241.

22. Bhure Lal, *TERRORISM INC. The Lethal Cocktail of ISI, TALIBAN & AL-QAIDA,* Siddharth Pub., New Delhi, 2002, p.57.

23. Ved Marwah, *Uncivil wars: Pathology of Terrorism in India*, Indus Harper Collins Pub., New Delhi, 1995, p. 352.
24. Wilson John & Swati Prashar, *Terrorism in South East Asia,* p. 29.
25. Steve Bowman, "Weapons of Mass Destruction: The Terrorist Threat", *CRS Report for Congress,* March 2002, p.7.
26. Lloyd Pettiford, David Harding, *Terrorism and the New World War,* Areturus Pub, London, 2003, p. 206.
27. Naunihal Singh, *World Terrorism and New Age Movement,* Authors Press, p. 173.
28. P.R. Chari & D. Suba Chandran, *Bio-terrorism and Bio-defence,* Manohar Publishers, 2005, pp. 53- 54.
29. *Ibid.*, p. 84.
30 Steve Bowman, "Weapons of Mass Destruction: The Terrorist Threat", *CRS Report for Congress,* March 2002, p.9.
31. Ved Marwah, *Uncivil wars: Pathology of Terrorism in India*, Indus Harper Collins Pub., New Delhi, 1995, p. 352.
32. Ranjit K. Prachnanda, *Terrorism and Response to Terrorist Threat,* UBS Pub, 2002, p. 23.
33. M.L. Sodhi, *Terrorism and Political Violence: A Sourcebook,* Har-Anand Pub., 2000, p. 107.
34. Steve Bowman, "Weapons of Mass Destruction: The Terrorist Threat", *CRS Report for Congress,* March 2002. p. 9.

3

Causes of Terrorism

Terrorism is being taken as the most serious challenge by the civilized society. There exist abundant typologies of terrorist movements with the ethnic, religious, ideological, autonomous and separatist agenda. Investigating with the roots of terrorism is most important if one needs to understand and rectify it. There are many factors at the macro and micro level that affect terrorism. The political, historical, familial, and even purely accidental, coincidental factors directly or indirectly give rise to violence. Broadly stated, to rectify the problems of terrorism and to redress the grievances of the suffering population, it is necessary to understand the 'root cause' theory of terrorism which suggests that it is directly caused by certain social and economic conditions of deprivation, poverty, unemployment, illiteracy, legitimate political grievances, historical wrongs, etc.

If we peep into the chronology of terrorism, there were different reasons which were responsible for its origin and growth. But in different periods, one or more cause was predominant. In the early 20th century, terrorists justified violence in the name of socialism and communism. Socialism was becoming a dominant way for many people to explain the political and economic injustice they witnessed in capitalist societies. In the latter half of the century, terrorist violence tended to have a nationalist component. Terrorist reflected a trend in which suppressed populations became violent against states that had not given them a say in the political process. In the 1980s and 1990s, terrorism began to appear with the emergence of right-wing, neo-Nazi or neo-fascist, racist groups. White men grew apprehensive of granting recognition and political rights to ethnic minorities. The bombing of the Oklahoma City Federal Building, the most lethal terrorist attack in the U.S. until the 9/11 attacks, gives an instance. In the Middle East too, religious and cultural extremism resulted in the rise of terrorism. Thus, both West and East saw an increase in fundamentalism in the turn of the century. The Japanese Aum Shinrikyo, Islamic Jihad and other groups were enthusiastic to use religion to justify violence.[1]

Thus the causes of terrorism have changed over time. The ideas of scholars, who explain terrorism, also change over time with the new trends in academic thinking. Terrorism is not a scientific phenomenon whose characteristics are fixed for all time. Terrorism isn't a natural phenomenon. It is name given by people about other people's actions in the social world. Terrorists are people who threaten or use violence against civilians with the hope of changing the status quo, perceive the status quo in ways that accord with the era they live in.

Crenshaw discusses the difficulty of finding general explanations for terrorism and emphasizes the idea that terrorism is 'a product of rational political choice'. Whereas Horgan and Taylor have noted: "What we know of actual terrorists suggests that there is rarely a conscious decision made to become a terrorist. Most involvement in terrorism results from gradual exposure and socialization towards extreme behaviour." It is generally argued that terrorists do not become terrorists over night. They follow a general sequence from social alienation to monotony and protest, and finally turning to terrorism."[2]

Jeffrey Ian Ross in "Structural Causes of Oppositional Political Terrorism: Towards a Causal Model", identifies three categories of causes of terrorism, namely structural and psychological causes, and the concept of 'rational choice.' Dipak Gupta seeks to understand why people engage in such action in the name of a group based on ethnicity, religion, nationalism or ideology. Gupta presents arguments that are rooted in economic and socio-psychological dimensions of human motivations. He points out that "political violence takes place when a leader gives voice to the frustration by formulating a well-defined social construction of collective identity and paints in vivid colour the images of 'us'and 'them.'[3]

The causes of the terrorist movements can be attributed to certain factors. Every militant or terrorist outfit embraces one of the factor as a dominant one which is used as its ideology.

POLITICAL CAUSES

Terrorism is an "intrinsically political" phenomenon. To say that terrorism is political suggests that terrorists are responding to their environment, rather than acting out of an internally coherent belief system. The political causes of terrorism are international as well as domestic. It may include overturning the international order, as perceived by the Muslim world to fight back the western domination. It may also concern the state weakness at the level of the international system. Some weak unstable states with prolonged civil conflicts and instability give rise to terrorism with a political cause. Political repression may also contribute to immigration which in turn leads to cultural clashes and a feeling of separatism among the immigrants. These conditions are thus a serious problem for the international community. Diasporas may also promote terrorist tactics. Gabriel Sheffer observes that 27 of the 50 most active terrorist organizations today are ethno-national and religious diasporas. Kurds, Palestinians, Sikhs, Tamils, and many other migrant peoples are motivated by discrimination and repression against them.[4] Ted Robert Gurr has argued in *Why Men Rebel,* that political violence is an outcome of a significant division developing between the value expectations of a given group of people and the value capabilities of the group.

Terrorism is not a monolithic phenomenon but rather quite assorted, not only in terms of ideas but in organization and foundation. Sometimes terrorism is associated with a social movement or political party that enjoys significant popular support. Such movements or parties employ terrorism because it is a convenient means of pressuring a government. Other types of groups which use the tactics of terrorism are more socially isolated. They may be small groups that have formed in order to use terrorism. Groups of both types are subject to internal tensions and splits, and factionalism is common. Their leaders struggle to maintain cohesion and allegiance.[5]

Terrorism can also be seen as valid by people, when they are discriminated against and access to power is blocked. It cannot be denied that in some circumstances the public may not only support the goals behind terrorism but the means itself. The charismatic leaders are able to transform grievances into a political agenda for violent struggle is a crucial factor behind the emergence of a terrorist movement or group. The existence of grievances alone is not enough. It needs to be translated into a coherent programme for violent action.

In most of the cases a terrorist act is an outcome of political inspiration and motivation instead of poverty or illiteracy. None of the 9/11 terrorists suffered from poverty, lack of education or lack of exposure to the privileged lifestyle of the western world. The reason they took part in this action is because they felt inspired.[6]

Relationship with Democracy

The relationship between terrorism and democracy has been widely discussed. A democratic government is supposed to represent the people and provide political means to voice grievances. To quote Wilkinson, there 'cannot' be an aggrieved group that is not adequately represented; otherwise, it is a "violation of the doctrines of democracy and constitutionalism." However, in the case of the minority whose rights and liberties are taken away by arbitrary action of the government or its agencies or when one minority is attacked by majority group of the country or another minority, and does not receive adequate protection from the state, then, it takes the route of terrorism. Thus, one can attribute the cause to the absence of a 'correct' implementation of democratic ideals and not democracy.[7]

It has often been argued that not all democracies respect minority rights. Majorities may discriminate methodically against minorities. Many of the world's established democracies are limited or partial. In the case of terrorism that is generated within a democracy, the degree of social, ethnic, and political heterogeneity or fragmentation within the state is critical. Controversial polities and fragmented societies are likely to be associated with a greater risk of terrorism. They are typically associated with other forms of political violence also.[8]

It is generally agreed that lack of democracy and civil liberties are reasons behind domestic terrorism. The most democratic and the most totalitarian societies have the lowest levels of oppositional violence. Failed or weak states on the other hand, lack the capacity, or will, to exercise territorial control. This often leaves a power vacuum that can be exploited by terrorist organizations to maintain safe havens, training facilities or serve as bases for launching terrorist campaigns. However, this should not be perceived as simply a lack of democracy or democratic processes. Long standing liberal democracies with established traditions of free speech and tolerance have been the targets of both domestic and foreign terrorism. Disenchanted with the political leaders, frustrated with the existing conditions and suffering under the misrule of the self seeking politicians and bureaucrats, people are attracted to the rhetoric of the militant.

Ethnicity and Seperatism

Terrorism is generally viewed as an expression of the political and ideological resistance against imperialism and colonialism. The most debated cause of terrorism is an aggrieved group resorting to violence for nationalist or separatist reasons. An alienated population is a prerequisite for terrorism to take roots in any society. Terrorism skillfully articulates the demands of the marginalised people, portraying itself as an emancipation struggle and its operations as a part of the strategy in the struggle for liberation. The occurrence of discrimination on the basis of ethnic origin is the chief root cause of ethno-nationalist terrorism. When sizeable minorities are systematically deprived of their rights to equal social and economic opportunities, hindered from expressing their cultural identities or excluded from political influence, this can give rise to secessionist movements that may turn to terrorism or other forms of violent struggle. The presence of sub cultures in a country is a common factor giving rise to separatist tendencies.[9] It justifies the overthrow of an unjust regime by any means. For terrorists, any means justifies the end. Ethnic nationalisms are more likely to give rise to terrorism than are moderate and inclusive civic nationalisms. In most colonized states "nationalism movements commonly turned to terrorism", it being "the resort of an extremist faction of this broader movement" within an ethnic minority.[10] Williams provides an overview on the relation between ethnic minorities and the likelihood of conflict, for example to establish or assert language rights and religious beliefs, but he also includes factors like "civil and political rights and privileges. What then generates perceptions of unfairness is competition or rivalry when an ethnicity is subordinated or disadvantaged in economic opportunity, social status, political voice and rights, or cultural expressions." However, the cited factors are not unique for ethnic minorities. To generalize it further, ethnic conflict arises from a "complex combination" of class, inequality, political opportunity, mobilization resources and "ethnic strength".[11] Few instances which present a picture of separatist and ethnic struggle for a separate homeland are — a Jewish Zionists who bombed British targets in 1930s mandate Palestine felt they must do so in order to create state. The IRA (Irish Republican Army) bombed English targets in the 1980s to make the point that they felt their land was colonized by British imperialists. In the 1960s and 1970s, the Popular Front for the Liberation of Palestine felt that armed attacks in Israel were a justifiable response to the usurpation of their land. Uighur separatists in China today feel that Chinese religious repression (the Uighur Chinese are Muslims) justifies their terrorist tactics.

Role of Ideology

Radical doctrines can deeply affect people's viewpoint. The presence of magnetic ideological leaders who can alter prevalent complaints and frustrations into a political agenda for violent struggle is a crucial factor behind the emergence of a terrorist movement. Extreme nationalist ideologies frames disaffected people's ideas. In a transnational world, ideologies help members of far-flung groups to co-ordinate action. Hijackers of September 11, consisted of highly educated Muslim youth, rather than the poor Muslims who were thought to be behind the radical movement. Ideology, not poverty, wrote Pipes, was the driving force behind militant Islam. Poverty did not create Muslim radicals. Intelligent radical Muslim ideologues used poverty, intimidation, and brainwashing in the madrasas to help promote their cause.[12]

Ideologies connect dispersed communities in support of a common objective and also make possible the provision of international support. Similarly, *Jihadist* doctrine helps Islamist militants connect with marginalized people throughout the Muslim world. Thus ideologies are used to justify nationalist aspirations, calls for revolution, cultural purification.

Jerrold Post explains the risk factors which give rise to a terrorist. They include what he calls 'generational transmission' of extremist beliefs which begin early in life, a strong sense of victimization and alienation, the belief that moral violations by the enemy justify violence in pursuit of a higher moral condition, the belief that terrorist's ethnic, religious or nationalist group is special and in danger of extinction, and they lack the political power to effect change without violence.[13] Also, failure or unwillingness by the state to integrate dissident groups or emerging social classes may lead to their alienation from the political system. Some groups are excluded because they hold views or represent political traditions considered irreconcilable with the basic values of the state, thus giving rise to the clash of ideologies. Large groups of highly educated young people with few prospects of meaningful careers within a blocked system will tend to feel alienated and frustrated, and to turn up against the state. Excluded groups are likely to search for alternative channels through which to express and promote political influence and change. To some, terrorism can seem the most effective and tempting option.

Psychological Causes

Early writings on psychological dimensions of terrorist behaviour were dominated by psychoanalytic formulations that motives for terrorism are largely unconscious and arise from hostility toward one's parents and that terrorism is the product of early abuse and maltreatment. Psychohistorian Lloyd De Mause has observed that "the roots of terrorism lie not in this or that American foreign policy error, but in the extremely abusive families of the terrorists."

Another remarkable effort was made in the early 1980s by former CIA psychiatrist, Jerrold Post. Jerrold Post investigates the psychological thinking of individuals involved in terrorism, and builds a framework for analysis with regard to the extent of conditions and characteristics that can increase the risk that a radical group will shift to terrorism. Post argues that 'political terrorists are driven to commit acts of violence as a consequence of psychological forces. Post argued that two different forms of dysfunction produced two different patterns of terrorist behaviour. The first type was the Anarchic-ideologue. These individuals were assumed to come from severely dysfunctional families where they likely had suffered severe abuse or maltreatment, leading them to have hostile feelings toward their parents. Their extremist ideology was a displacement of their rebellion and hostility onto the "state" authority. That is, they acted out hostility by rebelling against the "state" of their parents. In contrast, the second type, the Nationalist-secessionist was not hostile, but loyal to his parents, and his extremism was motivated to avenge the wrongs done to his parents by the state. In essence, they rebelled against external society out of loyalty to their parents.'[14]

Bruce Hoffman analyzes the changes in terrorism, which is viewed as a means of communicating a message and using violence as a means to solidify the achievement of their cause. Hoffman establishes several common traits, including strategic targeting and the belief in the triumph over their enemies. According to Hoffman terrorists live in the divinely decreed future. A look into the psychology of terrorists and examination of their actions could give explanations that bring them to commit terrorist crimes.[15]

Deprivation

Terrorism may be considered a politics of extreme frustration, which is the feeling that one wants to change a situation, but has no power to do so. Frustration may be a response to material deprivation, but it may also be an answer to the long-term deprivation of a group or society from what it perceives to be rightfully its own. Terrorists may be powerfully motivated by existential frustration, the feeling of being unrecognized. For terrorist groups, the achievement of recognition is often their raison d'etre. National liberation movements, such as the Irish Republican Army or the National Liberation Front, a group that used terrorist tactics on behalf of Algerian independence from France in the mid-1950s, seek international recognition of the existence of a people.

Group Psychology

The collective identity has drawn much attention in recent years. Some well-known scholars have the opinion that individual members of terrorist groups subordinate their own identity to that of the group. Thus, to best understand how and why terrorist groups work, and how best to engage and ultimately counter them, a study of their group psychology is necessary. Jerrold Post, a prominent expert on political psychology writes that:

"A clear consensus exists that it is not individual psychology, but group, organizational and social psychology that provides the investigative power in understanding this complex phenomenon. Terrorists have subordinated their individual identity to the collective identity, so that what serves the group, organization or network is of primary importance. For some groups, especially separatist terrorist groups, this collective identity is established extremely early. This emphasizes the socio-cultural context, which determines the balance between collective and individual identity."[16] Justification for extremist action is greatly intensified by group dynamics. Marc Sageman, a former CIA profiler of Al Qaeda, says that only an understanding of group impact can give up the causes of the phenomenon. It has been argued that when people are in groups they are more likely to make risky decisions because the risk is perceived as shared and less frightening. As the group becomes more radical, so does the individual. A group may also provide solidarity and a sense of significance. The group can also become extremely unified under segregation and danger.[17]

Narcissism

The concept of narcissistic rage in psychology starts with the idea that terrorists are full of anger that developed because of their flawed psychological development in childhood. If they do not have the chance to test their power in reality, they do not tend to have control over events, nor do they live normally among other people. In adulthood, external threats are greeted with intense rage. Taking the-terrorists-as-mentally-ill approach, this hypothesis concerns the early development of the terrorist. Terrorism is an attempt to acquire or maintain power or control by bullying. The "meaningful high ideals" of the political terrorist group "protect the group members from experiencing shame."[18]

The linkage between narcissism and terrorism was first advanced by Morf and subsequently discussed by Lasch, Crayton, Post and Pearlstein. The premise was that terrorist behaviour was rooted in a personality defect that produced a damaged sense of self. The essence of pathological narcissism is an overvaluing of self and a devaluing of others. Narcissistically vulnerable persons are drawn to charismatic leaders and groups are held together by a shared high-flying sense of self. Narcissistic rage is what prompts an aggressive response to perceived injustice.

Indeed "narcissistic rage" has been described as the psychological outpour of terrorist resentment. It explains that as children the nascent terrorists are deeply traumatized, suffering physical abuse and emotional disgrace. This creates a deep sense of terror and personal helplessness. In 1971, American psychiatrist David Hubbard produced a study, *The Skyjacker* based on unstructured interviews. Hubbard concluded that hijackers were psychically unstable, or ill, and that all shared five traits: A violent father, a deeply religious mother, shy, timid and passive, younger sisters toward whom the terrorist acted protectively and poor social achievement. To eliminate this fear and create a more tolerable self-image, such individuals feel the need to not consider themselves as victims. They kill their own self-respect by devaluing others. The outcome of this devaluation of others eliminates their internal voice of rationality and morality. This makes the individual vulnerable to any insults or ideas that terrorize to destroy the self growth. Such insults are known as "narcissistic injuries" and are the triggers of narcissistic rage.[19] A study by Psychiatrist Marc Sageman presents a different picture which did not give an adequate reason for disorder. He compiled data from public sources on 172 individuals he identified as members of a "global *Salafi mujahedin,* meaning Muslims engaged in terrorist acts against the "far enemy" in the service of a new Islamic world order ... Sageman excluded terrorists engaged in local jihads, such as Chechnyans, Kashmiris, Afghans and Palestinians. Sageman drew a number of impressionistic conclusions, which he admits are of limited statistical value, because the sample group was so small and not controlled as a scientific study would be. Of the 61 cases including some childhood information, Sageman found that:

- "Only four had histories suggestive of conduct disorder"
- "Only 1 case (Habib Zacarias Moussaoui) was suggestive of a childhood trauma"
- "One-quarter of the group had histories of petty crime"
- On the evidence of ten of the cases, "Sageman claims that he found 'no evidence of pathological narcissism' and 'no pattern of paranoid personality disorder' . . . with the exception of possible traits of Al Qaeda leader Ayman Al Zawahiri."[20]

Vengeance

"One of the strongest motivations behind terrorism is vengeance, particularly the desire to avenge not oneself but others. Vengeance can be specific or diffuse, but it is an obsessive drive that is a powerful motive for violence toward others, especially people thought to be responsible for injustices", says Crenshaw. Perception of injustice may also be viewed as grievances, which can be the most important cause of terrorism. Such grievances may be economic, ethnic, racial, legal, political, religious, or social, and they may be targeted to individuals, groups, institutions or categories of people.

In making of a terrorist, the key psychological factors are motive and vulnerability. *Motive* is a sentiment, craving, physiological need, or desire that acts as a stimulation to action, and *vulnerability* refers to vulnerability or responsibility to surrender. One's motivation for engaging in terrorism has been acknowledged as the "cause" or ideology of the group. The accepted picture of the terrorist as an entity provoked by profound and stubborn political dedication obscures a more complex reality. That reality unfolds that motives to join a terrorist organization and to engage in terrorism fluctuate across different types of groups, and also within groups and they change over a period of time.[21] There are a number of personal motivations. Sometimes, it is to provide power to the powerless, or to take revenge. While sometimes, it is to gain worth.

Three motivational themes — injustice, identity, and belonging appear to be important and steady. These themes also relate to one's probable openness or susceptibility.[22]

Perceived injustice has long been recognized a central factor in understanding violence generally and terrorism specifically. Injustice is the basic motivation for terrorism. A desire for revenge or vengeance is a common response to redress a wrong done on another.

The formation of identity typically occurs in a crisis of adolescence and is confused and emotionally challenging. An individual's quest for identity may take him to radical or terrorist organizations. The "black and white" nature of most extremist ideologies is often attractive to those who are encountered with the stressful world. An individual defines his identity through group membership. One's individual personality is merged with a group identity, with no sense of individuality or distinctiveness. Association with a terrorist group provides a sense of identity or belonging for those personalities whose primary sense of identity is blemished.

For these individuals, belonging to the terrorist group becomes the most important component of their psychological and social identity.

In fundamental terrorist groups, many latent terrorists seek a sense of belonging, and association. Among potential terrorists the real cause or inspiration for joining is the great need for belonging. For these estranged individuals from the peripheries of society, joining a terrorist group represented the first real sense of belonging after facing rejection. This strong sense of belonging has critical importance as a motivating factor for joining, staying, and acting. Terrorist groups may provide a security of family by overpowering individuality to the group identity. An envelope is created that acts as a protection from an antagonistic world. Many people are influenced to join by seeking solidarity with family, friends or acquaintances and that for the individuals who become active terrorists, the initial attraction is often to the group, or community of believers, rather than to an abstract ideology or to violence. It is the image of such strong cohesiveness and solidarity among extremist groups that makes them more alluring.

These three factors have been found often to co-occur in terrorists and to strongly influence decisions to enter terrorist organizations and to engage in terrorist activity. The synergistic effect of these factors forms the real "root cause" of terrorism, regardless of ideology. The real cause or psychological motivation for joining is the great need for belonging, a need to consolidate one's identity. Jerrold Post has stated that "the need to belong, the need to have a stable identity, to resolve a split and be at one with oneself and with society ... is an important bridging concept which helps explain the similarity in behaviour of terrorists in groups of widely different espoused motivations and composition."

Suicide Attackers

The individuals who commit suicide attacks have social, cultural, religious and material incentives. Suicide attackers view their act as one of martyrdom for their faith, their people, or their cause. In the case of *jihadists*, the primary aim of suicide terrorists is not suicide, because to the terrorist group, suicide is simply a means to an end with motivation that comes from rage and a sense of self-righteousness. They see themselves as having a higher purpose and are convinced of an eternal reward through their action. People typically associate martyrdom with hopefulness about afterlife rewards in paradise and feelings of heroic sacrifice. A longing for religious purity and a strong commitment to the welfare of own people drive the individuals to engage in suicide terrorism. This explains the phenomenon and enthusiasm for martyrdom. The desire to further the cause of Islam and to answer the highest calling in that religion motivates the actor.

Interviews by Mia Bloom, of failed suicide bombers in Israeli prisons explain the connection between loss and revenge. When asked why they became martyrs, the interviewees responded with many personal accounts. One such prisoner replied, "Pictures of dead kids had a major affect on me. Many were killed (right) before me, like my friend (whose body) I had to carry in my own arms..... After the martyrdom of a friend of mine, and after the murder of the baby......These two causes made me think that human life is threatened every moment without good cause.... without distinction between those (of us) who are soldiers, civilians, adults, or kids. Another prisoner responded, "The truth is that beforehand I saw pictures of dead and wounded children on television."[23]

Family and loved ones also support the behaviour. If the event occurs, the family is honoured. The family of a martyr gains forgiveness of their sins in the afterlife but the supporting community often cares for them socially and financially. Sheikh Yussuf Al-Qaradhawi, a spiritual leader of the Muslim Brotherhood draws the distinction succinctly as follows: "He who commits suicide kills himself for his own benefit, he who commits martyrdom sacrifices himself for the sake of his religion and his nation.... The Mujahed is full of hope".[24] Another motivation for suicide bombers is the quest for personal significance, the desperate longing for a meaningful life that appears only to come with death.

Suicide terrorism also is not exclusively a tactic of the religious extremist. The Black Tigers (Liberation Tigers of Tamil Eelam —

LTTE) constitute the most significance proof that suicide terrorism is not merely a religious phenomenon and that under certain extreme political and psychological circumstances secular volunteers are fully capable of martyrdom. In fact, that group alone is responsible for nearly half of the suicide attacks worldwide that have occurred in the past decade.

Many attackers have often been drawn from widows or siblings who wish to take revenge for their loved one's violent death. In Chechnya, Palestine, and Sri Lanka suicide bombers have lost a family member to the 'unjust state' and feel that their only meaningful response to express their outrage is to perpetrate an act of suicide terror. There has been increase in the recruitment of volunteers for suicide mission due to the human right abuses by the state. This has further justified the use of violence. There have been allegations that Tamil women raped by the Sinhalese security services and Sinhalese military at check points join the LTTE as the 'Birds of Paradise' unit of female suicide bombers.[25]

It can be asserted that terrorists are psychologically 'normal' in the sense of not being clinically psychotic. They are not depressed, severely emotionally disturbed, or fanatics. In the most comparative research on the psychology of terrorists, it has come up that most terrorists are what we call normal human beings and who are very rational and have a humane approach. According to Martha Cranshew, 'the outstanding common characteristic of terrorists is their normality.' In fact, terrorist groups and organizations regularly screen out emotionally unstable individuals. They represent, after all, a security risk. United Nations relief worker Nasra Hassan interviewed about 250 Hamas and Islamic Jihad members from 1996 to 1999. She offered her results in a *New Yorker* article in 2001. Hassan offered that:

- Suicide bombers ranged from 18 to 28 years old
- Two were sons of millionaires
- None were depressed

This study clearly reflects the normality in the psychological nature of terrorists. John Horgan, terror expert at Pennsylvania

State University, believes a moral dimension produces what he calls the "internal limits" of terrorists. He argues that terrorists must inherently believe that violence against the enemy is not immoral, but that they have internal limits. Some terrorists are comfortable with only a limited number of casualties. When an IRA man was ordered to shoot a police officer whose mother was a widow, he said he felt he 'would have to pay for it.' David Rapoport says that the final common pathway is a moral calculus, driven by the conclusion that the terrorists' enemies have done something so bad, so terrible that they can't get away with it. He says many terrorists believe that the pathway to heaven is straight from the hell.

Ervin Staub, a University of Massachusetts psychology professor, has identified three types of terrorists. 1. Idealists, who identify with the sufferings of some group. 2. Respondents who react to the experience of their own group. 3. Lost Souls, who are isolated and disliked and find purpose with a radical group. Lost souls are 'ripe for plucking' by recruiters.[26]

Poverty & Globalization

It has been widely argued that a direct connection exists between terrorism and poverty. Poverty is the most important factor which is accountable for terrorism. It breeds terrorism. Many terrorist groups claim to act on behalf of the poorest of the poor. Shining Path movement in Peru was a movement of the poor. A more important factor may be the social stratification and inequalities in the distribution of scarce resources. When a group is relatively deprived of its resources, they revolt. A small fragment of the population consumes majority of the resources. In the third world countries, in particular in the Arab countries, the growing frustration about the social and economic stagnation of the Muslim world has contributed to further radicalization. Furthermore, terrorism has added to the pauperization of the region.

Globalization has also resulted in alienating the already alienated and marginal society of the third world. Terrorists are of the mindset that it is better for the youth to pick up arms than to yield to the humiliation of globalization and Western hegemony. Samuel

Huntington has also argued that during modernization, isolation of various ethnic groups from each other is broken down. Those new acquaintances between groups make them compare adversely their share in values such as wealth power and knowledge with those of other groups. Modernization also produces feelings of relative deprivation by changing the relationship between communal groups in different societies: a previously dominant group may find its position threatened by another group that is better able to take advantage of the social and political changes taking place.[27] Rapid modernization and urbanization in the form of high economic growth has also led to the emergence of reactionary terrorism.

The global jihadist movement is an indication of the era of globalization, spread through the internet and other global media, such as satellite television. In contrast to merely local groups, the global jihadi movement has emerged out of 'deculturation'. It is a consequence of globalization and its uprooting. Youth generally find their identity in a new, radical jihadi culture divorced from its cultural underpinnings. Indeed, a number of studies suggest that young people attracted to the global jihad may not be particularly religious when they join: they are recruited through social networks, and radicalization takes place within the group.

Poverty is not a direct cause of terrorism. Studies show that terrorism can occur anywhere, but is more common in developing societies, rather than in poor or rich countries, and is most likely to emerge in societies characterized by rapid modernization. Economic change creates conditions that are conducive for instability, the emergence of militant movements and extremist ideologies. A persistent risk factor in developing societies is the so-called youth age bulge, that is, a substantial increase in the proportional size of the young male population facing insecure employment prospects. A high percentage of youth unemployment can be found in developing world. Governments have failed to make any real effort to find jobs for the younger generation due to the uncontrolled demographic growth.

Within countries, the groups that support and give rise to terrorist movements usually are relatively disadvantaged because of class, ethnic, or religious cleavages. At the individual level, the leaders of militant movements are better educated and of higher status than most of the population from which they come. This, however, is true of leaders of almost all political organizations. A significant number of activists are similarly well educated, even though many face uncertain employment opportunities. Recruits are also drawn from among poorer and less-educated youth – those with a lack of opportunities to complete secondary or higher education, or unable to find good jobs.

The state of administration has a direct impact on the terrorist movement. An administration which fails to be effective when needed could be favorable to the growth of terrorism as a weak and bad administration.[28] Corrupt governments frequently give rise to opposition that may turn to terrorist means if other avenues are not seen as realistic options for replacing these regimes with a more credible and legitimate government or a regime which represents the values and interests of the opposition movement. Archana Upadhyay in her recent work, '*India's Fragile Borderlands*', argues that terrorism can also be seen as an index of the growing desperation of the militant outfits in the face of state terror at different levels and in different degrees as well as the overall shortcomings in distributive justice and the rule of law.

The status of women is especially important. Although women are sometimes recruited as suicide bombers, in general they seldom support terrorism. Cross-national studies show that the higher women's relative educational status and political participation, the less frequent are political violence and instability. In summary, structured inequalities within countries are breeding grounds for violent political movements in general and terrorism specifically.

Gary Becker, a professor at the University of Chicago Business School, has also argued there is a connection between wealth and terrorism, based on the observation that "nations or regions that are experiencing rapid growth appear to have lower occurrence of terrorism." Violent activity is less appealing to individuals when their economic opportunities expand. So, even if it were the case that poverty does not directly cause terrorism, it could still be true that economic growth reduces terrorism. Harvard public policy professor Alberto Abadie concluded poor countries do not experience more terrorism than wealthy countries, after he studied wealth, political liberty and other variables in relation to terrorism. He also concluded that political liberty is a better indicator than poverty of terrorist activity.

The experience of social injustice is a main motivating cause behind social revolutionary terrorism. Relative deprivation or great differences in income distribution in a society have in some studies even been found to correlate rather strongly with the emergence of social revolutionary political violence and ideological terrorism. Inequality driven by economic globalization has resulted into despair and hostility. When people are denied access to clean water, soil and air to meet their basic human needs, we see the rise of poverty, ill health and a sense of hopelessness. Desperate people can resort to desperate solutions. Former World Bank President James Wolfensohn emphasizes that 9/11 was a wake up call to the west about how urgently the poverty in the south and inequality between the two unequal halves of the world needed to be addressed.

Religious Causes

Religion has been a major factor in recent acts of terrorism. It has provided the ideological framework and justification for the heinous acts of terrorism. Religious ideologies, goals, and motivations are often interwoven with economic, social, and political ideologies. As John Esposito explained, usually 'political and economic grievances are primary causes or catalysts, and religion becomes a means to legitimate and mobilize'.

Religious terrorism has an undecided relationship to the state. Although religious terrorism tends to be an instrument of non-state groups, states have at times used religion to legitimate state violence and terrorism. The 'war on terrorism' has a religious dimension of holy war similar to the point of view adopted by terrorist acts. State efforts at counterterrorism sometimes created more terrorism in response. The war on terror has 'deteriorated the situation' and 'made enemies out of old friends'.[29]

Terrorism can be found in all religious tradition. No one religious tradition holds a monopoly on violence and all religious traditions can be used to justify acts of destruction and aggression. The orations in the 'gurudwaras' and the 'mosques' have played the crucial role in mobilizing the people behind the terrorists.[30] Samuel Peleg pointed out that the monotheistic religions have a tendency to authoritarianism and intolerance due to 'their centrist emphasis on a single deity'. Some strands of Hinduism, Sikhism and Buddhism have also been capable of acts of terror, and these acts have been anti-modernist. Acts of religious terrorism have been rebellious against the secularization of state and society, modernity and globalization. The critique is often in terms of the failure of modern states and societies and with the loss of religious identity and values. The global resurgence of religion has seen radical forms of religion become a primary vehicle for both government and anti-government legitimization.

The world's great religions all have both peaceful and violent messages from which believers can choose. Religious terrorists and violent extremists share the decision to interpret religion to justify violence, whether they are Buddhist, Christian, Hindu, Jewish, Muslim, or Sikh.

Budhhism and Terrorism

The edict not to kill or inflict pain on others is integral to Buddhist thought. Periodically, however, Buddhist monks have encouraged violence or initiated it. The primary example in the 20th and 21st century is in Sri Lanka, where Sinhala Buddhist groups have committed and encouraged violence against local Christians and Tamils. The leader of Aum Shinrikyo, a Japanese cult that committed a lethal sarin gas attack in the mid-1990s, drew on Buddhist as well as Hindu ideas to justify his beliefs.

Christianity and Terrorism

Christianity's teachings, like those of other religions, contain messages of love and peace, and those that can be used to justify violence. Church-sanctioned tribunals aimed to root out Jews and

Muslims who had not converted to Catholicism, often through severe torture. Today in the United States, reconstruction theology and the Christian Identity movement have provided justification for attacks on abortion providers.

Islam and Terrorism

Like those of Judaisim and Christianity, Islam's texts offer both peaceful and warring messages. In the late 20th century, groups motivated by religious and nationalist goals committed attacks such as suicide bombings in Israel. In the early 21st century, Al Qaeda "internationalized" jihad to attack targets in Europe and the United States. From an Islamic perspective, there are scholars who consider Western society, which is based on Christian theology, as the main cause of terrorism. Pape argues that the conflict with West is not only about the ideology but also about the troops stationed in Iraq and Afghanistan which are considered largely responsible for the vagaries of the Muslim population.

Judaism and Terrorism

Judaism's central tenets involve a respect for life's sanctity, but like other religions, its texts can be used to justify violence. Some consider the Sicarii, who used murder by dagger to protest Roman rule in first century Judea, to be the first Jewish terrorists. In the 1940s, Zionist militants such as Lehi carried out terrorist attacks against the British in Palestine. In the late 20th century, militant messianic Zionists use religious claims to the historical land of Israel to justify acts of violence.

Cultural Causes

Another factor that has contributed to the current wave of terrorism is increasing cultural identity. The principle ethnic, religious and racial violence have occurred in the areas which have been the meeting places of major cultures or races. A number of terrorist movements of the past decade grew out of these clashes of human civilization. Palestinian fidayeen grew out of the clash between Jews and Arabs over Palestine. The Front de Liberation de Quebec (FLQ) arose from tensions between French and English Canada.

The Eritrean Liberation Front was a result of the conflict between Christian and Muslims in Ethopia. The inability of the west to prevent this clash of civilizations has resulted in the spread of terrorism.[31] There has been a cultural clash between Islam and the West. However, Berke and Schneider argue that the clash we are witnessing today is not a clash of religions, nor a clash of civilizations. It is a clash between two opposites, between two eras. It is a clash between a mentality that belongs to the Middle Ages and another mentality that belongs to the twenty-first century. It is a clash between civilization and backwardness, between the civilized and the primitive, between barbarity and rationality.[32]

Bernard Lewis argues that Muslims have an endless list of grievances and accusations against the West, its colonialism, racism, imperialism, secularism, its exploitation of their oil, violation of their culture and above all, its support to Israel, the principal enemy of Arabs. Muslims are enraged for the shame and humiliations that the west has inflicted upon them. For a long time there has been a rising tide of rebellion against this western paramountcy, and the desire to reassert Muslim values and restore Muslim greatness.[33] In this cross cultural clash, radical Hindu nationalists are killing Muslims and Christians in India. Radical Jewish groups are murdering Palestinians. Neo-Nazis are preying on minorities in America and Europe. Terrorism often arises in response to a culture of alienation fuelled by cultural conflict rather than in response to any particular national culture. Mark Beissinger explains, alienation produced out of longstanding and deep cultural conflict constitutes an underlying condition for terrorism to flourish. Groups promoting a cultural or nationalist agenda simply 'sell' their cause to the global jihadist movement. The radicalization of Islam in Chechnya and the Ferghana valley in Central Asia suggests that global *jihadists* create global networks by relying in part, though not entirely, on connections with local groups that promote nationalist or local causes. Often, young children are socialized into cultural value systems that celebrate martyrdom, revenge and hatred of other ethnic or national groups, this is likely to increase their readiness to support or commit violent atrocities when they grow up.

Repression by foreign occupation or by colonial powers has given rise to a great many national liberation movements that have sought recourse in terrorist tactics and other political means. Despite their use of terrorist methods, some liberation movements enjoy considerable support and legitimacy among their own constituencies, and sometimes also from segments of international public opinion.

Conclusion

The accounts of the terrorists are difficult to verify. Researchers differ over the path to radicalization. Some boil it down to religion, others to politics and power, others to an array of psychological and social influences. Based on the prevailing scholarly literature, certain causes of terrorism, have been identified. To summarize, a direct cause of terrorism is the existence of concrete grievances among an identifiable subgroup of a larger population, such as an ethnic minority discriminated against by the majority. Lack of democracy, civil liberties and the rule of law give rise to despair. This is not to say, however, that the existence of a dissatisfied minority or majority is a necessary or even a sufficient cause for terrorism; for not all those who are discriminated against turn to terrorism. Contested elections, police brutality and even peace talks are all examples of triggering causes. Rapid modernization and urbanization are strongly correlated with the emergence of ideological terrorism. Presently, the name of religion is being exploited to justify violence and the intensity of terror strikes has gone up incredibly. The powerful attraction of religious and spiritual movements has overshadowed the nationalist or leftist revolutionary ethos of earlier terrorist phases and it has become the central characteristic of a growing international trend.

There is no doubt that the terrorists prospects are improving day by day as their destructive potential increases. The past few decades have witnessed the birth of dozens of aggressive movements espousing varieties of nationalism, religious fundamentalism, fascism etc. To rectify the problem, it is needed to employ a much broader array of longer-term policy tools to reshape the international environment, redress the problems of poverty, marginalization and injustice, and solving the ethnic tensions. Thus, it would not be wrong to say that terrorism is a by-product of broader historical shifts in the international distribution of power in all of its forms-political, economic, military, ideological, and cultural.

ROLE OF PAKISTAN

Much of the Global terrorism today emanates from Pakistan. On December 13, 2001, well-armed terrorists stormed India's parliament. Investigations reveal that they had come from Pakistan. One can ponder how Khalid Sheikh Mohammed, who masterminded the 9/11 operation of 2001, was captured in Pakistan, how terrorists are hiding and leading Al Qaeda from Pakistan, and how jihadi terrorist organizations are working from inside the country and enjoying considerable flexibility. The involvement of Pakistan-inspired elements in the bombing of the Indian embassy in Kabul and the shelter provided by the Pakistani security forces to Dawood Ibrahim clearly reflects that Pakistan is the hub of global terrorism.[34] The confessions of Ajmal Ameer Kasab, one of the terrorists caught alive during the 26/11 attack, are enough to expose Pakistan's involvement in the ghastly crime. It is now clear that Pakistan is the epicentre of terrorism. Pakistan created the Taliban and the jehadis to achieve the strategic depths in Afghanistan and Kashmir. Pakistan is the source of terrorist violence both in Afghanistan and India. The Kabul attack on the Indian embassy was masterminded by the ISI. After Mumbai carnage, there is international pressure on Islamabad to ban the terror outfits operating in Islamabad.[35] U.S. Secretary of State, Hillary Clinton has accused Pakistan of abdicating to the Taliban and the extremists.[36] British Prime Minister Gordon Brown told the Pakistani authorities that the 75 per cent of terror plots in the UK have trails leading to Pakistan and that included the London subway bombing.[37]

Pakistani authorities have long had ties to militant groups based on their soil that largely focused their efforts in Afghanistan and India. Leadership elements of Al Qaeda and the Afghan Taliban, along with other terrorist groups, have made Pakistan's tribal areas their home and work closely with a wide variety of Pakistani militant groups. Violence in Pakistan has been on the rise as more militant groups target the state. According to South Asia Terrorism Portal (SATP), a terrorism database, 2,155 civilians were killed in terrorist violence in 2008 and nearly 1800 civilians have been killed in the first ten months of 2009 as compared to around 1600 civilian deaths from 2003 to 2006. Security forces, especially the army and the police, have increasingly become the target of the militant groups. In October 2009, militants attacked the army headquarters in Rawalpindi and held around forty people hostage for over 20 hours.[38]

Indian Prime Minister Manmohan Singh described Pakistan as the "epicentre of terrorism in the world" and said it had failed to take effective action against militants. He said Islamabad was either "unable" or "unwilling" to control terrorist group Lashkar-e-Taiba, which New Delhi accuses of staging the November attacks on Mumbai. The Chief of Indian Army while speaking on Pakistan's terrorist training camps and Jihadi infiltration said that Pakistan maintains many terrorist training camps and Pakistani-backed terrorists have been making a concerted effort to cross over the LOC in J&K State. More than 2000 Jihadis are being trained in the camps in Pakistan. During July 2005, Lt. Gen Hari Prasad, Northern Command- Army Commander, in a number of media interactions reviewed the enlarged Pakistani phenomenon and came to the conclusion that infiltration of Jihadis from Pakistan has shown a sudden increase. The terrorist training camps in Pakistan are alive and active. Pakistan's reputed magazine "*The Herald*" and other sources point to the fact that Pakistan maintains at least 53 terrorist training camps in Pakistan. They are not confined to Pakistan Occupied Kashmir (PoK) but are spread all over the country.[39] When US-led coalition forces attacked and occupied Afghanistan, most of the mujahideens either fled to the autonomous regions of NWFP of Pakistan or to the other safer areas of the country.[40] Thus Pakistan became the hub of global terrorism.

Most analysts believe that the Pakistani army and the ISI continue some form of alliance with groups they want to use as a strategic circumvent against India and Afghanistan. The Muslim terrorism in India is often believed to be manipulated by them without having any local connection. The militants operating in Kashmir are Pakistani or belong to international Islamic outfits like LeT, JeM etc. Since 1989, Pakistan has funded, armed, trained and supported a host of Kashmiri organizations in their struggle against Indian rule. Pakistan's support for radicals in Kashmir is part of its overall effort to back various insurgent movements in Kashmir.[41] Members of Al Qaeda, its Taliban supporters, and other Islamist militants find safe haven in Pakistani cities such as Quetta and Peshawar, as well as in the rugged Pakistan-Afghanistan border region.

World is now reappraising Pakistan as a rogue state that must be tamed. The situation in Pakistan may go out of control if the world community fails to act jointly at this stage. Pakistan's dubious role in the fight against terrorism must be exposed. The treachery of Islamabad is clearly reflected in its efforts to protect terrorist masterminds like Hafiz Saeed of the Jamaat-ud-Dawa.[42]

Fear of continued turmoil in Pakistan reflects that the country could be a source of a terrorist attack on the western powers possibly with weapons of mass destruction. Increased attacks on well guarded military, police, and UN targets indicate that the Taliban, Al Qaeda, and other militant groups within Pakistan are a growing threat. The current trends, if left unchecked, will increase the risk that Al Qaeda will successfully develop and use a biological weapon or a nuclear device against the United States or its allies.[43]

Origin of Terrorism in Pakistan

The origin of state-sponsored terrorism in Pakistan could be traced to the Soviet military intervention in Afghanistan in 1979 and the involvement of Pakistan as a state supporting the Mujahideen groups in the Afghan civil war. It was a part of a grand alliance among the states made by the US to counter the Soviet Union in the context of the Cold War. Soviet military intervention in Afghanistan had weakened the US presence in the region. In these circumstances Saudi Arabia and Pakistan became US allies in its mission to repel the Soviet invasion of Afghanistan. The US provided technology and sophisticated weapons, Saudi Arabia provided money and Pakistan became a hub for recruiting and training Mujahideen groups. As a result, the involvement of staunch Islamic groups from Saudi Arabia, Afghanistan and Pakistan in the Afghan war paved the way for the rise and legitimisation of the forces of Islamic fundamentalism and terrorist violence in Pakistan's polity.[44]

Islam and jihad were deployed as the instruments of the domestic and foreign policy of the Zia regime. Islam and jihad together provided a breeding ground for terrorists because the former gave religious sanctity to their activities and the latter motivated them to unite Muslims wherever the existence of Islam was perceived to be threatened. The Zia regime financed madrasas. Most of them eventually join loose networks of groups motivated by religious ideologies, including terrorist organizations. Many of the militant groups associated with radical madrasas declared their plans to bring jihad to India, Russia, the central Asian countries and the western world.[45] These schools have become the new breeding ground for radical Islamic militants, where the next generation is trained and groomed. Their graduating classes form an integral recruiting pool for transnational terrorist and conflict networks. For example, both the Taliban and the more extreme Kashmiri terrorist groups found their roots in the young boys from crowded refugee camps taught at radical Madrassas. Such radicalized schools were originally allowed to flourish by the government because the militant groups were seen to serve Pakistani interests in Kashmir and Afghanistan. [46] In the midst of the dismal economic conditions of Pakistan, teenagers who are tempted to be Mujahideen enjoy lucrative job prospects.

Terrorist Organizations in Pakistan

In recent years, many new terrorist groups in Pakistan have emerged and several existing groups have reconstituted themselves. A new crop of militants has evolved which has become more violent. The most menacing development has been the growth of Taliban-linked radical armed groups within Pakistan. The Pakistani army has actively helped some of these groups by providing them with training camps and weapons.[47]Members of Al Qaeda, its Taliban supporters, and other Islamist militants have found safe haven in Pakistan. Al Qaeda militants also reportedly have made alliances with indigenous Pakistani terrorist groups that have been implicated in both anti-Western attacks in Pakistan and terrorism in India. Pakistan is a major supporter of the Taliban and of terrorists operating in Kashmir, both of which groups it regarded as freedom fighters. The Afghan and Kashmir terrorist operations strengthened domestic Islamic radicals. The secular movement for independence has become an increasingly Islamist crusade to bring all of Kashmir under Pakistani control. Pakistan-based Islamist groups are now significantly more important than the secular Kashmir-based ones. These Pakistani militant groups like Lashkar-i-Taiba and Harkat-ul-Mujahideen pose a long-term danger to international security, regional stability, and especially Pakistan itself. Their agenda is to "liberate" Kashmir, which they believe was annexed by India illegally.[48] These groups have developed an ability to raise resources and plan and conduct operations in Afghanistan and India, and increasingly within Pakistan.[49]

Pakistan has been funding the activities of terrorist outfits in Pakistan-Occupied Kashmir (PoK) as well as in J & K. Pakistan has sought to legitimise the existence of as well as its support to terrorist groups operating in J & K by calling them freedom fighters. Among these outfits, the activities of Jaish-e-Mohammad (JEM) and Lashkar-e-Taiba (LET) are worth noting. The jihad-related terrorist organisations have often been closely associated with the senior officials of the ISI.[50] The Pakistani Islamis and Jehadi organizations are the main source of external support to the jihadi terrorist elements in Thailand, Singapore, Malaysia, Bangladesh and Indonesia based Jehadi organizations.[51] Similarly, in Xinjiang province of China, which is predominantly populated by Uighur Muslims, Pakistan was allegedly pushing Taliban-trained youth to fight the Peoples' Liberation Army (PLA).

The groups operating in Kashmir can be classified as:

Sectarian: Groups such as the Sunni Sipah-e-Sahaba and the Shia Tehrik-e-Jafria, which are engaged in violence within Pakistan.

Both are under the influence of the Deobandi organization Jamiat-e-Ulema Islami (JUI) and funded by wealthy Arab individuals and organizations. There are also Sh'ia sectarian groups who target Sunni Muslims and obtain funding from Iran.

Anti-Indian: Terrorist groups that operate with the alleged support of the Pakistani military and the intelligence agency Inter-Services Intelligence (ISI), such as the Lashkar-e-Taiba (LeT), the Jaish-e-Muhammad (JeM), and the Harakat ul-Mujahadeen (HuM). This category includes Deobandi organizations such as Jaish-e-Mohammad (JM), Harkat-ul-Ansar/Harkat-ul-Mujahideen Ahle Hadith organizations such as Lashkar-e-Taiba (LeT); and those groups under the influence of the Jamaat-e-Islami (JI) such as Al Badr and Hizbul Mujahideen (HM).

Afghan Taliban: The original Taliban movement and especially its Kandahari leadership centered around Mullah Mohammad Omar, is believed to be active in training youth in Pakistan's tribal areas.

Al Qaeda and its affiliates: The organization formed by Osama bin Laden and other non-South Asian terrorists believed to be ensconced in the Federally Administered Tribal Areas (FATA). Rohan Gunaratna of the International Centre for Political Violence and Terrorism Research in Singapore says other foreign militant groups such as the Islamic Movement of Uzbekistan, Islamic Jihad group, the Libyan Islamic Fighters Group and the Eastern Turkistan Islamic Movement are also located in FATA.

The Pakistani Taliban: Groups consisting of extremist outfits in the FATA, led by individuals such as Hakimullah Mehsud, of the Mehsud tribe in South Waziristan, Maulana Faqir Muhammad of Bajaur, and Maulana Qazi Fazlullah of the Tehrik-e-Nafaz-e-Shariat-e-Mohammadi (TNSM).

The Punjabi Taliban: Punjabi Taliban has gained prominence after the major 2008 and 2009 attacks in the Punjabi cities of Lahore, Islamabad, and Rawalpindi. Hassan Abbas, a fellow at the Asia Society, writes the Punjabi Taliban network is a loose conglomeration of members of banned militant groups of Punjabi origin-sectarian as well as those focused on Kashmir that have developed strong connections with the Pakistani Taliban, Afghan Taliban, and other militant groups based in FATA and the North-West Frontier Province (NWFP). The Punjabi Taliban includes individuals or factions of groups such as Jaish-e-Mohammed, Sipah-i-Sahaba Pakistan, and Lashkar-i-Jhangvi and their various splinter groups. Abbas writes that many of these militants "directly benefited from state patronage in the 1990s and were professionally trained in asymmetrical warfare, guerrilla tactics, and sabotage." The Punjabi Taliban is distinct from the traditional Pashtun Taliban, experts say. They are usually more educated and more technologically savvy.

Each of these groups has received state support in various guises over the years.

Kashmir-focused outfits have enjoyed extensive and enduring patronage of the ISI and the Pakistan army. Sectarian groups have also been engaged by various state and central governments.

TTP: In December 2007, about thirteen militant groups came under the umbrella of Tehrik-i-Taliban Pakistan (TTP), also known as the Pakistani Taliban, with militant commander Baitullah Mehsud from South Waziristan as the leader. After Mehsud was killed in August 2009 in a U.S. missile strike, Hakimullah Mehsud took over as leader of the TTP. In the last few years people have begun to organize themselves around an ideology pursuing an agenda much similar to that of the Afghan Taliban in Afghanistan. TTP not only has representation from all of FATA's seven agencies but also from several settled districts of the NWFP. The TTP has announced a defensive jihad against the Pakistani army, enforcement of shariat, and a plan to unite against NATO forces in Afghanistan. Pakistani authorities accused the group's former leader, Baitullah Mehsud, of assassinating former Prime Minister Benazir Bhutto in December 2007. The group has proved that it poses a serious threat to the country's stability.[52]

Lashkar-e-Toiba: Lashkar-e-Toiba means the army of Toiba. Toiba is the old name of the holy city of Medina in Saudi Arabia. The group was found in 1990 to fight Indian rule in Kashmir. Its members include thousands of Afghan veterans. It was blamed for the coordinated attacks on Mumbai in November last year. It was banned in Pakistan in 2002. Of all the Pakistani based groups, it is widely believed to be the most closely leashed to the Pakistani ISI. Unlike the other Pakistani militant organizations, LeT had never targeted the Pakistani state or international targets within Pakistan. Seven LeT linked militants are being tried in Pakistan for suspected involvement in the Mumbai assault, but India is insisting Pakistan to prosecute its founder Hafiz Mohammed Saeed, who India says was the attack mastermind.[53] The confessions of Ajmal Ameer Qasab are enough to expose Pakistan's involvement in the crime committed by the persons trained in Pakistan. His father in Pakistani Punjab's Faridkot village has confirmed that the terrorist in India's custody is his son. The nine terrorists killed by security forces could also have been identified by their parents in Pakistan had they been alive. They were the men of the LeT, which had been functioning under the guise of the Jamaat-ud-Dawa.

Lashkar has also taken responsibility for attack on the Red Fort in Delhi and the airport in Srinagar. It does not confine its territorial ambitions to Jammu and Kashmir. It proclaims that 'Hyderabad Deccan' and Junagadh are parts of Pakistan and that his aim is to liberate the Muslims of India from Hindu oppression.[54] Willie Brigitte, a French national was arrested on charges of attempting to stage terrorist attacks in Australia. He is believed to have been given instructions by Sajid Mir, the Lashkar Commander who is alleged to have handled David Headley. Brigitte also confirmed that the Lashkar ran atleast one camp for foreign jihadis. French investigators established that another Paris based Lashkar operative, Ghulam Mustafa Rana, had links with Richard Reid- the jihadist who attempted to blow up a Paris-Miami flight with explosives planted in his shoes.[55] The rocket attacks of September 2009, in the border villages of Punjab, further proved the Pakistani hand in instigating violence. Sources also inform that in July, Pakistani security forces had seized a huge cache of arms, including 107 mm rockets, from militant organizations, including Lashker-e-Taiba, at Dera Ghazi Khan.

Lashkar's cadre joined in jihadist struggles across the world. The units participated in the civil war in Tajikistan, which ran from

1992 to 1997. They also fought in Bosnia and Herzegovina. Kashmir, where the Lashkar Mujahideen first began operating in 1993, was seen as a stepping stone for a global jihad. In the Lashkar's conception, the jihad in Kashmir marked just one part of a worldwide contestation between Islam and infidels. By the last decade, the Lashkar's transnational affiliations were apparent. Pakistan daily *Jang*, reported in 1999 that the jihadists from more than 50 countries had attended the lashkar's annual congregation at its Muridke headquarters. The Pakistani state, the Lashkar leadership believed, was an ally in its jihadist project. In 1998, Punjab Governor Shahid Hamid, accompanied by a group of ministers, visited Muridke to congratulate the LeT on the martyrdom of their 418 mujahid in Indian occupied Kashmir.[56] Lashkar leadership believed that the Pakistani state was an ally in its jihadist project and the organization with its patronage from Pakistan, turned its camps into factories feeding the global jihad. The recruits are known to have travelled to Pakistan to train with the LeT.[57] The Lashkar Jehadi Headley has revealed to the interrogators that Pakistan has sheltered in Karachi the major Lashkar leaders like Bhatkal brothers, Mufti Sufiyan and Rasool Parti. Pakistan had played a key role in the Lashkar's trans-Line of Control (LoC) operations, serving between 1997 and 2001 as the organisation's commander for the forward camps from where infiltrating groups of terrorists are launched into Jammu and Kashmir with Pakistani military support.

The Lashkar-e-Toiba has training camps spread across Pakistan and Pakistan occupied Kashmir (PoK). Its recruitment centres are spread across the length and breadth of Pakistan and PoK in Muzaffarabad, Lahore, Peshawar, Islamabad, Rawalpindi, Karachi, Multan, Quetta, Gujranwala, Sialkot, Gilgit etc. LeT reportedly has 2,200 offices across Pakistan. It also has branches in Saudi Arabia, United Kingdom, Bangladesh and South East Asia. Majority of LeT recruits are from the Hanaffi traditions.

Al Qaeda: The Arabic word *qaeda* can be translated as a "base of operation" or "foundation," It was formed in the late 1980s by Osama bin Laden, most famous for the 9/11 attacks on the U.S. It serves as an umbrella organization for worldwide network of Sunni Islamic groups. Members of Al Qaeda, have found safe haven in Pakistani cities such as Quetta and Peshawar, as well as in the rugged Pakistan-Afghanistan border region. Al Qaeda militants also reportedly have made alliances with indigenous Pakistani terrorist groups that have been implicated in both anti-Western attacks in Pakistan and terrorism in India.

Rohan Gunaratna, an expert on terrorism, says that bin Laden's group is training most of the terrorist groups in FATA. "Al Qaeda considers itself as the vanguard of the Islamic movement," Gunaratna says, and has introduced its practice of suicide bombings to both the Afghan and the Pakistani Taliban. Besides providing militant groups in Pakistan with technical expertise and capabilities, Al Qaeda is also promoting cooperation among a variety of them. Don Rassler, an associate at the Combating Terrorism Center, an independent research institution based at the U.S. military academy at West Point, writes Al Qaeda "has assumed a role as mediator and coalition builder among various Pakistani militant group factions by promoting the unification of entities that have opposed one another or had conflicting ideas about whether to target the Pakistani state."

Pakistani Taliban's attacks against the government and the security establishment have strained their relations with the Afghan Taliban who enjoy close relationship with the army and the ISI, the country's premier intelligence agency.[58]

Many observers have also come out with the warning that an American preoccupation with Iraq has contributed to allowing the emergence of new Al Qaeda safe havens in western Pakistan.

A study conducted by C. Cristine Fair on the military recruitment in Pakistan has come out with the conclusion that Al Qaeda depends upon a network of informal relations with groups based in Pakistan to gain access to collaborators and individuals to execute attacks within Pakistan. This article's findings also suggest that Al Qaeda does not have an explicit and dedicated recruiting infrastructure to recruit Pakistanis for its operations. The people who were interviewed were dubious that from the perspective of a demand for manpower

Pakistanis have the human capital endowments that may be of interest to an organization like Al Qaeda. One analyst interviewed believed that Pakistanis in the diaspora might be more attractive to Al Qaeda because such persons would likely have the skills and backgrounds would be attractive for a transnational enterprise like Al Qaeda. Although Al Qaeda does not appear to have a dedicated recruiting infrastructure in Pakistan, the group's informal connections with other militant groups and Pakistani state organizations provide the group at least proxy assistance and support for their operations. The reports of Sheikh Khalid Mohammed's arrest highlight the potential links between Al Qaeda, the Pakistan Army, and Pakistani religious organizations.[59]

Al Qaeda's connections with Pakistani groups enable Al Qaeda activists to become absorbed into Pakistani society. The activists of Al Qaeda and other groups did training in the camps in Afghanistan. Cadres of Al Qaeda and Pakistan also have developed personal ties through marriage. Sometimes the relationships are based on business interactions. Pakistani militants came into contact with Al Qaeda while sharing training camps in Afghanistan. Because of such related experiences, these groups have a greater affinity for the Taliban and Al Qaeda than groups without such common training opportunities.[60]

To summarize the connections between Al Qaeda and the Pakistan-based groups, it is widely believed that Al Qaeda has connections with the Pakistani militant and Islamist groups, including: JI, JUI, LeJ, JM, and SSP. Although there is some discord about the relationship between Al Qaeda and LeT, it is clear that at some level Al Qaeda is obtaining forms of assistance from LeT cadres. Moreover, Al Qaeda has a huge support base in the tribal areas of Waziristan, Baluchistan and Swat.

Sipah-e-Sahaba: Formerly known as Anjuman Sipah-e-Sahaba (ASS), this group is thought to be behind most of the attacks on Shiites. It came into prominence following the Iranian Revolution in 1980s. Maulana Haq Nawaz Jhangvi, Maulana Zia-ur-Rehman Farooqi, Maulana Eesar-ul-Haq Qasmi and Maulana Azam Tariq established the SSP, in September 1985 in an environment of increasing sectarian hostility in Pakistani Punjab. The origin of this outfit lie in the feudal set-up of Pakistani Punjab and politico-religious developments in the nineteen seventies and eighties. Political and economic power in Pakistani Punjab was a privilege of large landowners, mostly Shias, a minority as compared to the Sunni sect. Urban Punjab in contrast, was a non-feudalised middle-class society and largely from the Sunni sect. The SSP is also alleged to have been set up at the behest of the then Zia-ul-Haq regime as part of the efforts to build an Islamist counter to pro-democracy forces ranged against the military regime of the Eighties.

The socio-economic rationale for SSP's origin is explained largely from the economic profile of Jhang, the home base of SSP. This place has a considerably high proportion of large land holdings, supporting feudalism. Most large landlords, who are Shias, dominate both society and politics in the region.[61]

Sipah-e-Sahaba, has launched a terrorist campaign against Pakistan's Shia minority, killing more than 3,600 people over the last decade. The outfit has also operated as a political party. Its members were also suspected of involvement in burning to death of seven Christians on suspicions of blasphemy. There is another school of thought which says that the SSP phenomenon began from Jhang as a reaction to the socio-economic repression of the masses by Shia feudal structure in the area.

The SSP is reported to have approximately 3,000 - 6,000 trained activists who indulge in various kinds of violent sectarian activities, which are primarily directed against the Shias. Most SSP cadres hail from Punjab. Many SSP cadres have received arms training from the Harkat-ul-Mujahideen (HuM) and the erstwhile Taliban regime in Afghanistan. The SSP is also reported to be closely linked to the Jaish-e-Mohammed (JeM), a Pakistan-based terrorist outfit active in Jammu and Kashmir. The SSP draws support, inspiration and assistance from various political parties in Pakistan, particularly the Jamaat-e-Islam (JeI) and the Jamaat-Ulema-e-Islam (JuI). The JuI is associated with running a large number of Madrassas all over Pakistan from where recruits for the HuM, SSP and Taliban are provided. In the poor areas of southern Punjab, madrasahs funded by the Sunni sectarian political party Sipah-e Sahaba Pakistan (ssp) reportedly even pay parents for sending them their children.[62]

News reports have indicated that the SSP and other Sunni outfits hold Iran as the sponsor of Shia extremist outfits in Pakistan. Hence when any major Sunni leader is assassinated, Iranians in Pakistan are targeted for retribution. For instance, the Iranian Counsel General in Lahore, Sadeq Ganji, was killed in December 1990 in what was reported to be a retribution for the February 1990 killing of the SSP co-founder Maulana Haq Nawaz Jhangvi. Similarly, in January 1997, the Iranian Cultural Centre in Lahore was attacked and set on fire, while in Multan seven persons were killed including the Iranian diplomat Muhammad Ali Rahimi.

Jamaat-ud-Dawa: It is known to be the parent organization of LeT. Hafiz Mohammad Saeed, Hafiz Abdul Raḥman Makki and Zafar Iqbal, all teachers at Lahore's Islamic University of Engineering and Technology, separately set up the Jamaat-ud-Dawa, dedicated to religious campaigning. It draws its sponsorship from the ISI and though proscribed abroad, has a free run in Pakistan. It has branches all across the country and is famous for its terror activities. It sees itself as a movement and not an organization and has appealed to many rural and urban areas. The Jamaat-ud-Dawa has a wide base and operates 140 schools and 29 seminaries in different towns and cities of Pakistan. According to the Jamaat's website: "Islam does not mean following a few rituals like performing prayers, keeping fasts, performing the Haj, giving alms, or donating to charitable works, but in fact, it is a complete "code of life". Its appeal extends to urban professionals like doctors who were out in Muzaffarabad in 2005, after a devastating earthquake. Unlike the Taliban, the Jamaat is modeled after Hamas and is not merely an army with gun-toting members but a complex and intricate organization with a social and political agenda. It has a huge following.[63] It has been banned by the Pakistan after being declared a terrorist organization by the UN Security Council.

Role of Madrassas: The presence of many unregulated Madrassas throughout Pakistan is believed to contribute significantly to its terrorism problem. Although the madrassas were created to fill the hole left by the state in educating young people free of charge, some became recruiting centers for terrorists, as most of the financing for the institutions came from terrorist groups and not from the government. There is also lack of good education in these institutions, as their graduates are only good for Mosque services, and not for other fields of life. Thus, social and economic factors played a great role in helping to spread intolerance.

Today, there are as many such schools within Pakistan. These new schools tend to teach a more extreme version of Islam than what had been propagated before. The individual schools decide what to teach and preach. Many provide only religious subjects to their students, focusing on Arabic texts and excluding simple math, science, or geography. The primary worry with the explosion of Madrassa system is not with the schools in general, but with the hatred they preach. Around 10-15 per cent of the schools are affiliated with extremist religious/political groups, who have co-opted education for their own ends. These schools teach a distorted view of Islam. Many of the radical religious schools also include weapons and physical training in their regimen, as well as weekly lessons on political speechmaking. The students are uneducated, young, dependent on the schools, and cut off from contact with their parents for years at a time, and thus highly vulnerable to being programmed towards violence.[64]

These madrassas are supposed to provide military training. Former Pakistani President Pervez Musharraf acknowledged that some madrassas might be involved in extremism and terrorism. In Pakistan, as in many developing countries, education is not mandatory. The World Bank estimates that only 40 per cent of Pakistanis are literate, and many rural areas lack public schools. Islamic religious schools madrassas on the other hand, are located all over the country and provide not only free education, but also free food, housing, and clothing. In the poor areas of southern Punjab, madrasahs funded by the Sunni sectarian political party Sipah-e Sahaba Pakistan (SSP) reportedly even pay parents for sending them their children. In the 1980s, Pakistani dictator General Mohammad Zia-ul-Haq promoted the madrassas as a way to garner the religious parties' support for his rule and to recruit troops for the anti-Soviet war.[65]

Many madrassas are financed by the zakat. More and more religious schools are funded by wealthy Pakistani industrialists, by private and government-funded nongovernmental organizations. Without state supervision, these madrassas are free to preach a violent version of Islam. Most madrasahs offer only religious instruction, ignoring other subjects important for functioning in modern society. These schools encourage their graduates, who often cannot find work because of their lack of practical education, to fulfill their "spiritual obligations" by fighting against Hindus in Kashmir or against Muslims of other sects in Pakistan. Pakistani madrassas adopt such extremist ideologies. Pakistan's interior minister Moinuddin Haider recognizes these problems. "The brand of Islam they are teaching is not good for Pakistan," he says. "Some, in the garb of religious training, are busy fanning sectarian violence, poisoning people's minds." He also announced a reform plan that would require all madrassas to register with the government, expand their curricula, disclose their financial resources, seek permission for admitting foreign students, and stop sending students to militant training camps. But Haider's reforms have failed because of the regime's neglect or the madrassas' refusal to be regulated. Very few madrassas in Pakistan have been registered with the government. Moreover, some chancellors are unwilling to expand their curricula, arguing that madrassas are older than Pakistan itself having been "designed 1,200 years ago in Iraq," according to the chancellor of the Khudamudeen madrassas. The chancellor of Darul Uloom Haqqania objects to what he calls the government's attempt to "destroy the spirit of the madrassas under the cover of broadening their curriculum."[66]

Pakistani revolutionary groups are now spreading jihad all over the world. The alumni of the existing madrassas ultimately join networks of groups motivated by religious ideologies, including terrorist organisations. Drug trafficking, crime and illegal trade finance such groups. Endorsing jihad has become a flourishing business in Pakistan. It is run on the basis of labour supplied by the poorer families and capital provided by private sources including the Pakistani diaspora. Pakistani militant groups have also been exporting their version of jihad to other parts. They have been training students from diverse areas such as Myanmar, Nepal, Chechnya, Bangladesh, Afghanistan, Yemen, Mongolia and Kuwait. The Darul Uloom Haqqania, the madrassa that contributed to the making of Taliban, had a substantial proportion of students from Afghanistan. It has also been training students from Uzbekistan, Tajikistan, Russia and Turkey. Besides, many of the militant groups associated with radical madrassas unequivocally declare their plans to bring jihad to India, Russia, the central Asian countries and the western world.[67]

These schools have become the new breeding ground for radical Islamic militants, where the next generation is trained and groomed. Their graduating classes form an integral recruiting pool for transnational terrorist and conflict networks. For example, both the Taliban and the more extreme Kashmiri terrorist groups found their roots in the young boys from crowded refugee camps taught at radical Madrassas. The 55th Brigade, made of up foreigners recruited by Osama bin Laden's Al Qaeda terrorist organization to fight in Afghanistan, also drew from the schools. Such radicalized schools were originally allowed to flourish by the government because the militant groups were seen to serve Pakistani interests in Kashmir and Afghanistan. The situation has now changed. These recruits have dangerous implications for security both inside Pakistan and abroad. Rather than acting as religious centers of cooperation, the leaders of various schools have issued edicts against other groups, thus triggering violence. For example, within North West Frontier Province, Sind, and Baluchistan, their statements have played a key role in turning Shia-Sunni disputes into a dangerous threat.[68]

The recruits are regularly sent abroad to serve in conflicts in Kashmir, Afghanistan, Chechnya, and a number of other wars decided by the school leaders to be part of the jihad. Their influence at both the strategic and tactical level in these wars should not be understated. In 1997, when a Taliban offensive stalled, the Haqquania Madrassa completely shut down. It sent its entire student body across the border to fight, helping the attack to succeed. Similarly, their role in supporting groups fighting India over the Kashmir, including those thought responsible for the recent parliament attacks, has raised tensions between the two nuclear powers to dangerous levels.

An added concern is that the student pool in many of these radical Madrassas is made up of foreigners as well, and thus lays the seeds of conflict elsewhere. This internationalizes their virulent influence. As much as 10-50 per cent of the students in certain Madrassas are from abroad, coming from regions at war such as Afghanistan, Chechnya, and the Philippines. These students return with new influence and a changed outlook, helping to worsen the levels of violence in their home states.

NARCO Terrorism

The association of important political parties and leaders with drug syndicates and the successful intervention of the links between traders in narcotics and terrorists through the ISI has caused the rise of narco-terrorism and transformed Pakistan into the hub of narco-terrorism in Asia. Along with Iran and Afghanistan, Pakistan has become a part of the Golden Triangle notorious for poppy cultivation and illegal traffic in drugs. With the Soviet invasion of Afghanistan over three million refugees from Afghanistan fled to Pakistan and some of them were familiar with the production and processing of heroin. As a result, they were able to establish plants in Baluchistan and North-West Frontier Province (NWFP) to produce drugs. With the Iranian blockade under the revolutionary regime, the Indo-Pakistan border became vulnerable to transactions in arms and drugs. The drug barons in Pakistan rooted these items through the states of Punjab, Rajasthan and Gujarat. With the fencing of the border in Rajasthan and Punjab the ISI had to shift the bases of its operations. By now it has been able to establish bases in Myanmar, Bangladesh and Nepal through narcotic funds. India's north-eastern states have also become exposed to terrorist assault.[69]

The Karachi Project

This project is conceived by Pakistan's ISI in collaboration with 'non state' terror outfits. It uses Pakistan-trained Indian youth to leave behind bags filled with explosives in India. This joint venture is between the Pakistan Army, the ISI and terror groups like Lashkar-e-Taiba and HUJI. It is a part of the plan which uses militant groups to counter India. They use Indian youth to carry out terror strikes using locally available bomb material. The Karachi Project uses only Indian nationals recruited by Lashkar either in India, Pakistan or in Bangladesh and indoctrinated using propaganda videos showing the Babri Masjid demolition and Gujrat riots. This project has been directly responsible for the death of over 500 Indians in 10 bomb blasts since 2005.[70]

The Karachi project made its debut on July 28, 2005, at around 5:15 p.m. An IED was placed near the toilet of the Shramjeevi Express running from Patna to Delhi. The results were deadly. Ten passengers were killed and 79 injured when an IED blasted through the coach. After this, there was a bombing after every six months, targeting places of worship, public transport and shopping centres. In the same year, in October, before Diwali festival, three serial blasts killed 62 people in Delhi. In 2007, three explosions at Sankat Mochan temple and railway station, in Varanasi, further disclosed the misdeeds of Karachi project. The most horrified explosion occurred in Mumbai, in 2006, when 209 people were killed in seven bomb blasts in six local trains in Mumbai. The death trail continued further at Hyderabad where twin blasts at garden and snack stall killed 42 people. In Jaipur, in 2008, nine blasts in market placed killed 63 people which further strengthened the Karachi Project. The death toll kept on rising with the 2008 Delhi and Ahmedabad bomb blast. However with the Pune blast of February 13, 2010, which occurred in popular German Bakery, many new links and clues of the Karachi Project have been disclosed.

The youth who are recruited are trained by the ISI in the remote areas of Pakistan. They are given arms training across the border. The ISI began training such operatives in small groups of four to five. It has been estimated, that in a time span of two years, around 50-60 jihadis have been trained and infiltrated in India. The candidates were given one month training capsule in bomb making by the use of chemicals and locally available materials to fabricate IEDs. They often select unguarded targets to obtain maximum results. David Headley has revealed that the IM fugitives have been provided with houses. They were also given funds to draw youth from India who are trained in the use of arms and explosives by Lashkar commanders as well as officers of Pakistan army.

The connection between the LeT and Indian Mujahideen (IM), as part of this project has been established. The LeT pushed David Headley into India to get possible targets. Indian Mujahideens went to Pakistan and viewed videos shot by him, so that they could be sent to India to carry out attacks. According to Headley, the fugitive Bhatkal brothers Riaz and Iqbal who founded the IM were being sheltered by the LeT and the ISI in Pakistan. He also told that some serving and retired Pakistani Army officers were also part of the project.[71]

Pakistan's double standard in the fight against terrorism must be exposed. The duplicity of Islamabad is clearly reflected in its effort to protect terrorist masterminds like Hafiz Saeed of the Jamaat-ud-Dawa, a front for the Lashkar-e-Taiba. He would have been in jail today for his role in Mumbai terrorist attack if Pakistan had cooperated with India. Pakistan blamed 'non state actors' for the November 26 terrorist attack on Mumbai, but now it cannot deny their Pakistani identity. The confessions of Ajmal Qasab are enough to expose Pakistan's involvement. Due to the US pressure, Pakistan has banned JuD. Its offices are closed officially and bank accounts have been frozen. Some of its leaders too, have been either put under house arrest or taken in police custody. But there is no guarantee that the JuD will really stop functioning. Pakistan is used to taking such steps only for protecting the elements it ought to punish. It is indulging in deceptive tactics to prevent the declaration of Pakistan a terrorist state. When the so called crack down began on the Muridke near Lahore HQ of the JuD, there were few people at the premises. The orders to freeze its accounts were issued after allowing the terrorist outfit enough time to withdraw the enormous funds it had in its coffers. The United Jihad Council, headed by terrorist mastermind Syed Salahadduin has been allowed to temporarily dissolve itself with its leaders going underground. This is Pakistan's way of fighting terrorism. Similarly, Indian Mujahideen jehadi, Salman aka Chotu, who was arrested from the UP-Nepal border by UP's ATS, said that Pakistan has done nothing to turn off the terror tap and that plans devised as part of the Karachi Project, for fresh attack on Delhi and Mumbai are on course. Salman was instructed to reactivate the IM cells which have gone dormant since the crackdown on the gang in 2008. Thus, Salman's account establishes once again that Pakistan remains committed as ever to use terrorism to extract concessions from India.

The Pakistani army always supported the jehadi network. There was no attempt to stop the activities of these groups in Pakistan after they were banned. They were just allowed to sprout. Qasab's journey from a remote village Faridkot to Mumbai is a testimony to this. "There have been clear indications of Pakistan's ISI not toeing Islamabad's official line and allowing supplies to easily get through to the Taliban."[72] Retired ISI officers are also helping the Pakistani Taliban and they have become more deadly. Ex-ISI officers are still in the business because they have now attached themselves as advisors to militant organizations like LeT and the Jaish. Ex-servicemen are imparting arms training within the compounds of their homes. Different officials are attached with different groups.[73] Not only India, Pakistan's border guards have permitted a thousand strong armed Pakistani Jehadis to cross over into Afghanistan to join the Taliban forces.

TURMOIL IN WAZIRISTAN

After numerous suicide attacks that killed many innocent civilians and security personnel, the Pakistani army has finally started it's long awaited offensive in South Waziristan to fight back the Pakistani Taliban. After a two week spate of terrorism in late September and

October 2009, the Pakistani army launched Operation Rah-e- Nijat. Thousands of Pakistani soldiers are executing the movement to encircle the homeland of Mehsud tribe. These tribe men, with the help of Taliban, have launched a series of terrorist attacks to destabilize the state. A bloody attack, on November 13, 2009, claimed 18 lives and left more than 80 wounded by destroying the regional headquarters of Inter-Services Intelligence in North West Frontier Province, while in Balochistan, suspected Taliban militants set ablaze NATO supply trucks on their way to Afghanistan. Earlier in the day, a suicide bomber crashed an explosives- packed car into a police station in Bannu, killing 7 policemen. In another suicide blast on November 10th, in Charsadda city, over 20 people died as military killed 9 militants in South Waziristan. Dozens of soldiers and police officers have been killed in suicide attacks from October 5 to 15 that included a 22-hour siege of the Army headquarters in Rawalpindi and the death of 8 soldiers and three simultaneous attacks on police training camps in Lahore. Over 90 innocent civilians, many of them women and children, were killed in a car bomb explosion in a busy market area of Peshawar, the capital of the North-West Frontier Province (NWFP) of Pakistan, on October 28,2009. The explosion coincided with the visit of Hillary Clinton, US Secretary of State, to Pakistan, gave the explosion a political colour as meant to express the protest of the perpetrators against the continuing US drone strikes on Al Qaeda and Taliban hide-outs in the tribal belt and against Pakistan's continuing co-operation with the US in counter-terrorism. The other attack took place on October 9 in which over 50 persons were killed in a suicide explosion in a market place. In another series of attacks reported on October 15, two were against targets which were attacked earlier- the FIA office in Lahore and the police training academy at Manawan, a Lahore suburb. About 20 terrorists split into three groups are reported to have participated in the three attacks in the Lahore area on October 15 against the FIA office, the Manawan Police Academy and a commando school at Bedian on the outskirts of Lahore. The fourth attack of the day was on a police station at Kohat in the NWFP carried out by a lone vehicle-borne suicide bomber. There were 32 fatalities in the four attacks of security forces personnel as well as civilians caught in the firing or explosion.

These attacks aimed at removing the government and getting hold of Pakistan's nuclear weapons. These terrorist attacks were also a reaction to the army's build up and the indications of pending military action in South Waziristan. Suicide bombers, traced to South Waziristan, had killed over 100 people and wounded many, including 2 suicide bomb blasts at the Islamic University in Islamabad, and also assassinated a Brigadier General. Taliban fighters also crossed the border from Afghanistan into Pakistan. Several leaders within the military had direct connections to the Army or ISI. Dr.[74]

South Waziristan, a remote mountainous region bordering Afghanistan, is considered to be a global hub for Islamic militants. The Mehsud tribe of this region is reputed to be among the fiercest fighters in Pakistan. This region is the home base of TTP, responsible for 80% of Pakistan's terrorist violence. The TTP is a hotch-potch of the numerous Pakistani insurgent and terrorist groups, which were trained and armed in the past by Pakistan's Inter-Services Intelligence (ISI) and Special Services Group (SSG). The Mehsuds are the sons of the South Waziristan soil, but have repeatedly demonstrated a capability for action outside South Waziristan in areas such as the Orakzai agency of the Federally-Administered Tribal Areas (FATA) and in the Peshawar, Kohat and Dera Ismail Khan areas of the North-West Frontier Province. Hakeemullah Mehsud, who was chosen as the Amir of the TTP after the death of Baitullah Mehsud in a US Drone strike on August 5,2009, is reportedly still based in the Orakzai agency, where he has been supervising operations against the NATO's logistic convoys to Afghanistan while at the same time coordinating operations in Peshawar, Kohat and Dera Ismail Khan. The current military operations by the Pakistani Army against the Mehsud component of the TTP in South Waziristan is viewed by the Taliban and Al Qaeda elements as undertaken at the behest of the US.

Both Afghanistan and Pakistan are living an unsafe moment. Afghanistan, besides its ongoing war and violence, confronts a governance crisis. Pakistan has embarked on a high-risk military campaign to combat the growing terrorism that is destabilizing the state. But some argue that the military's aim may not be to eliminate the insurgency outright, but rather to disperse the rebels and destroy the leadership. The goal would be to cripple its capacity to commit terrorism at will throughout Pakistan, while keeping the insurgents alive as a geopolitical trump card. The army launched several brief offences in South Waziristan. The military launched in Jan 2008, operation Zalzala to dislodge Tehrik-I-Taliban Chief Mehsud from his sanctuary but could not succeed until August when Mehsud died in a drone attack. The army also came into action when militants advanced from the Swat valley in the NWFP into the districts of Dir and Buner. The army was able to extract back the Swat valley from the militants after a two month long campaign. This time it appears that army is moving more rapidly than the previous campaigns. It has retaken Koktai, the birth place of Hakimullah Mehsud and the home town of Qari Hussain Mehsood, a senior Taliban commander known as 'the mentor of suicide bombers'. After the first ten days of the present military campaign in South Waziristan, the military claims that over 200 jihadists have been killed. The army faces 10,000-12,000 hard core Taliban, including as many as 1500 tough Uzbek fighters, Al Qaeda members and elements of Punjabi militant groups. They are better armed than the militants army faced in Swat.[75] The Taliban's siege of Military Headquarters has spurred Pakistan forces to fight harder against them. A Pakistani Professor has given a statement, "By launching these attacks on the very citadel and symbol of the Pakistan Army, they have just crossed a red line, and there is no turning back as far as the Pakistan army is concerned. I think they will be made to pay for it."[76]

It appears that this time the political determination to counter the militants is strong in FATA. The government and army have agreed that the time is mature to deal with the terrorists to overcome the problem. Public emotion, which had previously favoured the militants as defenders of Islam and Pakistani nationalism, has turned against them since the events in Swat. But the threat which Pakistan is facing is deep. There are armed Islamist groups such as Lashkar-e-Taiba (LeT), its parent organization Jamat-ud-Dawa (JuD) and other terrorist organizations which are against the democratic process and believe in turning Pakistan into a fundamental Islamic state. There are also Taliban militants in the tribal areas on the Pakistan-Afghanistan border. These groups are inspired by the Afghan Taliban, which was created by Pakistan in the 1990s as a proxy army. In recent years, Punjabi militants have also provided training to their Taliban brothers.[77]

Pakistan is facing the most crucial moment of its existence. If the army ends up being satisfied with merely degrading the TTP as a terrorist threat, the latter will be left wounded. It will be more radicalized, with strengthened support from people as anti-Americanism is already rife among the Pakistanis who blame the U.S. for the current crises. Civilian casualties will further aggravate the problem of Pakistani population.

SURVEY REPORTS: SAMPLES FROM PANJAB UNIVERSITY

A field survey was conducted, in which forty questionnaires were circulated among different categories of people in 20-50 age group. Almost 70 per cent of the respondents were students (mostly research scholars), 15 per cent were University Professors and remaining respondents were from different walks of life. The questionnaire had 10 questions in all, out of which 9 were close-ended questions and 1 was open-ended. Close-ended questions were chosen because respondents were more willing to answer them instead of open ended questions as they are easier when compared to open ended ones. Therefore, the probability of correct information cannot be ruled out in this form of questionnaire.

Following conclusions have been drawn from the analysis of the respondents' feedback.

1. Do you feel safe when you listen to heinous terrorist crimes?

a. Yes	18%
b. No	82%
c. Can't say	0%

When it came to their personal safety, around 82 per cent of respondents felt that they are unsafe. After listening to any incident of terrorist attack occurring in common places like Coffee shops, market places, bus stands, railway stations, etc., the common man has become unsecure and thinks that he might be the next victim of terrorism. Whereas, only a small fraction of respondents feel secure about their environment and do not think that the foray of terrorist acts have anything to do with them.

2. Does any particular religious attire make you speculative or insecure?

a. Yes	18%
b. No	72%
c. Can't say	10%

Seventy two per cent of respondents claimed that particular dressing of people did not make them speculative or distinct. They do not relate to turban, beard or veils as something fishy, as has often been portrayed in the western societies. The distinct identities of different communities are as normal for the majority of the respondents. However, 18 % respondents feel insecure about the assertion of any particular identity and relate them to violent activities. A particular religious attire makes them speculative, whereas 10 % of respondents are in dilemma regarding the religious identity.

3. Do you think that Islam is responsible for the present turmoil?

a. Yes	2%
b. No	75%
c. Can't say	23%

Two thirds of the respondents feel that Islam has nothing to do with terrorism. Some respondents have strongly condemned the relation of Islam with terrorism. They say that terrorism has no colour, caste or religion and it is wrong to link it with Islam. They also believe that there is politics behind this false propaganda. Another portion of 23% respondents have linked Islam partially to violence after the 9/11 incident. Whereas 2% people believe that Islam is responsible for the present crisis as it has been nurturing violence in the form of jihad.

4. Is the government taking necessary steps to curb terrorism?

a. Yes	37%
b. No	48%
c. Can't say	15%

Almost half of the respondents think that the Government is shirking from its responsibility. It is not taking the required action to curb terrorism and has been proved a failure in protecting its citizens. A sizeable portion of respondents believe that Government is taking necessary measures to counter terrorist activities. They feel that the legislative Acts passed by the Government have helped in bringing down the violence. Whereas 15% people do not have any say regarding the role of Government in curbing the terrorist activities.

5. Is military playing a positive role in Kashmir?

a. Yes	55%
b. No	20%
c. Can't say	25%

More than half of the respondents believe that military is playing a constructive part in Kashmir. Military is not only curbing terrorism but is also helping in maintaining peace in the valley. Twenty per cent of respondents think that military has ruined the lives of Kashmiris by its interference. They have also blamed army for Human Rights violations and for acquiring unlimited powers. It has moved beyond its sphere. Twenty five per cent respondents do not have any opinion regarding the role of military in Kashmir.

6. Do you think technology has made the task of terrorism much easier?

a. Yes	99%
b. No	1%
c. Can't say	-%

Clearly, 99 per cent of respondents believe that technology has assisted terrorists in each and every sphere. Today, terrorists have become tech- savvy and use various hi-tech gadgets to accomplish their mission. Distances have shrunk and communication is now much easy. It has now proved itself a bane if we relate it to terrorism. Only 1 per cent believe that technology has not helped in nurturing terrorism.

7. Do you think that counter insurgency operations lead to Human Rights violations?

a. Yes	65%
b. No	12%
c. Can't say	23%

Majority of respondents feel that counter insurgency operations have resulted in violation of Human Rights. Masses have suffered due to these operations as government agencies have acquired unlimited powers. Only 12 % respondents believe that there is no violation of Human Rights in counter insurgency operations. Twenty three per cent do not have any say regarding this matter.

8. Do you blame United States of America for nurturing terrorism in Asia?

a. Yes	50%
b. No	37%
c. Can't say	23%

Half of the respondents are of the view that U.S.A. has played a diplomatic game and is responsible for the present turmoil. They believe that America has started it for its personal gains, to control the oil resources.

Thirty serven per cent feel that America has been a victim of terrorism and is a major actor in the war against terrorism. Twenty three per cent have fluctuating opinion and are dubious about U.S.'s role.

9. What do you think is the main cause of terrorism?

a. Poverty	12%
b. Unemployment	22%
c. Ideology	28%
d. Ethnicity/Religion	38%

Least number of respondents believed that poverty is the root cause of the problem. However 22 per cent felt that unemployment has given rise to violence as unemployed youth resort to terrorism when their grievances are not addressed by the state. Moreover, the terrorist outfits take advantage of their frustration and inculcate seeds of hatred in youth and also give them sufficient amount of money. Twenty eight per cent respondents think that ideology is the major culprit which has circulated false images of sufferings and exploitation. Maximum number of people *i.e.*, 38 per cent believes that the root cause behind all the troubles which terrorism has generated is Ethnicity and Religion. Ethnicity has become a major driving force for the people.

10. The respondents had different standpoints regarding the measures to be used to curb violence. Most of them are looking forward to a political solution of the problem. A political will is required, cutting across party, religious and regional divisions. There should be transparency in actions of government and increased participation of people in institutional mechanism is required. A few respondents have also suggested Rule of Law as an effective technique to

curb terrorism. Social, economic and political justice should not be denied and a true democratic system is an answer to all the political grievances. Some have also suggested that political parties and religious organizations should join hands with each other and take necessary action. Government should take people in confidence. Few respondents also believe in increasing the sphere of government and police's powers and activities. They think that the extremists should come behind the bars. Police should be given more powers and political interference should be stopped. Modernization of defence services has also been recommended.

A sizable number of respondents have also suggested for the increased role of U.N.O. They are of the opinion that U.N.O. should get rid of the undue interference of U.S.A. U.N.O. should have the power to enforce its decisions and should not be a silent spectator.

Thus, if the government does its work honestly, it would definitely help in curbing violence. The government should take adequate steps to eradicate poverty, unemployment and inequality because these are the weak points that make common man's mind vulnerable to the shallow ideology of any extremist thought.

For youngsters, who instead of earning with honest means, pick up guns and just go on killing thousands of innocent people, it is necessary to provide basic amenities in life. Education is also very important but some educated persons also waste away their lives in such heinous crime. So, proper awareness is necessary. Beyond everything else, justice must be provided to all and sundry. It is not that the terrorists are violent from their birth but one or the other circumstance forces them to become so.

The government, state apparatus and the individuals have to work in tandem to achieve this Herculean task. The chunk of the responsibility lies in the government's hands; it has to work both at the micro and macro levels, from adopting stringent counter terrorism policies, upgrading standards of living and facilitating necessary education to all classes of society and thereby targeting the root of the problem. People need to understand human relations and there is an urgent need to educate the people and create awareness in them.

REFERENCES

1. Amy Zalman, 'Causes of Terrorism-Why are the Causes of Terrorism So Hard to Identify?', www.about.com.
2. Randy Borum, *Psychology of Terrorism,* University of South Florida, 2004, p.27.
3. *Exploring Root and Trigger Causes of Terrorism,* case study, work package 3, 2007. www.transnationalterrorism.eu.
4. Club de Madrid International Summit on Democracy, Terrorism and Security, *Addressing the Causes of Terrorism, Volume I.* 2005. Spain. p.15.
5. *Ibid.* p.13.
6. *Ibid.*
7. Paul Wilkinson, *Terrorism and the liberal state*, London: Macmillan Press, 1977, pp. 39-40.
8. Club de Madrid International Summit on Democracy, Terrorism and Security, *Addressing the Causes of Terrorism, Volume I.* Spain. 2005, p. 14.
9. Ved Marwah, *Uncivil Wars Pathology of Terrorism in India,* Indus Publishers, New Delhi, 1995, p.10.
10. Crenshaw, Martha, 'The causes of terrorism', *Comparative politics*, 1981, p. 383.
11. Robin M. Williams, 'The Sociology of Ethnic Conflicts: Comparative International Perspectives', Annual Review of Sociology, 1994, p. 49-59.
12. Avner Falk, *Islamic Terror: Conscious and Unconscious Motives,* Pentagon Press, New Delhi, 2009, p. 119.
13. Sarah Kershaw, 'Mind of the Terrorist', *Hindustan Times,* Jan 17, 2010.
14. Randy Borum, *Psychology of Terrorism,* University of South Florida, 2004, p. 20.

15. *Exploring Root and Trigger Causes of Terrorism,* case study, work package 3, 2007, www.transnationalterrorism.eu.
16. Club de Madrid International Summit on Democracy, Terrorism and Security. *Addressing the Causes of Terrorism, Volume I.* Spain. 2005, p. 7.
17. Sarah Kershaw, 'Mind of the Terrorist', *Hindustan Times,* Jan 17, 2010.
18. R. Hudson, *The Sociology and Psychology of Terrorism: Who Becomes a Terrorist and Why?*, Report prepared by the Federal Research Division of the Library of Congress, 1999.
19. Randy Borum, *Psychology of Terrorism,* University of South Florida, 2004, pp. 19-20.
20. Jeff Victoroff, "The Mind of the Terrorist: A Review and Critique of Psychological Approaches," *Journal of Conflict Resolution,* February 2005.
21. Randy Borum, *Psychology of Terrorism,* University of South Florida, 2004, p. 24.
23. *Ibid.*, pp. 24-26.
24. Mia Bloom, 'Dying to Kill: motivations for suicide terrorism', in Ami Pedahzur, ed., *Root Causes of Suicide Terrorism: The globalization of martyrdom,* Routledge, New York, 2006, p. 36.
25. Randy Borum, *Psychology of Terrorism,* University of South Florida, 2004, p. 34.
26. Mia Bloom, 'Dying to Kill: motivations for suicide terrorism', in Ami Pedahzur, ed., *Root Causes of Suicide Terrorism: The globalization of martyrdom,* Routledge, New York, 2006, p. 37.
27. Sarah Kershaw, 'Mind of the Terrorist', *Hindustan Times,* Jan 17, 2010.
28. Naunihal Singh, *World Terrorism and New Age Movement,* Authors Press, New Delhi, 2002, p. 14.
29. Gen Virender Uberoy, *Combating Terrorism,* Intellectual Book Corner Publishers, New Delhi, 1992, p. 47.
30. Club de Madrid International Summit on Democracy, Terrorism and Security. *Addressing the Causes of Terrorism, Volume I.* Spain. 2005, p. 28.

31. Ved Marwah, *Uncivil Wars Pathology of Terrorism in India,* Indus Publishers, New Delhi, 1995, p. 10.
32. Walter Liqueur, *No End to War: Terrorism in the Twenty First Century*, Continuum, New York, 2003, p. 19.
33. Avner Falk, *Islamic Terror: Conscious and Unconscious Motives,* Pentagon Press, New Delhi, 2009, p.172.
34. *Ibid*, 173.
35. Gautam Adhikari, "Save Pakistan To Save Us All" *The Times of India*, November 29, 2008, New Delhi.
36. Maj-Gen Ashok K. Mehta, "Terrorism a common threat" *The Tribune,* December 22, 2008, Chandigarh.
37. Gurmeet Kanwal, "Fighting the Taliban" *The Tribune,* August 23, 2009, Chandigarh.
38 K. Subrahmanyam, "From Marja to Pune" *The Tribune,* February 15, 2009, Chandigarh.
39. Jayshree Bajoria, "Pakistan's New Generation of Terrorists" *Council on Foreign Relations*. October 6, 2009. March 4, 2010. http://www.cfr.org/publication/15422>.
40. Dr. Subhash Kapila, "Pakistan's State-sponsored Terrorism and Jihadi Infiltration Continues Unabated: *A Review", South Asia Analysis Group, August 11, 2005. March 4, 2010. <http://www.southasiaanalysis.org/%5Cpapers15%5Cpaper1495.html>*
41. Satish Chandra Pandey, *International Terrorism and the Contemporary World, Sarup &Sons Publishers, New Delhi.* 2006.
42. Daniel Byman, *Deadly Connections,* Cambridge University Press, 2005, p. 155.
43. "Call from Bangalore", *The Tribune*, October 29, 2009, Chandigarh.
44. Arun Kumar, "Pakistan remains the geographic crossroads for terrorism: U.S.", *Thaindian News, October 22, 2009. March 4, 2010. http://www.thaindian.com/newsportal/south-asia/pakistan-remains-the-geographic-crossroads-for-terrorism-us_100264296.html.*
45. Rajen Harshe, "Cross-Border Terrorism: Road Block to Peace Initiatives", *Economic and Political Weekly,* Vol. 38, No. 35, p. 3622.

46. *Ibid.*, p.3623.
47. Peter W. Singer, "Pakistan's Madrassah's: Ensuring a system of Education not Jihad", *Brookings, March 7, 2010. March 7, 2010.* http://www.brookings.edu/papers/2001/11pakistan_singer.aspx.
48. Anatol Lieven, "The Pressures on Pakistan", *Foreign Affairs,* Vol. 81, No. 1 (Jan. - Feb., 2002), p.109.
49. Jessica Stern, "Pakistan's Jihad Culture", *Foreign Affairs,* Vol. 79, No. 6 (Nov. - Dec., 2000), p.118.
50. Michael Moran, "Pakistan's Frankenstein", *Newsweek,* Dec 4, 2008.
51. Rajen Harshe, "Cross-Border Terrorism: Road Block to Peace Initiatives", *Economic and Political Weekly,* Vol. 38, No.35, p. 3624.
52. B.Raman, "Jehadi terrorism" in Wilson John & Swati Parashar edt. *Terrorism in South East Asia: Implications for South Asia, 2005,* Pearson Education (Singapore) Pte. Ltd. New Delhi. P.34

53 *Ibid.*

54 "Punjab-based Militant groups in Pak", *The Indian Express, October 16, 2009, Chandigarh.*

55 G. Parthasarathy, "The Home of Terror", *The Times of India,* December 8, 2008, New Delhi.

56 Praveen Swami, "Ties that bind: Lashkar and the global jihad", *The Hindu,* December 12, 2009, New Delhi.

57. *Ibid.*
58. *Ibid.*

59 Jayshree Bajoria, "Pakistan's New Generation of Terrorists" *Council on Foreign Relations*. October 6, 2009. March 4, 2010. http://www.cfr.org/publication/15422.

60. C. Cristine Fair, "Militant Recruitment in Pakistan: Implications for Al Qaeda and Other Organizations", *Studies in Conflict & Terrorism,* 27:489–504, 2004, Taylor & Francis Inc. p. 495.
61. *Ibid.* p. 497.
62. "Sipah-e-Sahaba Pakistan, Terrorist Group of Pakistan", *South Asia Terrorism Portal, March 12, 2010,* http://www.satp.org/satporgtp/countries/pakistan/terroristoutfits/ssp.html.

63. Jessica Stern, "Pakistan's Jihad Culture", *Foreign Affairs,* Vol. 79, No. 6 (Nov. - Dec., 2000), p.118.

64. Harinder Baweja, "Without doubt, India is the enemy", *The Hindustan Times,* December 13, 2008, Chandigarh.

65. Peter W. Singer, "Pakistan's Madrassah's: Ensuring a system of Education not Jihad", *Brookings, March 7, 2010. March 7, 2010.* http://www.brookings.edu/papers/2001/11pakistan_singer.aspx.

66. Jessica Stern, "Pakistan's Jihad Culture", *Foreign Affairs,* Vol. 79, No. 6 (Nov. - Dec., 2000), p.118.

67. Ibid. p.p.119-122.

68. Rajen Harshe, "Cross-Border Terrorism: Road Block to Peace Initiatives", *Economic and Political Weekly,* Vol. 38, No.35, p. 3621.

69. Peter W. Singer, "Pakistan's Madrassah's: Ensuring a system of Education not Jihad", *Brookings, March 7, 2010. March 7, 2010.* http://www.brookings.edu/papers/2001/11pakistan_singer.aspx.

70. Rajen Harshe, "Cross-Border Terrorism: Road Block to Peace Initiatives", *Economic and Political Weekly,* Vol. 38, No.35, p. 3621.

71. Sandeep Unnithan, "The Karachi Project", *India today,* March 1, 2010. pp. 21-25.

72. *Ibid.*

73. M.G. Chitkara, *Combating Terrorism,* APH Pub. House, New Delhi. 2003. p.273.

74. Harinder Baweja, "Without doubt, India is the enemy", *The Hindustan Times,* December 13, 2008, Chandigarh.

75. Ahmed Rashid , "South Waziristan fails to impress" *The Pioneer,* November 7, 2009, New Delhi.

76. Robert Matthews, "A risky gambit: The Pakistani army campaign in South Waziritan" Norwegian Peace Building Centre.

77. Zainab Jeewanjee, "Domestic Agenda: Battling Terrorism" October 13, 2009.

78. A.H. Nayyar, Zia Mian, "Enemies within" *Frontline,* January 30, 2009.

4

Dimensions of Terrorist Threat in India: Case Studies

The Present Crisis in Kashmir

Ever since June 11, when 17-year-old Tufail Mattoo was fatally hit by a teargas shell, the Jammu and Kashmir Police and the Central Reserve Police Force (CRPF) have made desperate attempts to obstruct the protests. By the first week of August, 49 civilians had died and hundreds of people, including police personnel, had been injured severely. Kashmir has never seen such fierce political unrest, with thousands of protesters forcing the police and the CRPF to retreat. They set fire to police stations, government buildings and vehicles. The use of force has been the only option with the government for which it has to pay a heavy price.

In the series of violent incidents in various parts of Kashmir, two people were killed as CRPF opened fire on protesters at Amargarh, near Sopore in North Kashmir. These people were protesting after the Friday prayers against the disappearance of 17 year old Farak Bashir of Kreeri, allegedly in police custody. In Pattan, 35 km north of Srinagar, another youth was killed by security forces, which fired to control a restive crowd. Burning tyres were thrown across the road at Palhan, a small town along the highway. Around fifty protesters there, threatened to throw rocks at any vehicle which dared to pass that way. In Barahmullah town also, hundreds of people gheraoed a police post and tried to set it on fire, but the police retaliated and scores of people were injured. In Tral town in south Kashmir, over 30 people were injured in clashes with the police. Two improvised explosive devices were defused by the security forces in Baramullah and Anantnag districts. On the eve of Independence Day, four civilians were killed in firing by the police at the three places in North Kashmir. In another incident in Pampore, CRPF opened fire on protesters while trying to control the mob that was planning to block the Srinagar-Jammu highway. This resulted in killing of two persons. This event in Pampore gave rise to violent demonstrations in which thousands of people attacked a police station in Srinagar. At least six police stations came under mob attack. The protesters also burned down the Special Operations Group's camp in Kreeri township in Baramulla. An outhouse of the police station in Pattan was also torched.[1]

According to official figures, as many as 872 incidents of stone-throwing took place in June and July, in which 1,456 police and CRPF personnel were injured. In just six days, from July 30 to August 4, the situation took a turn for the worse as a large number of public and private property was destroyed. In the wave of anger, nine police stations, police posts and SOG (special operations group) camps, eight government vehicles and a coach of a train, one railway station, two houses of political activists and 13 government offices were destroyed. In July, 355 of 500 clashes between police and protesters were concentrated in the districts of Srinagar, Baramulla and Anantnag — home to Kashmir's four largest cities. June saw 369 clashes, 318 took place in these three districts.[2] This data reveals that the violence has a disproportionate share. More than half of the 21 civilians killed in police action between January 1 and July 7, 2010 were Srinagar residents. Thirty two out of the 72 civilians injured in the clashes also belonged to the city. Under 45 per cent of the clashes took place in Srinagar, and most were concentrated in the limits of five police stations — Rainawari, Nowhatta, Maharajgunj, Khanyar and Safakadal. Urban pockets in northern Kashmir have also accounted for the bulk of violence outside Srinagar. The northern Kashmir trading town of Baramulla, accounted for 46 clashes. Nearby town of Sopore witnessed 21 clashes. These three towns of Sopore, Srinagar and Baramulla accounted for 69.5 per cent of all violent protests this summer. Last year too, the pattern was similar as violence was concentrated around these three places.[3] Thus these protests are not a Kashmir-wide mass uprising. The violence remains concentrated in the urban parts of the districts of Srinagar, Baramulla, Pulwama, and Anantnag — the historic heartlands of the anti-India movement in J & K.[4] But according to Omar Abdullah, "We had credible information that there was a concerted effort by some parties to spread the agitation out of the urban pockets it is concentrated in, out into Kashmir's interior."[5]

Since 1989, Kashmir has been passing through a painful period of violence and destruction. Thousands were killed and property worth billions of rupees was destroyed. In the direct conflict between the militants and the government forces, the civilians, too, got crushed. In fact, the support of the Kashmiri population sustained the armed rebellion to an extent. With militancy losing its sting, the Government of India tried to bring in a "democratic character" to its rule in the State by deciding to hold Assembly elections in 1996, ending a long spell of Central Rule. By 2002, the separatist movement had stepped into a non-violent mode. The peace initiatives between India and Pakistan, followed by confidence-building measures injected a sense of optimism all round. This was the time when people hoped that something serious was happening on Kashmir and they gave it a chance to succeed. Negotiations were also opened with moderates such as Mirwaiz Umar Farooq, who leads a faction of the All Parties Hurriyat Conference, and Yasin Malik.[6]

But gone are the days and once again Kashmir is boiling. In 2010, Kashmir has thrown up an entire generation of young men who have been brutalized, hardened and often, radicalized by perennial conflict and the changing nature of the separatist campaign.[7] Stone pelting, a new form of protest involving young men and others has evolved. There are reports of regular payments having been made to stone-pelters.[8] But what made the protests and strikes relevant on the ground was the continued cycle of killings by security forces. Without using any other option, they straightway opened fire. "What can you do when a group of stone-throwing youth is determined to lynch you?" asked a police officer, who was injured several times. "They are taking on the country and we are to face their wrath. It is not a simple law and order problem." In the past few weeks, no police personnel were ready to come on record, fearing reprisal from the agitating crowds. In fact, mainstream politicians also have been targeted for being on the "Indian side". Some political workers, fearing for their lives, joined the protests. Minister for Agriculture G.H. Mir's ancestral house in Tangmarg was spared by arsonists, thanks to the intervention of guards posted there and some local people. The local Kashmiris are of the opinion that it is not a question of any government failing, it is the state which has failed. It is the system which has collapsed. They accused the government of letting the situation to worsen by reimposing curfew and not allowing people to breathe. The Government of India should accept Kashmir as a political problem and not tag it with any other issue and then take some initiative, people believe.[9]

Presently, much of the killing on Kashmir's street came about not because the protesters were taking over the authorities, but the lethal force was indiscriminately used by police which was panicked by the situation. The bureaucratic officials in Kashmir have also failed to tackle the situation. Politicians are missing in this critical hour and only a few turned up in their constituencies. This violence constitutes the most serious challenge the state's fragile political system has confronted. The ugly violence demonstrated that substantial number of young people in Kashmir's cities feel disenfranchised by the political system and are hostile to India. The ongoing unrest is the result of a failure of politics. If Kashmir burns time and again, it is because politicians in New Delhi and Srinagar have failed to extend a powerful and convincing political argument to the Kashmiris. The hatred with which the people had "dismissed" the mainstream parties in the Valley poses a big challenge for New

Delhi as it tries to establish its writ over Kashmir. The violent protests that went "out of anybody's" control signaled a much larger trouble on the streets. Mirwaiz Umar Farooq and Yasin Malik, considered to be moderate voices, did not muster courage to call for a "refined and people-friendly" agitation calendar. Syed Salahuddin had to take back his statement that people's problems be taken into account while issuing a calendar for strikes. His effigies were burnt in Srinagar and Sopore, almost making the "powerful militant commander" irrelevant. The calendar of agitation throughout the two months has been the domain of the Syed Ali Geelani-led Hurriyat and his lieutenant Masrat Alam and Dukhtaran-e-Millat chief Asiya Andrabi. Sometimes, however, the situation looked as if it was out of even Geelani's hand.[10]

The hardline faction of the Hurriyat Conference, led by its leader Syed Ali Shah Geelani, had called for the shutdown in the valley to protest against the killing of several youths. Police stood by silently as motorcycle- borne squads linked to Geelani's Tehreek-i-Hurriyat brutally enforced a shutdown. There is evidence that leaders of this party have paid local activists to initiate clashes with police. This party does not have a huge political network but it has made young Islamists of the valley to act on its call, using everything from mosque public address to mobile phone text messaging.[11] The Hurriyat calander of protest has certainly been followed religiously by shopkeepers, but for Kashmir's Gen Next protesters, there has been little by way of coordinated planning. Even at 1 a.m., women accompanied by infants, join the march to chant slogans. But the police says that women and children are used as human shields to protect the mob from security forces.[12] These Kashmiris are fighting for the right to self-determination and the complete withdrawal of the occupational forces. According to them the Government of India has not even once touched the cause behind the protests and the anger of the people.[13] Geelani has proclaimed that the people are fighting for the complete withdrawal of the forces and for the right to self-determination and are using "Go India Go" as the slogan. He has turned down the latest offer of dialogue from the Prime Minister until conditions like the release of political prisoners, repeal of the AFSPA and gradual demilitarisation of populated areas are met. Currently under house arrest, he called for civil disobedience and endorsed the ongoing protests. Alam assumed a frontline role as Geelani was arrested and is now spearheading the "Quit Jammu and Kashmir" campaign. Recently, he created a stir by releasing a video of his appeal to the armed forces asking them to stop participating in "killing and repression" of the Kashmiris. He said, "We will never tire of struggling for our history and freedom. We can't forget. We will not forgive." He is also spearheading a cyber war with anti-government blogs, tweets and videos. A firebrand young woman activist, Andrabi heads the women separatist group Dukhtaran-e-Millat (Daughters of Community). She identifies with the Hurriyat Conference and regularly comes out in support of its position on Kashmir and the protest programmes. Her popular base is unclear but she is seen as a strand in the separatist stream of politics. She has been arrested several times but has now gone underground and issues regular statements supporting Hurriyat's "Quit Jammu and Kashmir" campaign.[14]

Kashmir's cities have seen a wave of clashes between the police and the protesters which has been fuelled by radical Islamism that has acquired ideological influence among the youth. Growing numbers are turning to Islamist hardliner Syed Ali Shah Geelani for leadership. The reality is that the Islamist extremists spearheading the anti-India protests that have lead to the loss of almost 60 lives have no interest in peace. The protests have allowed a new generation of radical Islamist leaders, like Massrat Alam Bhat and Asiya Andrabi, to seize leadership of the anti-India movement in Kashmir.

This movement has also entered cyberspace with the youth pelting stones during the day and creating solidarity networks over social networking websites like Facebook and Twitter during the night. The cyber-Intifada slowly turned into an almost new sharing system of information and mobilization. Kashmir's angry young men are shaping their own version of the Intifada. These Internet warriors have developed their own idiom. They discuss the rotating weekly separatist protest calendars and have started holding the separatist leadership accountable. This activity has become so remorseless and passionate that it now acts as an interface between the street and the separatist leaders. The Facebook activity in particular has also become a source of news followed by even journalists. The Kashmir street today is characterised by youth with a stone in one hand and a mobile phone camera in the other. They send stones flying into the contingents of police and CRPF and then shoot the action to upload on Facebook and YouTube for others to see and keep a record.[15]

Faith on Abdullah Government Shattered

It was hoped that the young and dynamic leadership of Omar Abdullah would lead the state to peace and prosperity. However this government has failed to keep up to its promises and has been unable to prevent the state from turmoil. This government in Jammu & Kashmir came to power pledging zero tolerance to human rights violations. The draconian provisions of the AFSPA are yet to get underway in a serious manner. The five working groups established by the Prime Minister to resolve state issues at the end of the second round table conference in 2006 have not been given adequate attention.[16] By constantly referring to job creation as a solution, leaders of the government are wrongly identifying the protests with unemployed frustration as this is not the cause which is bringing people out on the streets. The people of Kashmir await not an economic package but a political one from New Delhi.

Yet, the Chief Minister succeeded in sending a "strong signal" when he got an Army camp relocated in Bomai village in north Kashmir. The soldiers at the camp had been held responsible for the killing of two youth. But the alleged rape and murder of two women in Shopian in May 2009 marked the start of Omar Abdullah's troubles. Protests over the incident occurred throughout Kashmir. Tourist inflow, which had showed signs of revival, dwindled and the economy crumbled. Soon, the cries of "Azadi" grew loud once again, but just when the agitation seemed to be picking up, it died out. As a Kashmiri expert pointed out, all it needed was a spark of "disillusionment" to ignite a more volatile phase of agitation. It came in the form of a fake encounter in the Machil sector of Kupwara. The Army, allegedly for "rewards and promotions", killed three young boys from Rafiabad, dubbing them "terrorists". This was enough to kick-start a new uprising. But from the way the fire has engulfed Kashmir in the past two months, it is not difficult to say that the political drift in Kashmir is almost complete. Notwithstanding the fact that the political problem in Kashmir is beyond Omar Abdullah's diagnosis or treatment, it cannot be denied that the mishandling on the part of his government played a significant role in the deterioration of the situation. Except for tough measures like calling in the Army and getting reinforcements from the CRPF or calling for the Rapid Action Force, attempts at finding a political solution did not seem to be working on the ground. Also, for the first time since militants made their appearance in Kashmir, the rank and file of the Jammu and Kashmir Police started feeling "unsafe" in their own State. "This has been the worst crisis I have seen in the past 20 years," a senior police officer said. Police stations and other government property were pulled down in broad daylight and the houses of police personnel became the target of mobsters who took "everything into their own hands".[17]

Not surprisingly, Omar's inability to see a pattern in the protests and his administration's inadequacy in responding to them, has created an opportunity that separatists don't want to miss out. The protesters turned the discourse away from human rights violations firmly into the arena of the political right of self-determination. Their mobilisation centred around new slogans like "Go India Go Back" and "Quit Jammu and Kashmir" that captured public imagination, bringing out tens of thousands on the streets in defiance of even shoot-at-sight curfews. The debate has become virulently anti-India again. "The Government is mistaken that it will crush the genuine sentiments of masses by calling more soldiers to Kashmir. We will resist the occupation at any cost," Masarat Alam, one of the Hurriyat Conference leaders is quoted as having said. The anger is mainly directed at police stations that have also functioned as camps for the dreaded Special Operations Group (SOG). Numerous such police stations have been torched or attempted to be burnt down even in places as far as the garrison town of Uri near the Line of Control (LoC). "It has become a vicious cycle. Every death brings about more protests and more deaths," says a top police official.[18]

Today, the people are up in arms not just against the state but also the symbols of the state authority. Methods of crowd control have failed in the face of people overcoming their fear in their attempts to shake the political stability. Hopes from the Indo-Pakistan dialogue for delivering any change have also faded and people are now taking things into their own hands. If military comes to intervene, the situation could lead to a much higher cost in terms of human casualties.[19]

India has failed to bring the people of the valley into the mainstream and this has been the major failure at the political level. Article 370 has been the main stumbling block towards this assimilation. The nation must integrate the people of J and K into the national mainstream. The anger on the streets is necessarily the manifestation of a larger political disillusionment, but the State government's handling of the mobs has only widened the gap. While many people disapprove of the burning of public property, the "insensitive approach" towards the killings has angered the masses. The hard posturing by the Chief Minister of asking people to cooperate with the security forces, enforcing curfew and not condoling the deaths or reaching out to people soon enough injured his reliability.[20]

The government of India has also tried to cover these protests as something which was externally motivated. First, it blamed LeT which was allegedly coordinating them. Then the blame shifted to Hurriyat leadership and finally the government reports say that militants are mingling with the protesters and opening fire on the security forces.[21] But some promises were also made by the government this month, like, the decision to review the Armed Forces Special Powers Act (AFSPA), announced by Mr.

Chidambaram in Parliament. It would perhaps be the one with the most immediate impact. Mr. Abdullah also said that a collective effort was needed to restore normality. He said strict instructions had been issued to the security forces to avoid killing of innocents. "The forces have been asked to observe maximum restraint," he added. The Chief Minister also said that there was no move to repeal or amend the AFSPA. [22] But he maintained that efforts were on to make AFSPA more humane and to remove it from certain areas where there is no militancy. Despite more than 3 months of agitation, the protesters have not been armed with anything more than stones.[23]

According to Happymon Jacob, the ongoing unrest in Kashmir is the result of a failure of politics, political courage, conviction and empathy. If Kashmir burns, it is because politicians in New Delhi and Srinagar have failed to extend a powerful and convincing political argument to the Kashmiris. It is the National Conference led government in Jammu & Kashmir whose poverty of politics has set Kashmir alights again.[24] The reality is that the current eruption of violence is marginally affected by Pakistan. For the majority of Kashmiris, Pakistan does not even figure in their minds when they take to the streets protesting against injustice. Barring the radical leader of Hurriyat party, Syed Ali Shah Geelani, no other political leader talks about going to Pakistan.

Suggestions

At this stage, priority should be to stop the violent action-reaction cycle and it should be ensured that there are no more fatalities and no more 'unexplained disappearances'. Experts have made suggestions of the setting up of local citizens' bodies to liaise with administrators and police along with investments in education and entrepreneurship as well as non lethal crowd control technologies. And most important of all, state politicians should step in courageously. Jammu and Kashmir could start developing effective but non-lethal crowd control resources. Killing of unarmed protesters should be stopped which is a consequence of mismanaged training. Democratic political parties should forge an agenda for political action and development.[25]

Government of India is saying that it is holding quiet dialogue with all groups. It will have to be a conversation that is clear to the outside world, so that it has legitimacy and trustworthiness. But most important, the dialogue must reach into history, examine the commitments that have been made especially in recent years and ensure that the faith of ordinary people in the capacity of politics and in the political system is substantively renewed.[26] Prime Minister signaled his recognition of the inevitability of a dialogue with Pakistan on the historical dispute over Kashmir's status. He also admitted that what was needed was "a political solution that addresses the alienation and emotional needs of the people" which could only be achieved through "a sustained internal and external dialogue."[27]

Finally, it is the promise of dialogue with separatist leaders that must pick up speed. New Delhi has always interspersed talks with leaders like the Mirwaiz, Sajjad and Bilal Lone and Yasin Mallik with long spells of silence. It is that silence that scuttles all that is achieved in the talks. It is time for a new envoy to be appointed to continue the dialogue uninterruptedly, and with some degree of flexibility to engage others who reject talks like Mr. Geelani as well. It was, after all, the call for calm from Geelani that gave Kashmir its first day of peace in eight weeks on August 6th.[28]

The key point to recognise in approaching the Kashmir issue is that, it is possible to preserve the distinct Kashmiri cultural identity in an autonomous political framework that is not at odds with the idea of it being part of a larger Indian Union. Self determination should not be viewed as a limited or closed thing. We have to look at the broader concept of things.

TERRORISM IN J&K

Violent behaviour in the state of Jammu and Kashmir has been a vital part of the political science since 1947, but the terror campaign that we see today is of recent origin. Since 1989, Jammu and Kashmir has been entwined in militancy operations combating Indian Security Forces. During the past two decades, the trend of terrorism in Jammu and Kashmir has manifested distress of civil population, radicalization of Islam in society and culture of Kashmir, violation of Human Rights, demolition of property, ethnic religious sanitization of Hindu minorities, attacks on security forces, mines and bomb blasts, subverting the genuine civil and political authority in the State and undermining the egalitarian and pluralistic socio political order. The loss of life and property in the state has enlarged manifold. There has been mass migration of Kashmiri Pandits from the valley. Thousands of innocent lives have been lost. Cross border terrorism has been on the rise in the valley. In more recent times there has been substantial deterioration in the state of affairs.

The state has been the hub of clash among India, Pakistan, and Kashmiris themselves since 1947. The core of the argument is the question of dominion and the possibility of self fortitude by Kashmiris of whether to remain in India, join Pakistan, or form an independent state. The conflict thus represents the confluence of religious chauvinism, secular nationalism, and ethnic nationalism, personified in *Kashmiriyat*. For India, Kashmir is sign of secular nationalism. For Pakistan, Kashmir represents the breakdown of secular nationalism and the imperative of a Muslim homeland in the subcontinent, as well as the "incompleteness" of Pakistan.[29]

New Delhi consistently blames Pakistan-based militant groups for lethal attacks on Indian civilians, as well as on government security forces, in both Kashmir and in major Indian cities. India holds Pakistan responsible for providing material support and training facilities to Kashmiri militants. Whereas Pakistan denies that it feeds the terrorist organizations but at the same time supports the freedom movement of the Kashmiri people. For the two countries, the conflict over Kashmir is less a contest over tactical ground or resources as over competing visions of nationalism and state-building.[30]

The state of Jammu and Kashmir is the largest in India at 84,471 square miles, but is meagerly populated, with about 8 million people. It is bordered by Tibet to the northeast, the Sinkiang province of China to the north, Turkistan to the northwest, Pakistan to the west, and the Indian states of Himachal Pradesh and Punjab to the south. The Himalayas separate Jammu and Kashmir into three regions: Ladakh, the Kashmir Valley, and Jammu. Currently, 45 per cent of the former princely state of Jammu and Kashmir is administered by India (Ladakh, Jammu, and the Kashmir valley) and 35 per cent by Pakistan (Azad Kashmir, which Pakistan rules indirectly, and the Northern Areas, which acceded to Pakistan in October 1947). China also lays claim to a segment of land (20 per cent of the original territory) in the northeast of the state, Aksai Chin, which it annexed in 1962. Generally speaking, Ladakh is drifting towards Tibet, Jammu wants to merge with India, and the Kashmir Valley wants to join Pakistan.[31]

The present chapter of militancy in Jammu and Kashmir is the extremist face of anti-India political organizations that have their own sources of inspiration, strategies, financial backing and other infrastructural facilities for operationalising their plans and programmes. Pakistan's powerful and largely autonomous ISI is widely believed to have provided this support for militant Kashmiri separatists organizations over the past decade. Several anti-India militant groups fighting in Kashmir are based in Pakistan and are closely linked to Islamist groups there. According to the Indian position, the rise of violent ethno-religious fervor in 1989 in India's only Muslim-majority state is the result of Pakistani propaganda and support and training to the insurgents. Whereas, Pakistani apologists, in turn, argue that the insurgency represents the spontaneous rise of ethno-religious sentiment amongst the oppressed Muslim community of Jammu and Kashmir. Kashmir, with its Muslim-majority population, has long been an emblem of India's secular status; its very existence demonstrated that Muslims could thrive under the aegis of India's secular policy. Today, as India's secular fabric has faded, the country's leaders seek to maintain their hold on Kashmir because they fear that Kashmir's exit from the Indian Union would set off powerful centrifugal forces in other parts of the country. Thus, the stakes for both states involve far more than territorial claims: the question of control of Kashmir goes to the very basis of the state-building enterprise in South Asia.[32]

Recent Terrorist Attacks

The violence in Jammu & Kashmir threatens to go on the boil again. Defense Minister A. K. Antony warned, on January 13, "The incidents in the first week of January in the Valley are indicative of the shape of things to come." In the context of an escalating threat of infiltration of terrorists across the Line of Control from Pakistan occupied Kashmir, one of the biggest counter insurgency operations, codenamed *Operation Khoj*, was launched in the State. Between March 27 and April 2, 2010, a group of 16 Lashkar-e-Toiba militants and six soldiers were killed, as almost 1,000 troops spread out across an area of just over 50 square kilometres in the Rajouri District. The operation was launched following information that a large group of LeT militants, all equipped with maps, weapons and ammunition, had infiltrated along the Pallanwalla sector near Jammu in the night of March 22. The militants had then split into smaller groups of four to six, possibly to launch a major attack. Superintendent of Police disclosed that the militants were probably trying to sneak into Reasi, bordering Sadda, as 31 of them had been killed in the district since June 2009. The entire group was, however, eliminated in four different surgical strikes in Triyath and Kandi areas of Rajouri district.

It has been estimated that the terrorists have triggered 11,876 explosions which claimed 1,754 lives while 15,589 others were injured during the last two decades in Jammu and Kashmir. According to the South Asia Terrorism Portal database, as many as 65 infiltration attempts, 126 militancy-related incidents, 18 civilian and 18 Security Forces casualties and 45 encounters, which left 53 terrorists dead, have been recorded just between January 1 and March 30, 2010. During the corresponding period of 2009, 95 violent incidents, eight civilian killings, 18 SF killings, 41 encounters and 47 militant fatalities were recorded. There has also been a decline in grenade attacks over the past two years, with 79 attacks in 2009, as against 170 in 2008.[33] The Chief Minister of the state, Mr. Omar Abdullah has expressed satisfaction over the situation in 2009 and described it as the "most peaceful year" in 20 years of turmoil. However he said that 2010 saw a rise in infiltration.

The composition of militancy in J&K continues to be dominated by foreigners. Out of the 398 terrorists killed in 2008-09, 304 were foreigners. In 2008, of the 237 militants killed 171 were foreigners and in 2009 of the 161 militants killed, 133 were foreigners. Foreign militants generally come from the North Western Frontier Province (NWFP), Punjab, Pakistan-occupied Kashmir and other areas of Pakistan. Infiltration bids have gone up in 2010 but most of them have been foiled by Army. An estimated 485 attempts were made by armed militants in 2009, up by 143 against the previous year 2008. Since the last two decades the conditions in the valley have worsened and there has been large scale migration. The Jammu and Kashmir Government said 219 Kashmiri Pandits were killed by militants since 1989 while 24,202 families were among the total 38,119 families which migrated out of the Valley due to turmoil.

Terrorists have been resorting to various methods to disrupt the peace in the valley. Not much time ago, the Security Forces recovered arms and ammunition from Rutsuna village forest area in Budgam District of Jammu and Kashmir. At the same time, a self-styled LeT 'commander' was killed in an encounter with the Army in Poonch District. Violence in valley can also be witnessed from the fact that Block president, Ghulam Nabi Khan, of the ruling National Conference was shot at and killed by militants in the Sopore town of Baramulla District on May 23. Whereas a week before, a day-long gun battle occurred in a village of Doda District between Security Forces and two LeT militants, identified as Abdullah Annece alias Ans alias Faisal Hafiz and Abdullah Mohammad alias Abu Maaz, both belonging to Pakistan. Both the militants were shot dead. At the same time, two Army personnel were killed and three others injured when their vehicle was ambushed near the LoC either by Pakistan Army or by the militants from the border fencing at Nangi Tekri in the Krishna Ghati sector of Poonch District. Another catastrophic activity of the terrorists could be seen on 14th May 2010, when six persons, including four Security Force personnel, were injured when militants hurled a grenade towards a CRPF bunker in Saraf Kadal area of the old city in Srinagar in Jammu and Kashmir. A day before, militants blew up fencing wire with an Improvised Explosive Device in the forward village of Abdullian in the R. S. Pura sector of Jammu District. They also made an abortive bid to blow up a Central Reserve Police Force bunker in the Habba Kadal area of Srinagar but the hand grenade missed its intended target and landed in the residential compound. In another incident, Rail services were disrupted after an Improvised Explosive Device (IED) ripped through the only railway track connecting north Kashmir's Baramulla District to South Kashmir's Qazigund area on April 2. Though there was no loss of life, the railway track was damaged. The Hizb-ul-Mujahideen is said to have claimed responsibility for the attack. In yet another incident, a Central Reserve Police Force (CRPF) trooper was killed and five others including an officer were injured, in a grenade attack by militants in the Maharajgunj area of Srinagar. Where as in two separate incidents in Doda District, four persons, including two children, were injured in two grenade blasts and a CRPF trooper, Head Constable, was shot at and injured by unidentified militants.[34]

To spread fear among the people, the militants shot dead a 30-year old shopkeeper in Srinagar city. At the start of this year, a suicide attack by LeT militants occurred at Lal Chowk in Srinagar. The target was a CRPF camp but militants took refuge in a hotel across the road when retaliated by SFs (Security Forces). Both the holed up militants were killed in a 22- hour gun battle. A policeman and a civilian were also killed and at least 12 persons including three CRPF personnel and a photo-journalist were injured in the incident.

In its year-end review, the Union Ministry of Home Affairs stated that, during 2009, the number of terrorism-related incidents had dropped by 27 per cent, those of killing of civilians by 17 per cent and of Security Force (SF) personnel by 19 per cent, compared to the corresponding period of 2008. This was the lowest level of violence in two decades in J&K, as terror-related incidents, killings of civilians and SF personnel went below the 1990 figures. The civilian killings during 2009 went down by over 42 per cent as compared to 2008 while militancy-related incidents dropped by over 35 per cent.

Comparative Fatalities in J&K, 2001-2009

Year	*Civilians*	*SF personnel*	*Terrorists*	*Total*
2001	1067	590	2850	4507
2002	839	469	1714	3022
2003	658	338	1546	2542
2004	534	325	951	1810
2005	520	216	996	1732
2006	349	168	599	1116
2007	164	121	492	777
2008	69	90	382	541
2009	55	78	244	377

Source: South Asia Terrorism Portal Database

Although the fatalities have decreased, as data says, the terrorist events in the valley have become a matter of routine now. The local militants are increasingly getting involved in the disruptive activities with the support of ISI of Pakistan. The cross border infiltrations have been providing the terrorist movement in Kashmir with enough arms and weapons. Also, according to official figures released in Jammu and Kashmir assembly, there were 3,400 disappearance cases and the insurgency has left more than 47,000 people dead till July 2009. Pakistani infiltrators have stated that the activities of militants in Jammu and Kashmir have increased according to a "definite plan" and that the militants were continuing their "'war" against Security Forces. In the near future there appears no end to the insurgency in Kashmir. As long as violence prevails in the valley, a permanent solution is difficult to arrive at.

History of the State

The state of Jammu and Kashmir was one of the 556 princely states indirectly ruled by the

British Raj. It consisted of three distinct areas. A large Muslim majority area in the west, the Hindu dominated area of Jammu in the south, and the predominantly Buddhist area to the west of

Ladakh. The Kashmir valley, which had been predominantly Hindu, was converted to Sufi Islam in the 14th century. The synthesis of Hindu-Muslim culture formed the basis of Kashmiriyat which was a mixture of mystical Hindu Vedantism and Islamic Sufism. Kashmiriyat stresses the commonality between the Hindus and Muslims of the valley.

Kashmiriyat is thus a culture of synthesis, understanding and humanism. Thus whenever fundamentalists of either religion, have sought to enforce their habits on the people, the Kashmiris have rebelled. Also, Kashmir was the only part of India with a mixed Hindu-Muslim population which did not see communal rioting during the 1947 partition of the sub continent.[35]

Kashmir was incorporated into the Moghul Empire by the Emperor Akbar in 1586. With the disintegration of the Moghul Empire, it was briefly independent but was conquered in 1819 by the Sikh Maharaja Ranjit Singh, who had established his kingdom in the Punjab. By the early 19th century the British had conquered much of northern India. In 1846 they divested Kashmir from the Sikh kingdom with the help of a Kashmiri Hindu called Gulab Singh. They then sold Kashmir to Gulab Singh for 7.5 million rupees. This created the Dogra state of Kashmir, ruled indirectly by the British, which was to last till the granting of Indian Independence in 1947.

The rise of the freedom movement in India also spread to Kashmir. Its icon was Sheikh Abdullah. His grandfather was a Kashmiri Pandit. The family had converted to Islam. Abdullah was thus the personification of Kashmiriyat. He converted the sectarian Muslim Conference, into a more broad-based National Conference. This nationalist party, unlike its predecessor allowed anyone to join, "irrespective of their caste, creed or religion".

The National Conference joined the Indian nationalist struggle lead by the Congress party in India. Abdullah did not support the 'two nation' theory propounded by the Muslim League led by Jinnah.[36]

Origin of the Kashmir Dispute

The origin and evolution of militancy in Jammu and Kashmir State is deeply rooted in the anti Indian political forces within the state who wanted Kashmir to become either an independent country in itself or preferred to see it as a province of Pakistan.

The dispute arose when the British announced in early 1947 that they would depart on 15th August 1947, and be succeeded by the two successor states of India and Pakistan. The states were advised to accede to whichever of the successor states they wished. They also instructed a British judge Sir Cyril Radcliffe to draw up the boundary between the two successor states in six weeks. Most of the princely states acceded to one or the other state because of their territorial contiguity and the religious choice of both the population and the rulers to one or the other of the successor states. There were three exceptions. Junagadh, in Gujarat,which was one of the patchwork princely states surrounded by neighbours who had acceded to India, and which like Hyderabad in central India had a predominantly Hindu population but a Muslim ruler, and Kashmir which was also contiguous with both India and Pakistan and which had a Hindu ruler and a predominantly Muslim population. The Hindu Maharaja of Kashmir, Hari Singh did not accede to either of the two successor states at the date of partition. He hoped to create an independent kingdom. But soon after, Pakistan attacked Kashmir claiming its rights over the state. The infiltrators penetrated the valley. Pakistani troops disguised as local tribesmen attacked the western reaches of his state. Hari Singh appealed to New Delhi for military assistance. Prime Minister Nehru agreed to provide assistance only after two conditions were met: the maharaja had to sign the Instrument of Accession and join India, and Sheikh Mohammed Abdullah, the leader of the largest and most popular organization within the state, had to give his imprimatur to the accession. By September 1947 the Maharaja had realised the impracticability of an independent Kashmir, and decided to offer accession to India on the condition that, he not be asked to immediately institute the democratic reforms demanded by Abdullah and his National Conference. Under pressure from India he did release Abdullah from prison but dragged his feet on granting democratic rights and thus handing power to Abdullah. The impasse over accession continued till the end of October. These conditions were met, and in late October 1947 Indian troops were airlifted into the Valley. They halted the advancing invaders but till then a third of the Valley had fallen into Pakistani hands. The local Muslims, mostly members of the NC provided the logistical support for the Indian troops.

On January 1, 1948, India's Prime Minister Jawaharlal Nehru following the advice of British Governor General Lord Mountbatten and contrary to the wishes of his Deputy Prime Minister Sarder Patel, lodged a complaint with the UN Security Council invoking Articles 34 and 35 of the UN Charter that called for a peaceful settlement of disputes between India and Pakistan, suspecting that it was behind the invasion. In the complaint, as it had already been pledged by Mountbatten in his letter to Hari Singh on October 26, India reiterated its pledge of its conditional commitment to a "plebiscite or referendum under international auspices,"

On January 20, 1948, the Security Council established a three-member UN commission on India and Pakistan (UNCIP) to send them to Kashmir to investigate the situation and exercise mediation. On April 21, the Council expanded the commission to five and authorized it to restore peace and arrange for a plebiscite after the withdrawal of tribal troops. The UNCIP on August 13, passed a resolution calling both on India and Pakistan to conduct a plebiscite after they agreed to a cease-fire and after Pakistan's regular troops and tribesmen were completely withdrawn. The cease-fire went into effect on January 1, 1949, while Pakistan was still in control of one-third of the state. Based on its resolution of August 13, 1948, the UNCIP sent a Monitoring Group for India and Pakistan (UNMGIP) to the region on January 24, to monitor the cease-fire line (CFL). This line was renamed in 1972 as the line of control or line of actual control (LAC). The presence of the UNMIP was approved by India and Pakistan following by their agreement in Karachi on July 27, 1949. Between 1949 and 1960 the UN made a number of attempts to resolve the dispute, but none of its proposals proved acceptable to both sides.

Sheikh Abdullah had also been thinking of independence as another option for the people in the state. He had formally taken over the government from Justice Mahajan in March 1948. In an interview with *The Statesman* he said, "Accession to either side cannot bring peace. We want to live in friendship with both the dominions. Perhaps, a middle path between them, with economic cooperation with each, will be only way of doing it. But an independent Kashmir must be guaranteed not only by India and Pakistan, but also by Britain, the United States and other members of the United Nations." Many of his statements created uncertainty and doubt about his real motives.[37]

In 1950, Sir Owen Dixon, the UN representative for India and Pakistan, noted that the Kashmir conflict was so uncompromising because Kashmir was "not really a unit geographically, demographically or economically" so much as "an agglomeration of territories brought under the political power of One Maharaja".[38] The conflict remains inflexible both because India and Pakistan are equally immovable in their claims, and because Kashmiris themselves are so divided in their aims and loyalties. The Kashmir conflict represents a self-determination movement for Kashmiris; an irredentist movement for Pakistan and Pakistan-controlled Kashmir; and a civil insurgency for India. Although the majority of Kashmiris were Muslim, the state had had a Hindu ruler since the British gave Maharaja Gulab Singh domain over Kashmir in 1846. In September 1950, Dixon suggested a proposal limiting the plebiscite only to the Kashmir Valley of the predominantly Muslim population, which both countries rejected.

In the first two decades following the 1965 Indo-Pakistani war, Kashmir lay largely quiet. Even during the 1971 war, the majority of Kashmiris remained loyal to India. Furthermore, the breakup of Pakistan after the 1971 war dealt a significant blow to the Pakistani irredentist claim on Kashmir. Many Indian political commentators promptly questioned Pakistan's claim on the Muslims of Kashmir when it could not keep its two wings together on the basis of religious faith.

Between 1965 and 1989, however, the process of political mobilization and the undermining of political institutions throughout India, but particularly in Kashmir, accelerated. There was a brief interval in the mid-1970s, when the hopes of the politically aware Kashmiris were raised by the release and return of Sheikh Abdullah after years of house arrest. The government also agreed to review several pieces of central legislation that had been passed pertaining to Kashmir. Abdullah's return to Kashmir was nothing short of victory. He quickly assumed the chief ministership and the leadership of the National Conference, and his party won a majority of seats in the next election in 1977, one of Kashmir's few openly conducted and fairly contested elections.[39]

But this period was brief. Sheikh Abdullah died in September 1982. He was succeeded first by his son, Farooq, a political neophyte who had none of the political survival skills required by the rough-and-tumble politics of the state and none of his father's charisma and political stature. In the 1983 state assembly elections, which were also reasonably fair. Farooq rebuffed Indira Gandhi's efforts to counterfeit an electoral alliance with the National Conference in Kashmir, and contested the elections alone. The National Conference again triumphed. But determined to install a Congress regime in Kashmir, Gandhi dismissed Farooq Abdullah on questionable grounds in July 1984, replacing him with G.M. Shah, a disaffected member of the National Conference.

Shah's term in office was short and troubled. The abrupt dismissal of Abdullah had deeply offended a new generation of politically conscious Kashmiris. Shah, who commanded no wide following within the state, was seen as a central government stooge. During the next two years, a variety of political disturbances — strikes, demonstrations, and bombings — wracked the state.

G.M. Shah proved surprisingly incompetent at curbing the rising tide of violence. In 1986, he too was dismissed on the grounds of corruption and failure to maintain public order in the state. In

November of that same year, Rajiv Gandhi signed an accord with Farooq Abdullah, under the terms of which Farooq was returned to the chief ministership of Jammu and Kashmir. This accord forms yet another critical turning point in precipitating the insurgency. Whatever sympathy and legitimacy that Farooq had had in the eyes of the emergent Kashmiri youth was now lost. The accord reduced him to the stature of a mere stalking horse for the Congress Party in Kashmir.

In the 1987 election, considered to be the most compromised in Kashmir's recent history; the Congress Party and the National Conference jointly contested the state assembly elections; they were opposed by the Muslim United Front (MUF), a conglomeration of political parties. This election was ripped. Whereas previous generations of Kashmiris, whose political consciousness was low, had long tolerated all manner of electoral irregularities, the new generation that had emerged in Kashmir was not willing to tolerate such widespread electoral fraud. Indeed, it is rather telling that several key insurgent leaders, Shabir Shah, Yasin Malik, and Javed Mir, were polling agents for the Muslim United Front in the 1987 elections. These individuals, along with thousands of their peers, were well aware that most elections in India are largely free and fair. The extensive electoral malfeasances that they witnessed in 1987 convinced this younger generation of Kashmiris that the national government in New Delhi had scant regard for their political rights and reckless disregard for democratic procedures. With no other institutional recourse open for expressing their disenchantment with the flawed political process, they resorted to violence. The insurgency has taken the lives of tens of thousands, forced hundreds of thousands from their homes, and shows no sign of coming down.

This sensitivity alienated the Kashmiris. They became unhappy with the Rajiv Gandhi government. The Abdullah government's failure to promote economic development further provoked anguish among the Kashmiris. Pakistan too, worsened the situation by supporting the secessionist groups with funds, weapons, and training, as it continued to make claims over Kashmir. Three principal umbrella groups were involved in the uprising. One group, composed of

Muslim fundamentalists, was pro-Pakistan and had links with the fundamentalist Pakistan party, Jammait-I-Islam. The second umbrella group was tied to the Jammu and Kashmir Liberation Front (JKLF) established in 1965, and demanded an independent Kashmir. The third group was the Jammu and Kashmir Peoples' League that had a pro-Pakistan orientation. These groups demanded that a plebiscite as pledged by India and guaranteed by the UN Resolutions of 1948-49 be conducted so that the Kashmiris could exercise their right of self-determination. Their demands were supported by Pakistan. India, however, rejected their demands based on the argument that in 1956 the Kashmir constituent assembly acceded to India. It further contended that the plebiscite was outdated and that based on the July 1972 Simla agreement, Pakistan was obligated to resolve the Kashmir dispute bilaterally with her and not under the aegis of any international organization. Furthermore, India pointed out that Kashmir had been under a democratic Muslim leadership with an opportunity to rule itself, while Pakistan had been under a military dictatorship for more than twenty-five years since its independence in 1947. Therefore, India argued that for Pakistan to call for self determination in Kashmir was disingenuous and hypocritical. Besides, India had to consider that 110 million Indians were Muslim, the second largest Muslim population in the world, and that Kashmir being a predominantly Muslim state stood out as a test case of India's commitment to secularism. In addition, India was also concerned with the Hindus and Buddhists who live in Jammu and Ladakh respectively, represent 35% of the population and want to be part of the Indian Union. Hence, India rejected the demands of the secessionists. But the militants determined to realize their goal engaged the Indian security forces in armed struggle and terrorism. By intensifying their struggle they made the state ungovernable. The Indian government sent increasing numbers of military and paramilitary forces numbering more than 300,000 to help put down the militancy.[40]

It dismissed Abdullah's government in August 1990 and brought the state under central control. Under the July 1990 Jammu and Kashmir Disturbed Areas Act and Armed Forces Special Powers

Act (AFSPA), repealed in May 1995, the security forces allegedly committed a series of human right abuses. The encounter between the security forces and the militants resulted in more than 50,000 casualties. This number included many hundreds of innocent, civilian bystanders, as the militants used them as shields in their battles with the security forces. Militants have also been accused of committing many human rights violations. For example, they allegedly engaged in killing, raping women and bombing railway bridges, passenger buses, and public buildings.

By early 1996, the central government adopted a multi-pronged approach to deal with the insurgency. It lifted direct rule over the state and restored state government under Abdullah who had won a landslide victory in the September elections, although the 30-disparate party coalition, known as the All-Party Hurriyat (Freedom) Conference (APHC), had denounced and boycotted the elections. It also created several Muslim counterinsurgency groups to fight the insurgents along with its security forces. In February 1996, the central government released from jail the four Pro-Pakistani separatist leaders, Imran Rahi of the Hiz-Ul-Mujahideen, Bilal Lodhi of the Al-Barq, Babbar Badr of the Muslim Janbaz Force (MJF), and Ghulam Mohiuddin of the Muslim Mujahideen, and initiated talks with them. They agreed to talks with the government with no preconditions and without Pakistan's involvement. On February 10, another pro-Pakistani Master Ahsan Dar, the founder of the Hiz-Ul-Mujahideen, who was in jail, joined them by endorsing their stand. The Indian government welcomed their offer and accused the Hurriyat Conference of "failing the people of Kashmir and breaching their faith." The conference responded by denouncing them for excluding Pakistan and that its actions were "anti-movement," and asked that they be expelled from their organizations. The moderate separatist leader of the Peoples League, Shabir Ahmad Shah, also joined the conference by saying that the problem could not be solved without the inclusion of Pakistan in the talks. Meanwhile, inter-group clashes began to increase, thus undermining their cause. For example, in 1995 alone, 167 clashes took place and 107 militants were killed. Even the leaders have been targeted for murder. This included

Mohammed Yasin Malik, leader of the splinter group of the Jammu and Kashmir Liberation Front (JKLF) which espouses independence; Syed Ali Shah Geelani of the Jumat-I-Islami; and Abdul Ghani Lone of the Peoples Conference who are pro-Pakistani.

Ethno Religious and Political Mobilization

It can be argued that the Kashmiri insurgency arose out of a process of political mobilization that was unified with steady institutional decay. The political mobilization of Kashmiris started later than in the rest of the Indian state, but it accelerated dramatically after the 1970s. Institutional decay in Kashmir began as early as the 1950s, much earlier than in the rest of India. These two trends intersected as a new generation of Kashmiris emerged on the political scene. Significant political changes within India at large and within Kashmir itself transformed the politically passive Kashmiris into a highly mobilized population. Kashmiris denied their voting rights in deeply flawed elections as they witnessed the increasingly free exercise of franchise in other parts of India. Awareness of this division grew with the spread of education and mass media in Kashmir and contributed to a growing sense of anger against the Indian state.[41]

According to Sumit Ganguly, the mobilization in Kashmir took place along ethno-religious lines. Four factors are significant. First, the state is divided into districts that also produce a religious division. Srinagar and the surrounding Valley of Kashmir are predominantly Muslim. The districts of Leh and Kargil, have predominantly Buddhist and Muslim populations, respectively. Jammu is predominantly Hindu. The predominantly Muslim composition of the National Conference had little appeal among the Hindus of Jammu. Buddhist-dominated Leh was also outside the ambit of National Conference politics.

Second, the geographic isolation of the Valley separated Kashmiri Islam from the larger currents of Muslim politics in India. Indian Muslims rarely made common cause with fellow Muslims in the Valley, and the Muslims of the Valley never developed extensive ties with Muslim communities in the rest of India. Furthermore, divisions exist even among Kashmiri Muslims. They were divided, first and foremost, by geography. While the people of Jammu spoke Dogri, those of Srinagar spoke Kashmiri. Furthermore, Muslims face discrimination in the mainstream of Indian society, and there is no substantial Kashmiri Muslim expatriate community. Thus, the Muslims of the Valley were reluctant to venture into the rest of the country to seek their fortunes.

Third, when secular politics fails to give an outflow for the expression of discontent, political mobilization tends to follow ethno-religious lines. This avenue of protest had a long history in Kashmir. A fourth and final factor that was responsible for the ethno-religious direction of the movement was Pakistan, sensing an opportunity to weaken India's hold on Kashmir, funded, trained, and organized the loose, unstructured movement into a coherent, organized enterprise directed toward challenging the writ of the Indian state in Kashmir. The Soviet withdrawal from Afghanistan in 1990 and the subsequent collapse of the Soviet Union greatly facilitated Pakistan in arming and assisting the Kashmiri insurgents. Significant numbers of battle-hardened Afghan mujahideen could now be directed toward a new cause. These Afghans had more to offer than direct support; their experience of ousting the Soviets from Afghanistan provided a model of opposition and resistance to a powerful state and its well-organized military.[42]

A number of more specific explanations for the crisis offer partial explanations for the origins of the crisis. For example, Ashutosh Varshney has traced the origins of the crisis to the clash of three competing visions of nationalism: Kashmiri, secular, and Islamic. Prem Shankar Jha, an Indian journalist, has argued that the revolt in Kashmir can be traced to middle-class frustrations. He contends that employment opportunities have not kept pace with the growth of an educated middle class in Kashmir Consequently, the rebellion represents the expression of collective and growing frustration with the lack of economic opportunity. Furthermore, unlike Indians from other regions who seek employment in all parts of India, Kashmiris are unwilling to relocate.

Rise of Religious Extremism

Since last two decades, the state of Jammu and Kashmir has also witnessed the rise of religious extremism which has given rise to the insurgency. The militant movement in Kashmir has resulted into erosion of the secular Kashmiri character and a Muslim individuality with fundamentalist color has started emerging rapidly. Jamaat-i-Islami and other Muslim fundamentalist groups of Kashmir like Student Islamic Federation, Islami Jamiat Tulba, Muslim United Front etc. through their constant efforts of propaganda and preaching in mosques, madrasas, Friday congregations and social and political assemblies triggered the Islamic passions among the majority of Kashmiri Muslims and built the youth cadres to achieve the objective of 'Islamicisation of Kashmiri society.'[43] Flooded with foreign funds mainly from Saudi Arabia and Pakistan, Jamaat-i-Islami expanded its reach in the valley. The Islamic fundamentalist indoctrination of Kashmiri Muslims was channelized against India and anything that symbolized Indian culture, society and polity. Now the slogans of jihad and for the establishment of Nizam-e-Mustafa were openly raised in Kashmir. In mid-1988, Allahwale (the Islamic fundamentalist group based in North India) along with Jamaat-i-Islami held a conference in Srinagar in which Muslim delegates from various parts of India and also from some West Asian countries participated. The delegates while highlighting the doctrinal purity of Islam, stressed the need to carry out jihad. Soon after several Imams from the fundamentalist Allahwale group were inducted into various mosques in Kashmir for religious indoctrination, displacing the local Kashmiri Muslim Imams who still believed in local indigenous culture and tolerant view of Islam. In this manner the wide network of mosques was taken over by the Islamic extremists and consequently used to stimulate Kashmiri Muslims for jihad.[44]

The extent of Pakistani and Afghan influence on the 'Islamist transformation of Kashmir insurgency' has been well elucidated in a report of the Task Force on Terrorism and Unconventional Warfare set up by the US House Republican Research Committee. Relevant excerpts from the report titled *The New Islamist International* dated February 1, 1993 are cited:

"Kashmir was the only area in India where, as of the mid 1980s, Islamic revivalism had taken a radical political stance and where the slogans of the Islamic state have been publically raised and had been received with growing popularity. The population was increasingly adopting the leadership of Jamaat-i-Islami of Pakistan and Khomeynists. Consequently by 1984 an Islamic radicalization had developed that saw the rise of such movements as the Jammu and Kashmir Liberation Front, Mahaz-i-Azadi and the Liberation League." During the first phase of militancy in Kashmir which started in 1989, the Islamist militant groups strived to bring structural changes at cultural levels of Kashmir society, seeking to Islamicise the socio political set up in the valley to bring it in tune with the Islamic state of Pakistan and the Muslim Ummah. The term Azadi was now replaced with jihad. Various Islamist groups like Jamaat-i-Islami and its militant wing Hizbul Mujahideen, women's wing Dukhtaran-i-Millat, Jamiat-ul-Mujahideen, Allah Tigers, Jamiat-ul-Ulemma Islam, Al Badr, Ali Jihad Force, Muslim Mujahideen, Islamic Students League, Zia Tigers etc. proclaimed the objective of their struggle as Islmicisation of socio political and economic set up, merger of Kashmir with Pakistan, unification of Ummah and establishment of an Islamic Caliphate.[45]

The extremist and terrorist organizations in Kashmir gave an Islamist colour and direction to the militancy in the state. These organizations launched a religious campaign against the Non-Muslims of the valley and killed the minorities in the name of jihad. Through the sermons in mosques and by the periodic writings in the local newspapers, they sowed the seeds of hatred among both the communities and started the campaign against the Kashmiri Hindus. A final ultimatum was given to this minority community through Press on 14 April 1990 asking them to leave the valley within 2 days or face retribution or death. About one thousand members of the Hindu community were brutally murdered and the entire community of about 350,000 forced out of their hearts and homes. This forced displacement of Kashmiri Pandits, who have been the indigenous minority is a classic case of ethnic-religious cleansing with long term implications for the secular polity in Kashmir. There were open calls for establishment of an Islamic order. The liquidation of Central government officials, Kashmiri Pandits and other liberal intellectuals was described as necessary to empty the valley of un-Islamic elements. Simultaneously all the cinema houses, beauty parlours, bars, use of cosmetics, etc., were banned by militant groups. Al Barq issued an order on ban of cigarettes. Kashmiri girls were asked not to take part in any cultural programmes outside the valley. Allah Tigers threatened to throw bombs on houses where women would refuse to wear viels. Through the terror of their guns, the militants coerced the local newspapers to highlight their activities. The Hizbul Mujahideen imposed a ban on the national and Jammu newspapers in Kashmir valley. The terror groups used both terror tactics and Islamist ideology to control the local press, which now projected the Islamist viewpoint on society, politics as superior to the so called democratic and secular order prevalent in India.[46]

The Islamist organizations also banned certain non Islamic practices prevalent among the Kashmiri Muslims such as visiting ancient holy shrines of Sufis and Rishis. People have also resisted attempts by some militant groups to stop the celebration of annual Urs at Batmol Rishi. At the same time, many terrorist organizations such as Hizbul- Mujahideen, have been holding out public threats against participation by Hindu pilgrims to the annual pilgrimage to the holy Amar Nath cave. They have resorted to mine blast and firing upon the pilgrims. These holy shrines of Kashmir have been targeted by the Islamist terrorists in order to obliterate the indigenous ethno cultural and spiritual heritage of Kashmir and the traditional ethos of religious tolerance, harmony and peaceful co-existence, and to usher in the fundamentalist and radical Islamic practices.[47]The religious extremism and terrorism had various devastating consequences for the psychological, physical, socio-cultural and demographic profile of the displaced people. More than 30,000 houses belonging to Kashmiri Pandits, their business establishments, educational, cultural and religious institutions have been burnt to completely destroy the traces of their 5000 year old history.[48] Therefore the insurgency in Kashmir has not only lost its indigenous character, but has also been simultaneously taken over by the Islamist radicals.

Role of Pakistan in Supporting Cross Border Terrorism

India consistently blames Pakistan-based militant groups for lethal attacks on Indian civilians, as well as on government security forces, in both Kashmir and in major Indian cities. India holds Pakistan responsible for providing material support and training facilities to Kashmiri militants. Most often blamed for terrorism in India are Lashkar-e-Taiba, Jaish-e-Mohammed, and Harakat ul-Mujahideen, and Hizbul Mujahideen. These anti-India militant groups fighting in Kashmir are based in Pakistan and are closely linked to Islamist groups there. Pakistan's powerful and largely autonomous ISI is widely believed to have provided significant support for militant Kashmiri separatists over the past decade in what is perceived as a proxy war against India. The chief of India's Defense Intelligence Agency reported providing the "solid documentary proof" that 70 Islamic militant camps are operating in Pakistani Kashmir. He claimed that about 3,000 "terrorists" were being trained in camps on the Pakistani side of the LOC. The cross-border terrorism from Pakistan is making it difficult for India to maintain its peace initiative, and current infiltration rates are widely believed to be on the rise. [49]

Pakistan fought four wars on Kashmir- 1947-48, 1965, 1971 and Kargil war. Pakistani army understood the edge of Indian army over Pakistan army in conventional warfare. So it changed the modus operandi and waged proxy war against India. Pakistan supported, trained and financed the local kashmiri youth for jihad against India.

The most important long-term outcome of the first Indo-Pak war was that the cease-fire line established on January 1st 1949 has subsequently held for over 60 years as the de facto border in Kashmir, through subsequent periods of war and peace. This de facto extension of its borders has been of strategic importance for Pakistan. If the whole of Kashmir had gone to India, the essential rail and road link between its two major cities of Lahore and Rawalpindi would have been under threat. Also, with undivided Kashmir having a border contiguous with Afghanistan to the north, India could have intervened to prevent Pakistan from pacifying the tribes in the always unruly North West Frontier Province. But, Pakistan has not been satisfied with these strategic gains. Its domestic politics have ensured that it has continued in its attempts to secure the Kashmir valley.[50] In 1965, the Pakistani military dictator Ayub Khan carefully orchestrated a strategy for fomenting a rebellion in Kashmir. The ultimate goal of this strategy, code-named "Operation Gibraltar," was to take advantage of the disturbed conditions within the state and seize Kashmir in a sharp, short war. Despite this well-organized effort, no insurgency ensued. However, a series of events in India reinforced Pakistani elite perceptions that the moment was ripe for attempting to drift Kashmir away from India. First, in December 1963, riots that had a strong anti-Indian flavor had broken out in the Kashmir Valley following the theft of a holy relic, believed to be a hair of the Prophet Mohammed, from the Hazratbal mosque in Srinagar, the capital city of Jammu and Kashmir. The Pakistani leadership immediately took these demonstrations as signs of pro-Pakistani sentiment. Second, in the wake of the death of Prime Minister Jawaharlal Nehru in 1964, Pakistani decision-makers inferred that India's unity was in danger without Nehru's towering influence. It was expected that various centrifugal forces, including caste, class, and ethnic cleavages would tear India apart. Finally, a "limited probe" that the Pakistani military leadership conducted in April 1965 in an area known as the Rann of Kutch in the western Indian state of Gujarat failed to produce a vigorous response from the Indian military; the seemingly soft Indian response led the Pakistanis to believe that the Indians did wanted to avoid the battle. Pakistani leaders reinforced these beliefs by falling back on racial and ethnic imagery, conjured up by British administrators for the purposes of colonial administrative convenience, to explain India's lack of military prowess.

Based on this series of dubious assumptions, Pakistan began to infiltrate regular soldiers disguised as local tribesmen into the Kashmir Valley in the summer of 1965. However, the Kashmiris in the Valley did not rise up in revolt and did not make common cause with the infiltrators. Yet this cannot be attributed to a lack of anti-Indian sentiment on the part of the Kashmiris. As the demonstrations in the wake of the Hazaratbal theft had demonstrated, such sentiments were widespread within the Valley. However, these sentiments did not automatically translate into support for Pakistan and a willingness to resort to large-scale violence to express their discontent with Indian rule.[51]

Pakistan, which claims that the entire state should have come to it at the time of the partition of India by the British in 1947, encouraged its own militant organizations to fight against India and advocate the merger of the State with Pakistan. Pakistan also raised many terrorist factions to counter the monopoly of JKLF group which was demanding Kashmir as independent nation rather than joined Pakistan. So many terrorist factions were trained and supported by Pakistan like Harkat ul-Mujahedeen, Jaish-e-Muhammad, Lashkar-e-Taiba. These groups' philosophy was to merge Kashmir with Pakistan. By 1992-93, hardcore, fundamentalist, pro-Pakistani groups had proliferated. These groups had 20 to 25 per cent Afghan guerillas (expert in warfare) and were controlled completely by Pakistan from PoK. Not only Afghans but also the LTTE were brought into the Pakistani camps in PoK to train the selected men in use of IEDs, and for operating Stinger missiles and signal equipment for various makes and usage. Many training camps are being run along the international border. According to estimates nearly 450 to 475 militants are regularly taking part in weapons training in camps at Dallapur, Jalapur, Kunjah, Mahara, Chawinda and Musa in Sialkot and Zafarwal sectors of Pakistan. The interrogation reports of several militants arrested by security forces has brought out the fact that Refugee Maintenance Cell has been set up by ISI and is headed by one retired Pakistani Colonel Abdul Rehman. The organization provides daily allowances to militants of all outfits.[52] All this time Pakistan conducted a well planned 'psychological warfare' to alienate the locals against Indian government and win them over to the so called Pakistani propagated cause of Azadi.[53] Thousands of Islamist terrorists have been pushed inside Kashmir, and to facilitate the infiltration of Islamist mercenaries, Pakistani forces resort to firing at Indian pickets along the LoC, to divert attention and to provide cover to the armed intruders.[54]

The Islamist mercenaries have extended their operations from Kashmir to Poonch, Mendhar, Rajouri, Doda, Kishtwar and even made forays into Chamba in Himachal Pradesh. This signals the Pak strategy of terrorizing and forcing out the Hindu minorities from these hilly areas and to Islamicise the entire state. Pakistan also seeks to acquire control over the strategic and high altitude areas in Jammu and Kashmir for carrying out its future offensive against the Indian forces in the state by pushing border opposite RS Pura, Ramgarh and Hiranagar sub-sections of the Jammu-Kathua belt.

The ISI also spread its roots in the valley and around the Jammu and Poonch areas. Because the Kishtwar-Doda areas were initially free of militancy, they also moved into them. The ISI established and runs its own Kashmiri organizations. The most important among these are the Hizb-e-Islami, which is comprised of former Kashmiri mujahideen who were trained by the ISI and then fought with Gulbadin Hikmatyar's organization in Afghanistan. These terrorist organisations have often been closely associated with the senior officials of the ISI. President Musharraf himself had long-standing close links with fundamentalist organizations. During the Afghan war he had been assigned the job of training mercenary Mujahideen groups.[55]

Kashmir millitancy phase from 1995 to now comprises mostly foreign terrorists from Afghanistan, Pakistan etc. They were funded, armed and trained by Pakistan and pushed into the Indian Kashmir for jihad against Indian army. These foreigner mercenaries or terrorist get monthy salary and even lump sum payment to there family on death, so called martayr. These foreigner mercenaries launch fidayeen or suicidal attack on the security forces for maximum damage. These tactics used to boost the morale the new recruit terrorists. By bringing in mercenaries and simultaneously shelling the border areas along the LAC, Pakistan has sought to project Kashmir as a flashpoint in South Asia bringing it into the focus of world attention.[56]

After Kargil war, there have been several attacks on the security forces. These attacks represent the adoption of a high risk strategy by Pakistan and the induction into J&K of increasing firepower and a new generation of terrorists with greater experience and better training. There has also been a visible improvement in the firepower available to the terrorists. Missile launchers, anti aircraft guns, anti tank and anti personnel mines are being used.[57]

In December 2001, the United States designated LeT and JeM as Foreign Terrorist Organizations shortly after they were publically implicated by New Delhi for an attack on the Indian Parliament complex that killed nine and injured 18. This assault spurred India to fully mobilize its military along the India-Pakistan frontier. An ensuing 10-month-long standoff in 2002 involved one million Indian and Pakistani soldiers and was viewed as the closest the two countries had come to full-scale war since 1971, causing the U.S. government to become "deeply concerned ... that a conventional war ... could escalate into a nuclear confrontation."

The United States signaled increased pressure on Islamabad in October 2003 when the Treasury Department designated the Pakistan-based Al Akhtar Trust as a terrorist support organization under Executive Order 13224. Al Akhtar is said to be carrying on support for Al Qaeda and Taliban terrorist activities funded by the previously-designated Al Rashid Trust. The United States also that month identified Indian crime figure Dawood Ibrahim as a "global terrorist" with links to both Al Qaeda and Lashkar-e-Taiba. Ibrahim, wanted by the Indian government for 1993 Bombay bombings that killed and injured thousands, is believed to be in Pakistan. These moves by the U.S. government were welcomed in New Delhi, where officials continuously are urging greater U.S. attention to anti-India terrorism emanating from Pakistan.

The Pakistani viewpoint on Kashmir says that it has always looked at Kashmir struggle as a freedom struggle. Over the past six decades, Islamabad strongly supported the right of self-determination for the Kashmiris and pledged moral, political, and diplomatic support to the Kashmir cause. Ever since 1990, uprising in Kashmir, Pakistan stepped up its support for the Kashmiris that allegedly included material support to the fighters in Kashmir. After 9/11 Pakistan, drew a distinction between freedom struggle and terrorism and made concerted efforts that War on Terrorism should not affect the Kashmiris' fight. While India has questioned Pakistan's credentials in becoming partner in US counter-terrorism strategy.[58]

Pakistan has provided political, ideological, financial, military and logistical support to the Kashmiri separatists. For long, Pakistan denied its culpability in the militancy that was raging in Kashmir and maintained that its support was purely ideological and political. Gradually it reverted to the logic of the liberation struggle. Pakistani leaders say that Kashmiri militants are 'freedom fighters' or 'jihadis'.[59] Thus, Pakistan has sought to legitimise the existence of as well as its support to terrorist groups operating in J & K by calling them freedom fighters. The scope of Kashmiri terrorism does not stop at the boundaries of any single state. Pakistan targets every potential flashpoint in India and seeks to establish linkages with every subversive and criminal force that can be exploited.

Terrorist Organizations Operating in Kashmir

The terrorist organizations in Kashmir have largely been the product of Pakistani intelligence. Pakistan, which claims that the entire state should have come to it at the time of the partition of India by the British in 1947, encouraged the Jamaat-e-Islami (JEI) of J&K to form its own militant organization to advocate the merger of the State with Pakistan. Initially JKLF was the organization whose military operations were supported by Pakistan. But JKLF did not favour merger with Pakistan, instead claimed for independence of Kashmir. Thus Pakistan began to create several new organizations which advocated its cause. The ISI cut down assistance to the JKLF and other groups fighting for independence and stepped up assistance to the new smaller groups which advocated merger with Pakistan. They were given funds, training in Pakistan and arms and ammunition. Disturbed by the infiltration of these organizations, the pro-Independence organizations such as the JKLF gave up their violent armed struggle against the Government of India in 1995. However, they have not given up their objective of an independent Kashmir. They are now trying to achieve it through a political struggle.

The pro-Pakistan groups co-operated with the Pakistani jihadi organizations. Most of the acts of terrorism in J&K after 1993 were committed by these Pakistani organizations with the assistance of local groups. The more important of these Pakistani organizations are the Harkat-ul-Ansar (HUA) subsequently re-named in 1997 as the Harkat-ul-Mujahideen (HUM), the Harkat-ul-Jihad-al-Islami (HUJI), the Lashkar-e-Toiba (LET) and the Al Badr. The Jaish-e-Mohammad (JEM), which came into existence in 2000 following a split in the HUM, also joined them.

The indigenous organizations say their agenda is restricted to J&K. Once they achieve their aims in Kashmir, their quarrel with the Government of India will be over. The Pakistani organizations say Kashmir is the gateway to India. They want to "liberate" all Muslims—whether in Kashmir or elsewhere—and form Muslim "homelands". Since the Kargil conflict of 1999 between India and Pakistan, the Pakistani jihadi organizations have virtually taken over the leadership and control of the jihadi terrorist movement in J&K and other States of India. They are increasingly attacking soft targets such as shopping areas, trains etc in order to inflict mass casualties.

Jaish-e-Mohammad

Jaish-e-Mohammad, or army of the Prophet Mohammed, is a major militant group with links to the Taliban and Al Qaeda. The Jaish-e-Mohammed (JeM) has been held responsible for the December 13, 2001 terrorist attack on the Indian Parliament in New Delhi. It has also been involved in attack on the J&K legislative assembly on October 2001. The Jaish-e-Mohammed (JeM) is a relatively new terrorist outfit, compared to other major outfits active in Jammu and Kashmir (J&K). Like the Lashkar-e-Toiba (LeT), the JeM too is an outfit formed, controlled and manned by Pakistan. The outfit was launched on January 31, 2000, by Maulana Masood Azhar in Karachi after he was released from an Indian jail during the terrorists for hostage swap of December 31, 1999, following the hijacking of the Indian Airlines Flight IC 814. He was also reported to have received assistance in setting up the JeM from

Pakistan's Inter-Services Intelligence (ISI), the then Taliban regime in Afghanistan, Osama bin Laden and several Sunni sectarian outfits of Pakistan. The Jaish-e-Mohammed is part of the Islamist terror network with its base in Pakistan and active in the terrorist violence in J&K. The outfit, like other terrorist outfits in J&K, claims to using violence to force a withdrawal of Indian security forces from J&K.

The Jaish-e-Mohammed has largely confined its operations within J&K. The only recorded instance of its operations outside J&K has been the December 13, 2001, Parliament attack in New Delhi. However, several of its cadre have been arrested or killed by security forces in states other than J&K. Most Jaish-e-Mohammed attacks have been described as fidayeen attacks.

JeM was carved out as a strategy to keep the terrorist movement alive. One of the ISI officers who played a key role in the creation of JeM was Brigadier Abdullah, head of the Kashmir division in the agency. With Pakistan's intelligence and security agencies aiding and abetting the growth and expense of JeM, it was Omar Sheikh who planned and executed Ajhar's jihad in Kashmir. With Mushtaq Zargar helping him to recruit local youth and setting up a network of informers and active participants, Sheikh planned and executed a series of terrorist attacks in Kashmir and other parts of India. [60]

Al-Badr

The Al Badr was formed in June 1998 with the professed goal of strengthening the 'Kashmiri freedom struggle' and to 'liberate' the Indian State of Jammu and Kashmir and merge it with Pakistan. The outfit advocates that Kashmiris should be given the right of self-determination in accordance with the United Nations resolutions. While advocating the idea of a sovereign Kashmir it is also critical of the moderate Kashmiri organisations, such as the Jammu and Kashmir Liberation Front. The current Ai Badr leadership is also opposed to the United States, Israel and the regime of Saudi Arabia. The outfit has in the past indicated that it perceives Kashmir to be the 'gateway of India' and describes its objective as the 'liberation' of Muslims in the rest of India after 'occupying' Kashmir.

The Al Badr, according to official sources in Jammu and Kashmir, which was earlier operating under the banner of Hizb-ul-Mujahideen, was encouraged by the Inter Services Intelligence (ISI), Pakistan's external intelligence agency, to operate independently in the year 1998. Indian intelligence sources have indicated that a new version of the Al Badr was formed as part of this changed strategy, in 1998, through the induction of foreign mercenaries serving in several other terrorist outfits in Kashmir.

During the time of its formation, the Al Badr was led by Lukmaan, a resident of Pakistan occupied Kashmir (PoK). Bakht Zameen, a resident of Punjab province in Pakistan, is the present 'chief commander' of the outfit. Al Badr is reported to possess a cadre strength of approximately 200, including 120 foreign mercenaries. The outfit is headquartered at Mansehra in Pakistan. It is also reported to have a camp office in Muzaffarabad, PoK. Reportage of the past five years has indicated that the Al Badr is active in the Anantnag, Baramulla, Budgam, Srinagar and Kupwara districts of the Kashmir Valley. It also has a presence in the Poonch and Rajouri districts of Jammu region. The Al Badr is part of the United Jehad Council (UJC), a coalition of Pakistan-based terrorist groups active in Jammu and Kashmir. It is reported to have training camps in the Manshera area of North West Frontier Province (NWFP) in Pakistan, Kotli and Muzaffarabad in PoK.

It has launched attacks targeting Indian military installations and prominent government officials in Jammu and Kashmir. Al Badr has time and again been opposed to any process of dialogue between India and Pakistan. For instance, the outfit's chief Bakht Zameen said in an interview on September 5, 2001, that India was not honest about holding a dialogue for the harmonious settlement of the Kashmir issue. The outfit has also sought to enforce Islamist lifestyles in the areas in which it operates. For instance, reports of August 2003 indicated that the Al Badr ordered women in the rural areas of J&K to quit police jobs, wear veils, give up studies after the age of 14 and not to move out without a male. Posters carrying these diktats were seen pasted on street walls and mosques in the

Thannamandi and Darhal areas of Rajouri district. The posters warned of penalty if women failed to abide by. Earlier on December 20, 2002, in a major terrorist act against women across Jammu region, terrorists killed three young girls, including two college students, at Hasiot village in Rajouri district. The separate incidents were reportedly carried out by a group of three Pakistani terrorists belonging to the Al Badr led by the outfit's 'area commander' Zubair Gul.[61]

Harkat-ul-Ansar

It is another radical Islamist terrorist organization with its headquarters in Islamabad. It was carved out in Kashmir with the merger of two pan Islamic outfits, Harkat-ul-Jehad-e—Islami and Harkat-ul-Mujahideen. It aims at liberating the Muslim majority area and establishing the supremacy of Islam. It has its operation extending to Kashmir and other parts of India. This organization has been recruiting students from Muslim theological schools for arms training. The HUA strategy is to achieve its Islamist objectives by means of religious discourses and holy crusade. Most of the Harkat-ul-Ansar mercenaries infiltrated into Jammu and Kashmir have made their sanctuaries in the hilly areas of Baramulla, Anantnag, Udhampur, Kishtwar and Doda. These militants have been targeting the security forces and the minority groups.[62]

Human Rights Violations

Many human rights organizations such as Amnesty International and the Human Rights Watch (HRW) have condemned human rights abuses in Kashmir by Indians as "extra-judicial executions", "disappearances", and torture. The "Armed Forces Special Powers Act", provides a license to kill innocent people. The Armed Forces Special Powers Act (AFSPA) grants the military wide powers of arrest, the right to shoot to kill, and to occupy or destroy property in counterinsurgency operations. Indian officials claim that troops need such powers because the army is only deployed when national security is at serious risk from armed combatants.

A Human Rights Watch report has accused the Indian military and Indian-government of serious and widespread human rights violations at Sopore in Kashmir. One such alleged massacre occurred on 6 January 1993 in the town. In vengeance for the killing of one soldier, paramilitary forces rampaged through Sopore's market setting buildings ablaze and shooting bystanders. The Indian government pronounced the event 'unfortunate' and claimed that an ammunition dump had been hit by gunfire, setting off fires that killed most of the victims.

In an attempt to quash the violent insurgency in Jammu and Kashmir, some Indian security personnel have resorted to brutal tactics against the Kashmiri population. Portions of the capital Srinagar have been burned to the ground. Muslim neighborhoods that security forces suspected to be sympathetic to the separatist cause have been subjected to a collective punishment that includes indiscriminate shootings, beatings, and rape. Others suspected of militant activism often faced torture, execution, or a new "countermilitant" assignment to assassinate other alleged insurgents and local residents.

Under the July 1990 Jammu and Kashmir Disturbed Areas Act and Armed Forces Special Powers Act (AFSPA), repealed in May 1995, the security forces allegedly committed a series of human right abuses. The abuses included mock "encounters" with suspects to cover-up the deaths of victims who died in police custody, inhuman treatment of prisoners and suspects with beatings, burnings with cigarettes, suspension by the feet and electric shocks, arbitrary arrest and detention of the suspects for more than 12 months, searching and arresting suspects without a warrant, and using excessive force against mass demonstrations and militants. The encounter between the security forces and the militants resulted in more than 50,000 casualties. This number included many hundreds of innocent, civilian bystanders, as the militants used them as shields in their battles with the security forces. Militants have also been accused of committing many human rights violations. For example, they allegedly engaged in killing the moderate Muslim leadership, raping women and bombing the railway bridges, passenger buses, and public buildings.

Human Rights Watch also reports that abuses are not limited to one side, Muslim militants are also guilty of civilian massacres, summary executions, rape, and torture. With equally questionable standards for suspicion, they have kidnapped and assassinated government officials, civil servants, and suspected informers. In fact, the event that led the Indian government to send security forces to Jammu and Kashmir in 1989 was a kidnapping by militants of the home minister's daughter. Muslim militants have also targeted Hindu families, harassing, torturing, murdering, and threatening them in an attempt to drive them out of the valley. Foreign guerrillas in Kashmir fighting a "holy war" are responsible for some of the more brutal attacks on members of the Hindu minority.[63]

Human rights violations have also been reported in Pakistan-administered Kashmir. The Human rights organizations expressed concern over the human rights violation in Gilgit, Baltistan and urged the government of Pakistan to establish democratic institutions and rule of law in this area of northern Kashmir.

On 18 June 2010, a rally was organized by Mr. Yasin Malik, chief of Jammu and Kashmir Liberation Front (JKLF) to protest the increasing human rights violation by the army. 'Jail Bharo' agitation began in the valley to protest against the killing of the Kashmiri youth. Kashmir lost four teenagers at the hands of the police and the other forces in the past six months.[64]

Plight of Kashmiri Pandits

The Pandits, who are the Hindu community of Kashmir and have an ancient and a proud culture, have been amongst the most afflicted victims of the Pakistani-supported campaign of terrorism in Jammu and Kashmir. Their roots in the Kashmir Valley run very deep. They are the original inhabitants of this beautiful valley. Their number being small and peace-loving by nature, they have been the soft targets of terrorists. Virtually the entire population of 400,000 Kashmiri Pandits have been forced to leave their ancestral homes and property. Threatened with violence and intimidation by Muslim fundamentalists, they have been turned into refugees in their own country. As a matter of fact, Jammu and Kashmir has become a target of Pakistan, sponsored by religion-based terrorism. The persecution by Muslim extremists of the Hindu minority and the systematic religion-based extremism of terrorist elements has resulted in the migration of these Hindu/Pandits and other minorities from the Kashmir Valley to other parts of India. Fundamentalists and terrorists have also targeted and assassinated Muslim intellectuals and liberal Muslim leaders too, who spoke of Hindu-Muslim unity and brotherhood.

There has virtually no effort to make possible their return to the valley. The possibility of reversing the terrorists' ethnic cleansing of the valley remains remote and there are reports of the hidden migration of the minorities. This development has gained impetus after horrific killing of 24 Kashmiri Pandits in 2003. These people including 11 women and two children were brutally massacred at Nadimarg village in South Kashmir.[65]

Conclusion

The militancy in the state is deeply rooted in the contemporary history of the state as well as that of the Indo-Pak relations. During the past twenty years, the phenomenon of terrorism in Jammu and Kashmir has manifested in coercive intimidation of civil population, introduction of radical Islam in culture and society, violation of human rights, destruction of property, ethnic cleansing of hindu minorities, attacks on security forces, mines and bomb blasts and undermining the democratic and pluralistic socio political order. In this case, various police, army and paramilitary forces are engaged in a battle to retain control over large areas of the sovereign territory of the Indian Union, against a heavily armed enemy backed by an established neighbouring state that supports arms and trains them.

TERRORISM IN NORTH EAST

North-East region of India is the most diverse part of the country. The North-East consists of what is commonly known as 'Seven Sisters', namely Assam, Arunachal Pradesh, Manipur, Mizoram, Meghalaya, Nagaland and Tripura. North East has a total area of 2,55,083sq km *i.e.* 7.76 per cent of the geographical area of

India. The religious, linguistic and ethnic divides in this region are sharper and historical, geographical and cultural ties are not much visible. There are a number of scheduled tribes in the North East with different dialects. It has appropriately been described as 'Miniature Asia' a place where the brown and yellow races meet.[66]

In terms of colonial background, the British East India Company conquered Bengal in 1757. To the northeast of Bengal was the Brahmaputra River valley, heavily populated by ethnic Assamese. The valley was incorporated into the company's holdings in 1826 through war with Burma. Company control extended more gradually into hill areas surrounding the Bengal and Assam plains. After the British crown took over these regions, many of these hill areas and some zones in the plains were designated "tribal," closed to immigration, and kept under distinct administrative regimes.[67] This area was never fully colonized by the British. At the time of Indian independence there was an attempt to institutionalize some local autonomy for the region's people, most notably through the creation of autonomous district councils under the sixth schedule of the constitution. Since that time, numerous ethnic groups in the area have called for greater autonomy or independence and the 'sons of the soil' movements have developed in response to migration within the region.[68]

Northeast India after independence has a history of long-running and violent autonomy movements of different ethnic groups. The region has been caught in a vicious cycle of inadequate economic development and insufficient job opportunities, causing unrest and militancy. The region is an ethnic minefield, as it comprises different Scheduled Tribes. Turbulence in India's Northeast is, therefore, not caused just by armed separatist groups fighting the federal or local governments for some form of autonomy, but also by the recurring battles for territorial supremacy among the different ethnic groups. Moreover, the location of the eight north-eastern Indian states itself goes to explain why it has always been a hotbed of militancy with trans-border ramifications. This region is vital to India's security. 99 per cent of its external boundary represents international border. This region spreading over 263,000 square kilometres shares a highly porous and sensitive frontier with China to the north, Myanmar to the east, Bangladesh to the southwest and Bhutan to the northwest. This region has therefore become of crucial importance to India's national security. India has 4200 km long international border with China of which 1500 km lie in North East India. The partition of the country in 1947 altered the geo strategic situation of the whole of the North East India in a profound way. All communication channels that once passed through that region were disrupted and India's North East was cut-off from the rest of the country, connected only by a narrow strip of land near Siliguri, the famous 'Chicken's Neck', which is a strategic passageway, just a few kilometers from Bhutan, Bangladesh, Nepal as well as the Indian state of Sikkim. This is the region where India's longest-running insurgency is located. This has made the region periphery. Another geographical area which has largely influenced the history of North East is Patkai range. This forms the watershed between India and Myanmar and is of strategic importance. Indeed, North East India shares only 2 per cent of its boundary with India, the rest 98 per cent of its borderlands abut alien lands. The geographical location of North East makes it strategically important.

The many ethnic groups inhabiting this region consider themselves as separate people, having little in common with the rest of the country. The lack of physical, cultural and emotional links has encouraged this feeling of separation. The emotional distance between North East and mainland India is larger than the physical distance. North East India exhibits a tradition that isn't remotely close to any 'ideal Indian tradition'. The communities in the North East claim for their respectable identities. This can be witnessed among the Meiti `Manipuris and a large section of Assam's varied communities. These communities claim to possess a civilizational heritage and refuse to become part of India.[69] 'It has been rightly said when people in Delhi think of the North East, they think of the distance and that translates into a mental gap. When the people of the North East think of Delhi, they think in terms of different levels of development, and this translates into an emotional gap.'[70] 'More important than the geographical isolation and seeds of separation is the cultural chasm and lack of psychological integration with the rest of the country that makes for the distinctiveness of the region. The nationalist struggle for freedom which unified diverse Indian population did not touch North East. The region remained immune to the process of 'Indianness'. There is complete lack of knowledge and awareness of the North East, reinforcing the psychological distance. New Delhi has done almost nothing to assimilate the region into the greater Indian ideal, and has certainly not made any efforts to include North East India into its nation building enterprise. Indeed unrest has erupted in the region due to the insensitivity of New Delhi towards the region. It must also be noted that the vigilant attitude towards the region is also because of the generalized understanding in New Delhi about North East India. For example, the appearance, culinary tradition, attire and custom of much of the region, when exhibited in New Delhi or the rest of India, seem alien to the mainstream Indian. At times, the population from the North East in the metropolitan cities of India is termed as '*chinkies*'. Such aspects have led to alienation.'[71] The racial approach of mainstream India has had an impact on the victims which has resulted into radical and anti-Indian ethos. They are asking for autonomy, redressal of problems such as underdevelopment, unemployment, draconian laws and corruption. In certain parts of North East India, earlier Hinduized populations are beginning to retrace their roots to their age old ancestry.

The insurgency in North East has been waged on ethnic lines, with every insurgent organization owing its origins to an ethnic distinctiveness. The ethnic components of the region have sought to wage small wars in order to assert their own identities. Northeast of India is witnessing its ethno-national groups' uprising to fulfill their sub-national aspirations. For instance, the movement for greater autonomy by the Bodos, Assam's largest plains tribal community, led to the group securing a new politico-administrative structure within the existing state of Assam following a memorandum of understanding (MoU) with the central government on 10 February 2003.[72] This ethnic debate in North East is further complexed by the tribal identity. Indeed more than ethnicity, it is tribal identity that provides a sense of belongingness to the people of North East.[73] North East is not a homogenous area and it cannot be seen as constituting a single, indivisible, geographical whole. People do not have a common historical and inherited problem.

Tribal insurgencies in North East erupted in Nagaland, Mizoram, Manipur and Tripura. In Nagaland, it has been in suspended animation for the last ten years through a cease-fire but the conflict has not been yet resolved. The tribal insurgency in Mizoram was resolved through a political settlement, with Laldenga, the undisputed Mizo insurgent leader, joining the nation's political mainstream. Manipur continues to boil and is today the most violent state in the North-East. There is conflict between different segments of people on the basis of ethnic differences. Insurgency in Tripura is more of a 'civil war' between the tribal population and the Bengali immigrants after independence. These immigrants have reduced the original population to minority. Assam is the most important state in the North East, strategically, economically and demographically. Bodo insurgency has erupted there demanding a separate state of Bodoland. The insurgent movement in Assam has also been cultural with the bulk of population from plains seeking a separate cultural and historical identity. The insurgents in Nagaland, Manipur and some parts of Assam are running parallel governments. Taxes are levied not only on villages but also on private industries. In Nagaland and Manipur government employees with the exception of armed forces pay regular taxes to the one or the other insurgent groups.

Background of North Eastern Insurgency

The geographical remoteness of the region is the main determinant of the violence. The British made little efforts to integrate these areas into the country's mainstream. The Naga and Mizo territories of North East were categorized as 'Excluded Areas', during the British colonial rule and this limited their contact with the rest of India and as a consequence, isolated them from the political developments occurring in the rest of the country. When India got independence, these areas became part of the Indian Union and both these territories were given a special administrative status that allowed them a substantial degree of autonomy.[74]

The problem of ethnic violence dominates the North East. Ethnic components of the region have moved to separatist tendencies to assert their distinct identities. Nirmal Nibedon has written about the ethnic violence in his book 'North East India: The Ethnic Explosion', that "it is the ethnic explosion. Make no mistake about it. Have no doubts about it. The ethnic minorities are wielding sophisticated weapons and engaging national armies in combat, unceasingly. In brief they are all zealously guarding their ethnic identity." There is lack of homogeneity in the North East even at a micro level. The formation of Autonomous Council were primarily aimed at granting autonomy to various ethnic groups. Unfortunately the ethnic group for which such an arrangement is made often do not exclusively live in that particular Autonomous Council area. For instance, the formation of Autonomous Council for Nagas excluded vast number of Nagas who lived outside the Council. When the Council was transformed into a separate state of Nagaland, the problem persisted and sizable number of Nagas continue to live in the areas outside the Naga homeland. The ethnic linkages do not have a clear demarcation and often spill over into neighbouring states creating tension and conflicting situations. Manipur has sizable population of Nagas, Kukis and allied Mizo tribes. The formation of Nagaland and Mizoram states has generated a sense of affinity and loyalties of those clans to their ethnic community outside Manipur. This has sharpened and intensified the internal divisions in Manipur with rival ethnic communities. The tussle between Hmars and Kukis also highlights this dichotomy. Spread over in Assam, Manipur, Meghalaya and Mizoram, the Hmars refuse to identify themselves with the Kukis and emphasizing their distinct character, they demand a separate Autonomous Council in Assam.[75]Even the bigger groups are searching for their ethnic identity. In the case of Assam, who earlier boasted of their cultural superiority and regarded tribal as inferiors are now reconstructing their own tribal identity and searching for their roots.

There has been emergence of sub nationalism and political struggle against the presence of foreigners and outsiders. These sub national movements in the North East have been evolutionary. The success of one ethnic group gives rise to hope of the other ethnic groups. They also start demanding for autonomy. If Nagas can have a separate state carved out, then even Nagaland should grant similar demands of the Kukis in Nagaland. The example of Bodo nationalism is a notable example of this emerging sub national trends in the North East. Following India's independence, cultural and social activities were the prime concerns of the Bodo movement and their demands were confined to greater educational opportunities and developmental assistance. The establishment of Bodo Sahitya Sabha in 1952 led to the demand for the introduction of Bodo as an optional language in schools of Assam. Successful achievement of this linguistic struggle escalated into the demand for a separate non Assamese Bodo script. All these developments eventually formed a demand for a separate state of Bodoland.[76]

The demographic attack is also for the insurgency in North East India. Beginning with the British rule, North East has been witnessing migration from neighbouring regions. This influx from within and outside India and the demographic changes brought about by the immigration often is the immediate source of conflict. One of the primary reasons for the emergence of insurgency in Tripura and Assam is the demographic changes brought about by Bangladesh that has overwhelmed Tripura, and is close to transforming Assam's population patterns.[77]Increased population pressure on land intensified the problem of landlessness among the indigenous people. Trade was dominated by the migrants. This presence of migrations gave rise to the 'son of the soil' solidarity among the Assamese. Bengali speaking people in Assam are considerably rising while the percentage of Assamese speaking people is on the decline. Division became more prominent between the indigenous Assamese and tribal population. The demographic changes resulted in heightened conflicts over language, education and employment policies. This invasion of migrants and discouragement of economic interest of the native population gradually changed the demographic profile of the region and led to political tensions. This tension emerged in different forms like violent struggle to insurgency. Ethnic groups compete with each other for property rights, employment, educational opportunities, linguistic rights, governmental assistance and developmental projects. Unequal distribution of resources creates social imbalance and ferments ethnic conflicts. Moreover, people of the region are of the view that Union government does not want to check this pouring in of illegal migrants and is actually encouraging them to increase their vote bank. Much of the anti-foreigners agitation in Assam revolves around Bangladesh migrants. In Tripura also anti outsider feeling is against the immigrants from Bangladesh. The Chakmas who originally migrated from CHT, are the focus of anti-foreigners agitation in Mizoram. As they had migrated long before the partition of the Indian subcontinent, the Chakmas in Mizoram are official Indian citizens but ethnic dynamics of Mizoram still considers them as foreigners. However, the most widely known anti foreign agitation took place in Assam when it became an election issue in 1978. Asom Gana Parishad, a regional party of Assam came into power through this issue of anti-foreigners, primarily Bangladeshis.

It has been identified that economic backwardness is the root cause of the problem. Separatists have also blamed India for the economic backwardness and woes of North East. The region lags behind the rest of the country, particularly those parts of the country with comparable resources. The colonial interests dictates its economy and the region has become an exporter of primary raw materials. Economic activities got concentrated in selected pockets.

Vast areas still remain inaccessible and backward today. North East has loads of natural resources but still it is backward. It has a huge potential of hydel electricity, oil reserves, tea, coal and jute production. Some of these resources have been explored while others remain under-utilized. High rates of population growth, a restricted range of resources, labour immobility, restricted land market, poor infrastructure and stagnant economy are the defining features of this region.[78] The region thus remains mainly agricultural with a low level of cultivation and the prospects of industry also do not seem bright. One of the important reasons to explain the poor growth of North East is the resistance of the people to socio economic changes and the structural rigidity of a traditional society. The restricted movement of the outsiders has stripped off the region from investment which is considered a boon for the economic growth. Development has been a major casualty of insurgency, and violence has disrupted economic development projects to keep off the outsiders or protest against the exploitative nature of developmental project. The region lags behind the rest of the country. Despite a large geographical area, the land available for cultivation is limited. The arable land in the states of North East India is less than 50 per cent. Jhoom cultivation is practiced there which further results into deforestation and soil erosion. Also irrigation facility is not available widely. Moreover there is less scope for employment opportunities. Trade, industry and private sector are not much developed there, so all the pressure is on public employment. Therefore there is unrest among the youth who fail to acquire employment for themselves.

Modernity has also lightened up the pursuit for ethnic identity in the region. It has integrated the community and offered a social mobilization along the ethnic lines.[79] Modernity has also highlighted the stratificational inequalities among different communities or ethnic groups.

Buddhadeb Ghosh and Prabir De have argued that four deficits confront the North East:[80]

- A basic locational deficit
- An infrastructural deficit
- A resource deficit
- A two-way deficit in understanding with the rest of the country, which compounds the others.

For deeper understanding of the problem, separate study of each state of North East which is infected by insurgency, is being done.

Nagaland

Nagaland is the only all tribal state in India. Lakhs of Nagas live outside Nagaland in the neighbouring states of Manipur, Assam, Arunachal Pradesh, and in the Somra tract along the international border with Myanmar. Though only a few tribes have been dominating the political scene there are 16 major and 20 smaller tribes living in Nagaland.

The roots of Naga separatism precede India's Independence. As far back as 1929, under the banner of the 'Naga Club', the Nagas petitioned the Simon Commission, which was examining the possibility of future self-governance in India, that they be left alone to determine their own future as they had in the past, and not be forced to be ruled by Indians who had 'never conquered them'.[81]

They opted for independence at the time of partition. Infact the Naga leader Z.A. Phizo, had started agitating for independence even before India got independent. He led a delegation to meet Mahatma Gandhi in Delhi in 1947 to press for Naga's claim to independence. Sir Akbar Hydari, the then Governor of Assam, signed a nine point accord with the Naga National Council to develop themselves according to their own wishes. The last clause of the accord fixed that after the end of ten year term, the Naga Council will be asked whether they require the above agreement to be extended for a further period, or a new agreement regarding the future of the Naga people be arrived at. This clause has been the subject of controversy.The Naga National Council formed in 1946, proclaimed independence on August 14, 1947 and maintained that the Nagas have never acceded to India, and they were not an Indian entity.[82]

By 1953, insurgency in Nagaland had started. Under the leadership of Angami Zapu Phizo, Nagas began an armed rebellion in 1955, which made Indian Army step into the Naga Hills in 1956. In response to the demands from moderate Nagas, New Delhi formed a new administrative unit called the Naga Hills-Tuensang Area (NHTA) in 1957, carving out the Naga Hills District from Assam and placing it directly under central administration. Nagaland became a full fledged state in 1963. But this also did not solve the problem. The Naga demand is for the greater Naga state comprising of all the Naga inhabited areas in the region including North Myanmar. 'The spread of Christianity gave Nagas a sense of identity or a sense of 'separateness' from the people of the plains. This sense of separateness was exploited by Phizo to politicize the Nagas on a separatist platform.'[83] In March 1956 Phizo created an underground government called the Naga Federal Government (NFG) and a Naga Federal Army.

To work out a permanent peace in the Naga Hills, negotiations were restarted between the GOI and the underground Naga leaders without Phizo as he was inflexible in his demands. However these negotiations could not make much progress and once again hostilities erupted. The five year period of peace was shattered by new terrorist groups, better trained and equipped with sophisticated weapons. They continued their violent activities. But the underground leaders were founding it difficult to sustain a high level of insurgency without active foreign help which they stopped getting after the defeat of Pakistani army.

In 1972, New Delhi declared the NNC as an unlawful organization under the Unlawful Activities (Prevention) Act of 1967 and launched a massive counter-insurgency offensive. The insurgents agreed to hold peace talks with the Union Government. This led to the signing of the controversial Shillong Accord on 11 November 1975 between a section of the NNC and its 'underground government', the Naga Federal Government (NFG), and the Union Government. The signatories to this agreement accepted the Indian Constitution and agreed to surrender their weapons and join the Indian national mainstream. The underground leaders agreed to surrender their arms. However a section of leaders who had gone to China to receive training and were ideologically communists, repudiated the Accord. They shifted their base to North Burma Hills under the leadership of Muivah, a Tangkhul Naga from Manipur, and Issac Swu. Thus there was a vertical split in the underground movement. This faction was named National Socialist Council of Nagaland. Their aim was to establish a pan-Mangoloid state committed to the ideals of socialism. The other faction called itself the Naga Federal Government. This accord was also repudiated by Phizo while Phizo's leadership was challenged by Muivah and Issac.

> "With the passage of time this group became more active than the NFG. NSCN set up its training camps in the northern parts of Burma. However, this group suffered a split in 1988 and the NSCN (Muivah & Issac) faction was driven out of its sanctuaries in North West Myanmar by the Khaplang faction. It has then regrouped itself and built sanctuaries in Bangladesh. Now the activists have extended their activity to Nagaland and all the three hill districts of Manipur. The tribes in Nagaland support NSCN (IM) and Konyaks tribe still support NSCN (K)."[84]

After a continuous struggle with the Indian security forces, the NSCN-IM signed a ceasefire agreement that came into effect on 1 August 1997. In 2001 a similar ceasefire was carried on with the Khaplang faction of the NSCN. Since then the Central Government held three rounds of talks with the Naga leaders. The Centre's allowing of the ban on NSCN to lapse on November 26, 2002 has allowed for positive movement of the Naga imbroglio. On the one hand Indian government has realized the need to factor in the aspirations of a minuscule nationality and make them willing partners in the future deliberations towards a settlement and on the other the Nagas have started believing in negotiations.[85]

> "If one analyses the peace negotiations between the NSCN-IM and the Indian government during the past decade, it appears that the rebels may be willing to give up their demand for an independent Naga homeland but not their dream of the different Naga tribes to 'live together in one land as one family'. The NSCN-IM wants something like a 'Greater Nagaland' to be formed by the merger of Naga-inhabited areas in the adjoining states of Manipur, Assam and Arunachal Pradesh, and if possible those in Myanmar, into the present state of Nagaland. Indeed the NSCN-IM has made it clear that it has an expansionist plan. Although the NSCN-IM is engaged in bitter inter-group rivalry with the Khaplang faction of the NSCN as well as the Naga National Council, all these groups are in direct confrontation with the Indian nation-state."[86]

The NSCN has extended its control over more areas of North East and has formed alliances with the other insurgent groups. They have also acquired modern and sophisticated weapons. But the character of Naga insurgency has undergone a change over the years. What was a rural guerrilla movement has now entered the domain of urban centers. The commitment to the earlier cause is absent now. Naga insurgency has been marked by rivalries between insurgent groups. Today militancy is a way to make easy money. Extortion, kidnapping and killing has replaced the guerilla warfare. Drug trafficking has increased. Nexus between corrupt politicians and militants has misused the government funds. NSCN has also developed links with other organizations. It has been extending its control over other parts of North East. Money is also extracted by NSCN from tea gardens along the Nagaland Assam border. They have acquired sophisticated weapons with the external support.

People in Nagaland are now fed up of violence and bloodshed. Naga Kuki confrontation has further complicated the problem. The insistence of Nagas to incorporate Naga dominated parts of Manipur in the 'Greater Nagaland' will be a major hurdle in the final settlement of the problem. The insurgency in the North East started first in Nagaland and cannot be controlled without first controlling it in Nagaland. Nagas have always considered themselves to be an independent nation. 'We are Nagas by birth, Indians by accident', is a common refrain among these indigenous tribal people.

But the peace negotiations are going and on 23rd July, 2010, NSCN-IM 'general secretary' Thuingaleng Muivah met Union Home Minister P. Chidambaram in New Delhi and discussed with him issues related to the Naga peace process. Muivah apprised Chidambaram about his nearly one-and-a-half-month-long 'peace mission' across Nagaland and its outcome. It is hoped that a positive development will soon come up.

Manipur

The genesis of insurgency in Manipur has its roots in the instrument of accession to India on August 11, 1947. The absence of state of Manipur in the initial years spurred Meiti sub-nationalism which gave a cry for the formation of separate independent republic. The economic unrest among the youth has given rise to terrorism in Manipur. This terrorist movement in Manipur was guided by Bisheshwar. He had gone to East Pakistan in the mid-60s and set up a revolutionary government from there. He felt that the only way Meiteis can get a fair deal is by taking up arms.

Manipur is also witnessing clashes between the Nagas and Kukis. These two tribes inhabit the Manipur Hills and the other tribe, Meitis inhabit the valley. The Tangkhul Nagas are mostly supporters of NSCN (M) which has been committing terrorist acts in Manipur. While Kukis are ethnically more closer to Mizos. They dominate the southern hills of Manipur and have maintained links with the Mizo underground. Smuggling etc. in this region has been profitable for them which has generated income for the Kukis. This has been the bone of contention between them and the Tangkhuls as they do not want to share this income with Tangkhuls. The Meiteis on the other hand has a strong grievance against the Union government for alleged discrimination against them. They have not been declared scheduled tribes while the hill tribes have been. This has kept them aloof from employment and educational opportunities. To assert their identity, they have now revived the practices of old Meitei religion.

With the formation of United National Liberation Front (UNLF) in 1964, Manipuri rebels forged links with militant and underground groups both within North East and Burma and erstwhile East Pakistan. By 1990s, UNLF emerged as the most dreaded underground group with strong ideological orientation and organizational capabilities.

The government of India started the peace process and declared cease fire with the NSCN (IM) in 1997. The NSCN (IM) has been demanding the extension of cease fire to hill districts of Manipur, and the Naga inhabited areas of Assam and Arunachal. There have been demonstrations by Meiteis against extending the cease fire to Manipur. The Manipuris are very sensitive to any suggestion by the government to bifurcate Manipur to meet the demands of NSCN (IM). The Naga desire for a homeland that would bring together all

Nagas into one political unit can come into being only at the expense of Manipur.[87]

In 2001, the Central Government announced the extension of cease fire with Naga militants without territorial limits which caused a massive outburst of anger in Manipur. Imphal burned with violence and 18 young Manipuris lost their lives in agitation. In July 2005, Manipur was once again on the boil as All Naga Students' Association of Manipur had blocked NH 39 and NH 53 — the two lifelines of the state.

Manipur's disorder is a product of Nagaland's and Mizoram's virtual stability, stimulated by militants there who have moved their operations out of their home areas. The centre has often used Armed Forces Special Powers Act, which has been opposed by the people.[88]

Present Crisis

The current situation in Manipur is a complex amalgam of factors. There are longstanding conflicts among ethnic, tribal, plains and hill groups. The Meitei people who constitute the majority in the State have a deeply felt historical perspective of Manipuri territorial and cultural unity. The nexus between crime and politics on one hand, and foreign involvement through funds, arms, and sanctuaries on the other, make for a highly volatile security situation. Over the years, the nature of insurgency in Manipur has shifted to acts of terrorism, extortion, coercion of the population giving rise to a situation of internal disorder. In the last two decades the numbers of militant groups, their arsenals and lethality have grown immensely. Civil society in Imphal and across the nine administrative districts of the state has been squeezed out between insurgent groups who have found an opportunity to continue to ply their 'hafta' or protection money trade under the cover of ideology, and the total absence of law and order that the authorities have decided to leave unrepaired and leave conditions ripe for perpetual exploition. To put it bluntly, Manipur is in ruins. The situation, it appears, cannot be managed by the State law and order machinery.

Even as the north-eastern states reported an overall decline in the number of violent incidents, Manipur continues to be the hotbed of insurgency. Manipur, which has the highest number of banned outfits in the north-east, reported the maximum 88 incidents in the year, that claimed the lives of two security personnel, six civilians and 38 extremists. In 2009, 435 people, including 81 civilians and 336 militants, were killed in 659 incidents in Manipur. As many as 517 people, including 364 extremists, were killed in 2008 in Manipur.[89]

As many as 20 different insurgent groups in Manipur are engaged in war with the security forces, and the worst victims of it are the average Manipuri citizens. The insurgency-ridden state is characterised by scenes of heavily armed militants, sheltered in villages. The security forces round them up at the dead of night and subject them to hours of interrogation and various forms of mental and physical torture to extract information about the militants. There is widespread extortion by underground outfits. Right from an ordinary shop owner to a senior government employee, everyone has to pay "protection money" regularly, which the militant groups term as "contribution for the revolution". Even Ministers and police personnel have not been spared. Some government departments allegedly pay a fixed percentage of their revenues to insurgent groups every month.[90]

Manorama Case

On the night of July 11, 2004, the Assam Rifles arrested a young Manipuri woman named Manorama Devi from her home. The next morning, villagers found her bullet-ridden, lifeless body. The Assam Rifles claimed she had been shot dead while trying to escape. The State went up in flames over the issue. Apart from calling for the prosecution of the soldiers involved in Manorama's arrest and killing, people demanded that the Armed Forces (Special Powers) Act (AFSPA) — the draconian 1958 law under which the armed forces enjoy broad immunity from prosecution, be done away with.[91] Repeated attempts to identify and punish those responsible for her death have been stalled by the army, which has received protection under the immunity provisions of the AFSPA.

In 2004, elderly Manipuri women staged an unprecedented protest over Manorama's killing by stripping off their clothes and raising a banner calling for the army to come rape them, too. One of the women, L. Gyaneshori, told an eminent Human Rights Organization:

> "Manorama's killing broke our hearts. We mothers were weeping, 'Now our daughters can be raped. They can be subjected to such cruelty. Every girl is at risk.' We shed our clothes and stood before the army. We said, 'We mothers have come. Drink our blood. Eat our flesh. Maybe this way you can spare our daughters.' But nothing has been done to punish those soldiers. The women of Manipur were disrobed by AFSPA. We are still naked."[92]

The movement, spearheaded by 32 social organisations under the banner of 'Apunba Lup', had spiralled into a "civil disobedience" movement, which became violent after a student leader Pebam Chittaranjan immolated himself on Independence Day. The adviser of the Bishenpur unit of the Manipuri Students' Federation, Pebam Chittaranjan left a suicide note, which says: "It is better to self-immolate than die at the hands of security forces under this Act. With this conviction I am marching ahead of the people as a human torch." Pebam Chittaranjan had run for about 100 metres with his body in flames before falling to the ground in Bishenpur Bazaar.

Demand for Abolition of AFSPA

The current debate over the use of the Armed Forces (Special Powers) Act (AFSPA) has fumed the hill state. The Army argued that the AFSPA was the cornerstone of its functioning in terroism-hit areas, and that fighting low-intensity wars without it was near impossible. Human rights groups, in turn, said that the Act offered a licence to kill and rape. It has long been clear that the Indian Army sees the AFSPA as the keystone of security management in terrorism-hit States.[93] While the actions of the security forces often gives rise to allegations of excesses and atrocities, the rise in the incidence of extortion, kidnapping for ransom, looting and intimidation by militants has given some degree of legitimacy to harsh laws such as the Armed Forces (Special Powers) Act, 1958.[94]

Human rights violations by Indian security forces have fueled the armed opposition in Manipur as armed groups have carried out torture, killings, indiscriminately used bombs and land mines, engaged in forced recruitment, and conducted widespread extortion. The 79-page report, "'These Fellows Must Be Eliminated': Relentless Violence and Impunity in Manipur," of the Human Rights Watch, documents the failure of justice in the state, where for 50 years the army, empowered and protected by the Armed Forces (Special Powers) Act (AFSPA), has committed numerous serious human rights violations. These laws perpetuate human rights abuses, which drive civilians to seek the protection of one or other armed group. The report details the failure of justice in the killing and possible rape of alleged militant Thangjam Manorama Devi by the paramilitary Assam Rifles in 2004. The report documents specific cases of extrajudicial executions and torture by soldiers, paramilitaries, and police in Manipur since 2006, and the Indian government's failure to curb the abuses. Torture of detainees, in particular severe beatings during interrogations of suspected militants and their supporters, remains common. Torture victims have also how they were arbitrarily arrested, beaten, and subjected to electric shocks.

Extrajudicial killings often followed a consistent pattern in which the military or police took a person into custody, often in front of eyewitnesses, who was later declared to have been killed in an armed encounter with militants. Such faked "encounter killings" often occurred when security forces suspected someone to be a militant, but did not have enough evidence to ensure a conviction. On occasion, government officials or members of the armed forces would later admit to relatives that a person had been killed by "mistake." This claim is never made officially, so in police records the victim remains identified as a militant, and avenues for redress remain closed. In the name of national security and armed forces morale, the state protects abusers and leaves Manipuris with no remedy to secure justice.

Prime Minister Manmohan Singh appointed a committee to review the AFSPA in Manipur. Created after weeks of protests in

Manipur following the killing of Manorama in 2004, the committee led by Justice B.P. Jeevan Reddy recommended in 2005 that the AFSPA be repealed. Referring to the committee reports, Mr. Singh had stated that there were genuine grievances of the people of Manipur.[95] The Indian government has failed to take action on the committee's recommendation.

Mohammad Abdul Hakim described the killing of his 15-year-old son, Razak Khan, on September 13, 2007 by a joint team of police and members of the 32nd Assam Rifles.

> "We were beaten and told to collect in the courtyard. Soldiers went inside to search the house. Suddenly, I heard my son's voice shouting, 'I am not Khajing!' One of the neighbors later told me that he saw the soldiers push my son to the ground. He was crying. They shot him as he lay on the ground. We only heard the gunshots and then my son stopped shouting." Elangbam Sanayaima was detained by members of the 21st Assam Rifles on November 29, 2007, and accused of being a member of the separatist United National Liberation Front (UNLF). He was taken to an Assam Rifles camp. According to Sanayaima: "At the camp, I was blindfolded and my hands were tied behind my back. Then they started interrogating me. They insisted over and over again that I was Sanayaima of UNLF. They asked me about my training and my colleagues. When I said that I was innocent, they beat me. Then they pushed my head back until I was almost upside down. They poured water into my nose and mouth until I could not breathe."[96]

The people of Manipur has done everything humanely conceivable to register their protest against the AFSPA — naked protest by mothers, self immolation by student leader, mass demonstrations, petition to the Supreme Court, complaints to the United Nations, etc.

To control the situation, Okram Ibobi Singh government withdrew the disturbed area status of a 20-square-kilometre area falling in seven Assembly segments in Imphal municipal limits, in order to render the AFSPA ineffective there. However, the delayed decision, despite the fact that it was against the wishes of the United Progressive Alliance government at the Centre, failed to assuage the public anger. The Apunba Lup rejected the Chief Minister's gesture and intensified the movement; it refused to accept anything short of a withdrawal of the Act from the whole of Manipur. This prompted the State government to book more than 30 leaders of the movement under the National Security Act (NSA).

In keeping with the Centre's offer to hold unconditional talks with all groups including the militant outfits, Ibobi Singh urged social bodies such as Meira Paibis (Women Torchbearers) to help defuse the crisis and arrive at a permanent solution. He also sought the help of the editors of local newspapers to convince leaders of the Apunba Lup to respond to the Union Home Minister's offer to hold unconditional talks.[97]

Sharmila Case

Today Manipur is up in arms, echoing the demand raised by 33-year-old Sharmila, who, under judicial detention, continues to be nose-fed forcibly at the Jawaharlal Nehru Hospital in Imphal for refusing to end her "fast unto death" until the Act is withdrawn from the whole of Manipur. Sharmila started her fast on 5 November 2000, three days after the Malom massacre in Manipur. On that day, the Assam Rifles, a paramilitary unit stationed in the state, killed 10 civilians including women and children in an inhuman and vengeful act of retaliation, responding to an earlier ambush staged by the armed insurgents against the Assam Rifles. A decade since the massacre, while the justice system of India is dragging its feet and has failed to finish even a preliminary inquiry into the incident.

Even now, however, it is not too late for the government to retrieve the situation. There can be few measures which can be taken up urgently. It must ensure that justice is done in the Manorama case. The government should punish not just the soldiers involved in her murder but also those officers who have conspired to cover up the murder. Since what the soldiers committed appears to be nothing other than murder, plain and simple, they should not be allowed to shield themselves behind the immunity provided by the AFSPA. The government must appreciate the depth of popular resentment against the AFSPA and examine ways in which the law can either be repealed or modified drastically. The AFSPA has been in operation in the whole State of Manipur since 1980, and in Tamenglong and the hill regions since 1961. But the number of insurgent groups has only increased, as have the sphere of their operations. It is never advisable to have a situation where the enforcers of the law are exempt from any kind of judicial oversight. In the best of situations, such exemptions breed disregard for the life and liberty of ordinary people. The UPA government should visit Manipur and look into the actual operation of the law on the ground. The Centre should think seriously about the proposal made by Rishang Keishing and four other former Chief Ministers of Manipur for the initiation of unconditional dialogue with the major insurgent groups in the State. If dialogue is being seen as the way forward in neighbouring Nagaland, and actually helped resolve the decades-long insurgency in Mizoram, there is no reason why attempts should not be made to bring about a political solution to Manipur's insurgency problem.[98]

Tripura

The conflict in Tripura has been confined to protecting minority tribes in the state. Since 1947, the state has witnessed the influx of refugees from Bengal pushing the tribal population further. This continuous movement of Bengali Muslim refugees had alienated the native tribes. The flow of these migrants into the state has made the preservation of tribal population difficult. They have been reduced to minority in their own land. Insurgent groups in Tripura such as All Tripura Tiger Force (ATTF) have been demanding separate tribal homeland. The Tripura Upjati Juva Samiti was formed to protect the rights of the tribal. This group took to underground activities and committed violent acts. At the same time their supporters organized demonstration and agitations to protect their rights. The TUJS extremists started a training camp in Chittagong Hill Tract for their armed wing. Their ideology is built around their separate ethnic identity and socialism and their goal is to drive out non-tribal from Tripura and re-establish tribal supremacy. This polarization between tribal and non tribal is the major problem of

Tripura.[99] However, the signing of peace accord in 1998 partly reduced the frequency of insurgency.

Assam

The situation in Assam is quite different from the other parts of the North East. Unlike the hill areas, the Assamese took an active part in the freedom struggle and are proud of their Indian heritage. But over the period they got alienated and feared the loss of their identity.

The terrorist movement in Assam revolves around the major issue of transportation of illegal immigrants. Large scale migration had started in Assam, immediately after independence. Hindus migrated from Sylhet district of the then East Pakistan to India being insecured about Pakistan's drive of Islamisation. However, these migrants flooded in the land of Assam and pressure on resources increased. This is attributed as a major reason for the economic slowdown. The state of Assam has witnessed various tribal movements. The movement led by All Assam Students Union felt that the presence of foreigners was the danger to Assam. As a result of population movement from Bangladesh, the indigenous people of Assam reduced to minority in their home state. Illegal migration into Assam has been taking place primarily for economic reasons. The influx of the Bangladeshi population in India has created insecurity among the indigenous people. Their cultural security will be in danger, their political control will be weakened and their employment opportunities will be undermined. Due to the problem of infiltration, Assam movement took place in Assam. It was initially a mass agitation against the infiltration of foreigners, particularly the Bengalis into the land of Assam. They wore down the cultural identity of Assam and posed a serious threat to the politics and economy. The indigenous tribal and Muslims were part of the agitation.[100]

The anti-foreigner rebellion caused by the All Assam Students' Union (AASU), from 1979 to 1985, was triggered by the native Assamese community's fear of the invasion of illegal Bangladeshi migrants from across the border. There was the signing of an agreement, called the Assam Accord. Rajiv Gandhi negotiated with the student leaders which resulted in Assam Accord of 1985. The government decided to drop all the cases against AASU and other agitators, the draconian laws which gave unlimited powers to the government officials and armed forces were lifted and the government pledged to check illegal migrants who had settled in the state after 1971. The central government also promised to hold elections in the state. AASU agreed to take part in the elections. The elections were held soon after the Accord in which Asom Gana Parishad (AGP) came out victorious.[101]

There are several organizations which advocate the independence of Assam. The most prominent of which is the ULFA (United Liberation Front of Asom). ULFA has two main goals, the independence of Assam and the establishment of a socialist government. The ULFA founded in 1979 attributed to the colonial rule of India responsibility of Assam's underdevelopment and sufferings. It was founded by Paresh Baruah who had close links with the Pakistani ISI. They did a number of terrorist acts to pressurize the government to accede to their demands. It has now established itself as a parallel government extracting taxes from the people. It has also indulged in violence and terror against the security forces. The ULFA has carried out several terrorist attacks in the region targeting the Indian Military and non-combatants. The ULFA is believed to have strong links with Nationalist Socialist Council of Nagaland (NSCN), Maoists and the Naxalites. It is also believed that they carry out most of their operations from the Kingdom of Bhutan.

The region also has insufficient economic development and deficient job opportunities, causing unrest and militancy which has further retarded economic growth. The feeling of step motherly treatment of Assam in economic development by the Centre was highlighted by the decision to build the first oil refinery in public sector at Barauni in Bihar, which would process crude oil from Assam carried over hundreds of kilometers of pipeline from the Upper Assam oil fields.[102]

In the recent years Islamic fundamentalism has also grown in Assam. It is linked to the rise of fundamentalism in Bangladesh.

Bodos

The Bodos belong to Indo-Mongoloid tribe who migrated to North East India from China and Tibet and spread over Assam, North Bengal and parts of Eastern Bengal. Bodo problem lies in occupation of tribal lands by Bengalis and Assamese, neglect of Bodo language and their economic exploitation. Their demand for a separate state is due to the fear of domination by non- Bodo majority. Bodo lives in majority in the parts of Kokrajhar and Goalpara districts in Assam. They are near the strategic corridor which connects the North East by rail or road with the rest of the country. The demand for the separate state of Bodoland encompasses the whole of northern bank of Brahmputra, even though the Bodos do not command majority in any of the districts in Assam. They are scattered.[103]

Initially Bodos were demanding an autonomous council like other tribes but after 1987 they began to seek a separate state of Bodoland. The Bodo movement took to insurgency after 1988 incident when nine Bodo women were gang raped by some Assam policemen. The movement slowly began to turn violent.The tribal violence was met by hard brutality which further aggravated their anger. Bodo militants especially those belonging to National Democratic Front of Bodoland (NDFB) forged links with other extremist organizations in North East and have even managed to set up training camps in Bhutan and Bangladesh. After that the Bodo militancy has been on the rise. They have also developed strong bases in the Manas sanctuary, bordering Bhutan. The Bodos feel that their bargaining power in demanding a separate state of Bodoland has been subverted by continues migration from other parts of Assam. Therefore they have adopted a violent campaign of terror against ethnic groups such as Santhals, Hajongs, and Muslims.[104] In a violent move by Bodo Security Force, a refugee camp at Barpeta was struck at in July 1994. They killed 50 inmates all Muslims. Most of them were migrants from Bangladesh. This act has also been seen as an attempt of ethnic cleansing of all non-Bodos. This insurgent group has managed to polarize the situation between the Bodos, the Assamese and the Bengalis. So far the Bodo militancy has not assumed a separatist dimension. They are demanding only a separate state within India, but the NSCN and the ISI meddling in the region can give it a separatist colour.[105]

The Bodo insurgency is the result of Assamese chauvinism and lack of vision on the part of their leaders. There was neglect of Bodo grievances. They were afraid of Assamese hegemony. But when the Assam Accord was signed the Bodos became hopeful that they would not be alienated and their land would be restored back to them. But nothing positive happened to them, thus adding to their woes. The creation of Bodo Territorial Area in 2004 has been welcomed but it has not satisfied all sections of Bodo militants.

Mizoram

In 1959, the Mizo hills suffered one of the worst famines. The state government failed to make adequate arrangements. As a protest against the inadequate relief measures, Mizo National Famine Front was formed in 1960 as a voluntary social welfare organization to help the famine victims. The front was able to mobilize a strong public support. Later, the word 'Famine' was removed and it became 'Mizo National Front'. Laldenga assumed its leadership and formed an armed wing called 'Mizo National Army'. They demanded independence for Mizoram and committed violent acts. Mizos were aware of their rights and were prepared to fight for them. Insurgency in the area started on Feb 28, 1966 when armed MNF volunteers attacked a number of government installations in Aizwal, Lunglei, Vairangte etc. The situation went so much out of control that IAF bombers had to be called for to strafe the MNF positions. Some bombs were also dropped to frighten the MNF. Property was destroyed in the air raids. The people of Aizwal till today have not forgiven India for bombarding the whole population. These raids have left a prominent mark on the psyche of the people.[106]

Violence continued when in 1986, Mizo accord was signed between the Centre and the MNF. Under this, MNF and other insurgent groups decided to give up their arms and secessionist policy. They also agreed not to give support to other insurgent groups in the North East. Thus Centre granted statehood to Mizoram and also agreed not to amend Inner Line regulations without the consent of the state government.[107]

Over the past decade, 35,000 Reangs, also known as Brus, have been fighting for autonomy from the state of Mizoram from their base in relief camps in North Tripura. In October 1997 these tribals were forced to leave Mizoram after the Mizos, led by the influential student organisations the Mizo Zirlai Pawl and the Young Mizo Association, allegedly burnt several Bru villages and killed and raped a number of Bru men and women. Since then the Bru National Liberation Front (BNLF) has been negotiating the status of the refugees with the Mizoram state government.

The Mizo Accord has been a success story and provides a useful model for the successful resolution of ethnic conflicts in North East. Though post-conflict Mizoram has experienced its share of group mobilization and ethnic contestations, at no time has the violence in this state paralleled that in other parts of the state. Mizoram has largely remained, in the words of its Chief Minister Zoramthanga, 'an island of peace in a sea of turmoil'.[108]

Meghalaya and Arunachal Pradesh

The tribes of Meghalaya also agitated for separation from Assam as the migrants from Bangladesh and Nepal made them insecure. Arunachal Pradesh has remained peaceful in the region but it can outpour its grievances if the resentment against the Chakma refugees is not addressed soon.

Terrorist Organizations

In India's North East, two terrorist organizations have come out to be more important: the United Liberation Front of Asom (ULFA) that seeks the secession of Assam, and the National Socialist Council of Nagalim (Isak-Muivah) [NSCN-IM] that has been seeking Naga independence. They run widespread networks of extortion, drug smuggling and other criminal activities, and also control significant business operations. The NSCN-IM has been engaged in negotiations with the Union Government under a ceasefire agreement that has been in place since August 1997. The ULFA has constantly rejected possibilities of a negotiated settlement. The ULFA and the NSCN-IM have sustained to extend their influence in the Northeast region through violence as well as by training and arming a large number of other terrorist and proxy groups, and are supported by the ISI in their activities. However, no North Eastern terrorist organisation has, till now, sought to extend its sphere of operations outside the region.[109]

Christian terrorists are also active in India's North-East. Funds are collected in the form of donations in various church establishments. Some of this money is spent in spreading education and healthcare. However, it has been suspected for a long time that a part of this fund gets diverted for buying arms for the Baptist terrorists of the North-East. Ex-Chief Election Commissioner, T.N. Seshan, gave voice to this suspicion in a television panel discussion on Doordarshan as early as in 1993. It is also suspected that the funds come from Islamic sources such as the Inter-Services Intelligence (ISI) of Pakistan, the Gulf states etc. and Christian sources such as the Baptist Church in southern USA and the UK. NLFT (National Liberation Front of Tripura) employs terror tactics to effect mass conversion to Christianity and is a predominantly Baptist organisation.[110]

United Liberation Front of Assam

There are several organizations which advocate the independence of Assam. The most prominent of which is the ULFA (United Liberation Front of Assam). ULFA has two main goals, the independence of Assam and the establishment of a socialist government. The ULFA has carried out several terrorist attacks in the region targeting the Indian Military and non-combatants. The ULFA is believed to have strong links with Nationalist Socialist Council of Nagaland (NSCN), Maoists and the Naxalites. It is also believed that they carry out most of their operations from the Kingdom of Bhutan.

United Liberation Front of Assam (ULFA) was formed on April 7, 1979 by Bhimakanta Buragohain, Rajiv Rajkonwar alias Arabinda Rajkhowa, Golap Baruah alias Anup Chetia, Samiran Gogoi alias Pradip Gogoi, Bhadreshwar Gohain and Paresh Baruah at the Rang Ghar in Sibsagar to establish a "sovereign socialist Assam" through an armed struggle.

Its declared objectives are:

- To achieve Assam's independence by armed struggle.
- To safeguard Assam's interests.
- To have full control over the natural resources of Assam.
- To spread widespread support against Indian exploitation.

The ULFA constitution also stated that it would maintain close links with the other like minded organizations. It had close links with UNLF, PLA and PREPAK of Manipur. ULFA maintained close links with AASU and during the first few years of its founding maintained a low profile. It concentrated on building the organization on a sound base, establishing foreign links and securing support of other militant groups of the North East.

The ULFA sought shelter in the forests on the Indo-Bhutan border from the early 1990s and established several camps in the forest areas of southern Bhutan. Most camps and other establishment of the ULFA were in Sandrup Jongkhar, a district in southern Bhutan that borders Assam's Nalbari district. The RBA is reported to have destroyed all the outfit's camps and observation posts during the military operations launched in December 2003.

In 1986, ULFA first established contacts with the then unified National Socialist Council of Nagaland (NSCN) and the Kachin Independence Army (KIA) of Myanmar for training and arms. Subsequently, links were established with Pakistan's Inter Services Intelligence (ISI. Reports indicate that at least 200 ULFA activists received training in Pakistan and Afghanistan ULFA also has a number of camps in Bangladesh. The ISI and the Directorate General of Field Intelligence (DGFI) of Bangladesh are agencies which reportedly facilitate the ULFA's presence and operations. Apart from running training camps, ULFA launched several income generating projects in Bangladesh. It has set up a number of firms in Dhaka, including media consultancies and soft drink manufacturing units.

To start with, initially using Bangladesh as a safe haven and training location, ULFA gradually expanded its network to include operational control of activities and the receipt and shipment of arms in transit before they finally entered India. The Muslim United Liberation Tigers of Assam (MULTA) and Muslim United Liberation Front of Assam (MULFA) are the chief suppliers of arms for the ULFA through Bangladesh. Owing to greater vigil along the known routes of ULFA arms flow, the group has, in recent times, been making attempts to set up bases in Meghalaya, especially in the West Garo Hills to coordinate the transit of arms coming through Bangladesh.

ULFA also runs profitable narcotics business in Myanmar and Thailand. A close nexus between ULFA and the Liberation Tigers of Tamil Eelam (LTTE) had also been reported. The LTTE is reported to have trained various ULFA cadres in explosives handling.

Split in ULFA

In the absence of top leaders aligned to Paresh Baruah, Munim Nobis, Sunil Nath and Kalpajyoti Neog signed a statement opposing armed struggle and advocating peace talks with the government. The ULFA had split into pro and anti-peace talk faction. The pro-talks faction gave up their demand for 'SwadhinAsom' or independence and favoured autonomy. They were expelled from the organization and many came overground.[111]

Shift in Ideology

One of the reasons for the diminishing public support for ULFA has been its U-turn on the question of illegal Bangladeshi immigrants. In a 15 page booklet issued in July 1992, ULFA states that the immigrants from Bangladesh have now become a part of national life and Assam's struggle for freedom can never be successful without them. Another significant point in the booklet is that English would be the link language of Swadhin Asom, thus nullifying almost a century-old struggle to give the Assamese language its rightful place in the state. The document was also critical of AASU and termed the Assam Movement as one based on emotion.[112] Another episode of interest is that the ULFA is now reportedly tutoring the 'intending infiltrator' in Assamese so that the absorption into the Assamese population is quicker. ULFA runs a school in Bangladesh that teaches Assamese to people from Bangladesh who desire to illegally migrate into Assam.[113]

There have been reports of links between tea companies and ULFA. Almost all tea companies in Assam are paying protection money to ULFA. During the Kargil war in 1999, it was also reported that ULFA gave the information to ISI regarding the movement of troops from Assam. These anti-national activities of Assam have been criticized by the Assamese. They have responded with anger against the ULFA leadership. ULFA has now lost much of its support base. ULFA has also been inspired by the Islamic religious fundamentalism. It is now fraternizing with the same people it wanted to be deported. ULFA is now focusing on religious propaganda and enlarging their area of influence.

The popularity of ULFA is on downslide. One of the reasons for this shrinking support base is the dual role it plays as the champion of the Assamese aspirations and supporting Bangladeshi immigrants. But it continues to garner some support amongst the middle class Assamese because they fear that they will be marginalized.

The ULFA's efforts currently revolves around re-establishing its camps in Bangladesh and increasing its bases in Bhutan and Myanmar with assured supplies of arms and ammunition from across the international borders. Though ULFA leaders are linking with other militant groups in North East especially NSCN(K), their promise to smaller rebel factions to provide them with arms and logistic support is feared to shoot up militant related violence in the area.[114]

United National Liberation Front

The United National Liberation Front (UNLF), the oldest Meitei insurgent group in the State was formed under the leadership of

Areambam Samrendra Singh on November 24, 1964 to achieve independence and a socialist society. Samrendra Singh sought to spread ideological consciousness before launching an armed struggle. Samarendra Singh was killed by unidentified terrorists in Imphal on June 10, 2001. In the seventies and eighties, the UNLF concentrated mainly on mobilisation and recruitment. In 1990, it decided to launch an armed struggle for the 'liberation' of Manipur from India. In the same year, it formed an armed wing called Manipur People's Army (MPA). The UNLF aims to establish an independent socialist Manipur.[115] The outfit operates in the Jiribam valley and Cachar district of Assam. Soon after its formation, the UNLF leaders established a political relationship with the authority of the then East Pakistan, and underwent military training in that country in 1969. On June 14, 1975, UNLF leader N. Bisheswar Singh and 16 other Meitei rebels proceeded to Lhasa to seek Chinese assistance. The UNLF has training camps in Myanmar and Bangladesh.Recent moves by central government to establish peace and harmony in the North East is a welcome step as it brings Bodos and Assam to the negotiating table and strike a balance in the vulnerable state.

External Interference

Providing insurgents of enemy country with safe havens, arms, training, is a phenomenon that is rooted in the post colonial state policy and diplomacy of South Asia. According to Subir Bhaumik, 'South Asia possesses ideal conditions for sponsored insurgencies — its constituent parts are incomplete and artificially formed nation states consisting of ethnic religious groups in uneasy cohabitation and has also witnessed a certain institutionalization of the phenomenon.'[116] Many ethnic groups in the region especially the areas bordering other countries, have more in common with the population living across the boundary than with their own nationals. Thus, this cross border nature of the ethnic and religious affinities provides a fertile ground for external involvement.

The North East insurgents have found sanctuaries in Bhutan and China in the North, Bangladesh in the South and Myanmar in the East. They have received moral and material support from China, Pakistan and Bangladesh.

The Naga were the first to seek and receive aid from foreign country. Pakistani support was given when the Naga leader Phizo crossed the border and reached Eastern Pakistan. Pakistan also negotiated with China for arms, aid and training. On return from China, underground Brigadier Thinusellie was sent to East Pakistan in the late 1968 to coordinate arrangements for training of guerillas in bases in Pakistan. 'The Chinese therefore opened a guerilla-training centre in East Pakistan to train North East insurgents. It was almost a strategic compulsion for Pakistan to tie down maximum Indian troops in the North East.'[117] Pakistan also helped Mizos as it had long border with the then East Pakistan. It provided ingress and exit routes.

The support given by Pakistan and China to North East insurgents was a consequence of antagonistic relations of India with China and Pakistan. Apart from Nagas, Chinese also helped ULFA of Assam in training and provision of arms. Paresh Baruah has often talked about Operation Chilarai and Lachit, in which ULFA went on missions to the province of Yunnan in 1986.[118] Infact the arms with 'made in China' tags are found very commonly in North East. For China, the protracted militancy and demands for separation provide an opportunity to contain and restrain India within the sub continent. In April 2000, Arunachal Pradesh government pointed out that 2000 Chinese personnel have been spotted laying the road track opposite Asaphila area in the Tawang district. The Chinese People's Liberation Army was busy building an unmetalled road track heading towards the Line of Actual Control across Arunachal Pradesh.

Pakistan launches its operations in India from Pakistan. Pakistan has launched its second front against Kashmir from Bangladesh. 'The strategic encirclement of North East India and the attendant problem of New Delhi's insensitivity has made the region into a veritable 'proxy war' playfield.'[119] ISI is training cadets belonging to ULFA, ATTF and Islamist groups in various insurgency tactics. It has emerged as an important front for terrorism, both domestic and international. There are over hundred camps in Bangladesh that belong to the insurgent groups of North East India. It is from these camps that most anti-India operations are carried out. Bangladesh has given official patronage to these insurgent groups ever since 1950s.[120] 'An unfamiliar programme from Bangladesh is beginning to appear in North East India. The agenda has a pan Islamic bearing. It has the illegal migrant population and has begun to take roots primarily as a result of the illegal access of Bangladeshis into Assam and the other parts of the North East, and the pan Islamist motivations that are provoking them to take part in the global Salafi movement. During the course of their training in Pakistan, they were imparted lessons about Shahadat for the cause of Islam and the creation of Nizam-e- Mustafa in Assam.'[121] Indeed Bangladesh houses the ULFA's training and liaison camps. Leaders of ULFA permanently reside in the Bangladeshi cities of Chittagong and Dhaka, *e.g.*, Paresh Baruah. These leaders are running lucrative businesses in Bangladesh and are living a life of luxury. Also the consignments which are dispatched to ULFA come through Bangladesh, especially via the port city of Cox's Bazaar and Chittagong. Seized documents and interrogation of some arrested activists revealed that the Defense Forces Intelligence (DFI) of Bangladesh had also trained ULFA cadres in the Sylhet district.

Myanmar cradled most of the insurgent groups in North East India, with training, safe havens and arms. The Mizos and Tripuris were also able to establish links with the Burmese insurgents and found safe sanctuaries in the lightly administered areas in Myanmar. The insurgent groups there have found no problem in crossing the border because of unchecked passage between the border towns of Moreh in Manipur and Tamu in Myanmar. This has facilitated drug trafficking from the golden triangle through the North Eastern region. Unlike China and Pakistan, the sanctuaries of North East insurgents in Myanmar are not due to the antagonistic relations between India and Myanmar but by its inability to administer the hilly terrain of the country, along India's border.

ULFA reportedly developed linkages with several officers and personnel of the Royal Bhutan Army (RBA) and Police – which ensured, among other things, a steady flow of rations, logistical support as well as aid and contacts for money laundering. However Bhutan Army took a decisive action against the ULFA sanctuaries and they had to flee. This should be taken as an example by other countries' governments

Thailand is also slowly turning into a base of operations for the various militant groups operating in the North East. Thailand has a flourishing clandestine arms bazaar. These arms are shipped from southern Thailand and Myanmar to Bangladesh through fishing vessels operated by Burmese insurgents. The recovery of arms during Operation Leech by Indian armed forces off the Andaman Coast is the biggest proof. ULFA activists are also known to have visited Thailand for negotiating purchase of arms and communication equipment.

ISI also carried out 'Operation Tehsad' in North East India. It supplied sixty kilograms of RDX in Assam in order to destroy area's oil industry and surface transport. The ISI gave ULFA the first installment of the explosives by which they could begin their operations.[122] ISI has also organized training camps for the ULFA cadres in association with the DGFI of Bangladesh in CHT: ULFA has for long maintained close linkages with the Pakistan's ISI. Several ULFA cadres have also received arms training from the ISI at various training centres in Pakistan, close to the Afghanistan border. The top ULFA leadership was also in close touch with certain officers of the Pakistani High Commission in Bangladesh, who have arranged for their passport in various names and travel to Karachi, from where they have been taken to the terrorist training centres run by the ISI and its affiliates. ULFA had also announced its support for Pakistan during the Kargil war. ULFA's a website newsletter Swadhinata also known as 'Freedom', receives editorial support from ISI agents inside Pakistan. It was in 'Freedom' that the ULFA first supported the Pakistanis during the Kargil war. The ISI has provided ULFA cadres with arms training, safe havens, funds, arms and ammunition. Training has been given at camps in Pakistan, Bangladesh and Bhutan. At least 300 ULFA cadres were also trained at Rawalpindi and other locations in Pakistan. The training included courses in the use of rocket launchers, explosives and assault weapons. Paresh Baruah has been regularly visiting Karachi since 1992-93. He is also reported to have met Osama bin Laden in 1996 during a visit to Karachi. The ULFA leader was reportedly taken to a camp on the Pakistan-Afghanistan border, where he not only received assurance of military help in the form of arms and ammunition, but also assurances of co-operation and logistical support of all international organisations owing allegiance to bin Laden, including the International Jehad Council, the Tehrik-ul-Jehad, Harkat-ul-Jehadi-e-Islami (HuJI), apart from the Al Qaeda.

The ISI has also trained ULFA terrorists in counter intelligence, disinformation and use of sophisticated weapons and explosives. Pakistan has facilitated the visits of Paresh Baruah and other ULFA leaders to Singapore, Thailand and other countries, and a channel for the transfer of funds and arms has been created. Several *Madrassas* (seminaries) and mosques sponsored by the ISI in the Sylhet and Cox's Bazaar areas are being used to hoard and transfer arms procured by the ULFA from Thailand and Myanmar. The ISI largesse enabled ULFA to buy arms in Cambodia, paying for these in hard currency routed through Nepal. The ISI also 'introduced' ULFA to LTTE transporters who, for a fee, undertook to transport arms from Southeast Asia into Myanmar.

The activities of ISI of Pakistan are concentrated in following areas:

- Promoting indiscriminate violence in the state by providing active support to the local militant outfits.
- Creating new militant outfits along the ethnic and communal lines.
- Supplying explosives and sophisticated arms to various terrorist groups.
- Promoting fundamentalism and militancy among local Muslim youth by misleading them in the name of jihad.
- It has sought to unite various insurgent groups and make Indian counter-insurgency operations ineffective.

Co-operation between various terrorist organisations in India's north-east and foreign groups was formalised with the formation of the Indo-Burmese Revolutionary Front (IBRF) in 1989. The IBRF was made up initially of the NSCN-K, ULFA, United Liberation Front of Bodoland, Kuki National Front (KNF) (all from India) and Chin National Front (Myanmar). Paresh Baruah is reported to have paid a substantial sum of money to the Kachins for the first large consignment of weapons from Thailand.

Funding

Terror tactics of the terrorist organizations give surprising amount of wealth. For large scale extortion weapons are needed. Arms license are given freely in Nagaland. With these weapons, ULFA has been known to raise huge amount of money, mainly through extortion. In its 'fund raising drive', crores of rupees have been generated. The big multinational companies have also been known to provide protection money to ULFA. Businessmen were also required to invest ULFA money and multiply it.[123] The involvement of Naga politicians in providing weapons is well known as weapons are crucial to funding.

The illicit trade in narcotics is the best source to raise funds. However the insurgents in the North East have so far relied on other means to raise funds. ULFA raised money through extortion, robbing and collecting protection money from tea gardens. In Nagaland and Manipur too, insurgents collect taxes from every household, contractors, employees and even government officials including ministers. However, this trend is changing fast and insurgent groups have begun to trade in illicit narcotics to raise funds to keep the insurgency going. Rumours are also there of drug dealing in which senior leadership of ULFA is involved. The NSCN (K) faction has also been known to be trading in drugs, especially heroin.

The Role of Narcotics and Arms Trafficking

The illegal narcotics trade is one of the major reasons for the insurgency in the North East. This is a major source of funding.

Earlier it was believed that states of Manipur, Mizoram and Nagaland are only links in the smuggling route, but it should be remembered that poppy cultivation in Manipur and Tripura is also quite well spread. Ukhrul and Senapati districts of Manipur produce high quality cannabis, which moves to Bihar and U.P. and then to Nepal for its final destination in western countries. Poppy cultivation is prevalent in Eastern Mizoram along Myanmar border. It is also prevalent in Lungleigh along the border with Bangladesh. There is also evidence of poppy cultivation in Behiang in Churachandpur district of Manipur. Poppy is also grown illicitly in Tirap, Chaglang, Lohit and Upper Siang districts of Arunachal Pradesh and Chandel districts of Manipur.[124] Domestic heroine base originates in India and is usually trafficked to Nepal, Bangladesh, Sri Lanka and Maldives.

The three states of North-East — Manipur, Mizoram and Nagaland — have a common border with Myanmar and thus fall on the transit route of smuggling of narcotics. The major routes in the region are Behiang on the Churachandpur-Imphal route, Moreh, Kanjong in Ukhrul district and Somrah. Manipur, Nagaland and Mizoram bordering Myanmar are the most susceptible areas along the new drug trafficking route. The insurgent group of Manipur is also involved in trafficking of drugs. Some analysts who see the violent clashes between Kukis and Nagas to control Moreh, a trading centre on Indo-Myanmar border, as a life and death struggle to control the trade in narcotics.[125]

After its formation, the NSCN emerged as the most powerful insurgent group in the North East. It has collected huge assets of arms with its market in South East Asia. It also controls the route through which such arms are smuggled into North East. Most of the smuggled weapons that flow into North East originate in Cambodia, which has a surplus of such weapons.[126]

ULFA bought sophisticated weapons from NSCN and KIA and built up an arms depot located on the Assam-Nagaland border. Besides M-20, pistols, M-21/22/23 rifles, G1, G2 and G3 rifles, SLRs and stenguns, the ULFA procured Chinese bombs using pressure devices.[127]

Drug trafficking and gun running go hand in hand. While drug money is used to procure arms, arms sale in turn go to finance drug trafficking.

Present Scenario in Assam and Nagaland

Manipur, which recorded 380 fatalities according to the *South Asia Terrorism Portal* database, remained the most troubled region in the North East.

With at least 371 fatalities in the year, Assam remained the second most violent theatre of conflict in India's Northeast. Data for the year demonstrates a significant increase in militant fatalities and a corresponding decline in civilian deaths. A decline of nearly 32 per cent was recorded in the civilian category, while militant fatalities increased by 45 per cent. SF fatalities rose marginally by under 17 per cent.

Assam: Militancy-related Fatalities, 2005-2009

Year	*Incidents*	*Civilians*	*SFs*	*Militants*	*Total*
2005	398	173	7	74	254
2006	413	164	32	46	242
2007	500	286	24	129	439
2008	491	244	18	125	387
2009*	728	167	21	183	371

Source: South Asia Terrorism Portal

* Data till December 5, 2009

There has been a substantial increase in number of incidents, with 728 reported till December 6, the highest in the last five years, All 27 Districts of the State reported militant activity in 2009, with the Karbi Anglong and North Cachar Hills Districts being the worst affected. In terms of activity, the BW was the most effective outfit in 2009, with ULFA and the National Democratic Front of Bodoland following close behind. Further, the ethnic clash between the Zeme Naga (supported by the Nagaland-based NSCN-IM) and Dimasa (backed by the BW) tribes claimed the life of 43 civilians in the North Cachar Hills District in 2009. However, the surrender of a large number of BW militants in the second half of 2009 provided some respite in this troubled District. At least 28 major incidents of militant violence were reported from Assam in 2009. On November 22, suspected ULFA militants triggered two powerful bomb blasts barely 50 meters from the Sadar Police Station in Nalbari town, killing eight people and injuring 53. In another shocking incident on October 4, at least 11 persons were killed and ten injured in an attack by suspected militants of the anti-talks faction of the NDFB at Balichand area in the Sonitpur District. Similarly, on July 1, the unidentified militants shot dead four children and a 25 year-old woman at Semkhor village in the North Cachar Hills District. In another dreadful incident, suspected BW militants shot dead 12 persons, including eight children, and set ablaze 20 houses at Michidui village in the North Cachar Hills District and a month back from this heinous incident, BW militants shot dead five persons, including two children, and set ablaze 54 houses when they attacked Borchenam Basti, a Zeme Naga inhabited village under Haflong Police Station in the North Cachar Hills District. In an incident of ethnic clash between the two groups, violence between the Zeliangrong community and Cacharis in North Cachar Hills District continued for over two days, claiming 10 lives. The clashes between the two communities, the Zeme sub-tribe of the Zeliangrong tribe and the Cacharis (Dimasas) started after suspected BW militants killed nine Zemes on April 28. An incident which hit the news channels on January 1, 2009 was that ULFA militants triggered serial bomb blasts in three different areas of Guwahati city, killing five persons, including a minor, and injuring fifty. The first explosion took place around 2:25 pm (IST) in Birubari, followed by high-intensity explosions in the Bhootnath area (5:25 pm) and Bhangagarh area (5:40 pm).

The Naga insurgency in India's troubled northeast has, over the years, lapsed into turf wars, and trends in 2009 demonstrated the consistency in events, though the steady acceleration of violence since 2001 appears to have been dramatically reversed. From a peak of 201 fatalities in 2008 - overwhelmingly resulting from clashes between the various militant factions - fell to just 17 in

2009. Nevertheless, even at this diminished intensity, Nagaland retains its third place in terms of violence among the States of India's troubled Northeast, behind Manipur (360) and Assam (336).

Insurgency-related Fatalities in Nagaland: 2001-2009

Year	*Civilians*	*SFs*	*Insurgents*	*Total*
2001*	16	01	65	82
2002*	16	03	71	90
2003*	13	03	70	86
2004*	42	00	55	97
2005*	28	1	70	99
2006*	29	02	116	147
2007 *	44	01	109	154
2008 *	68	03	130	201
2009***	7	0	10	17

*Union Ministry of Home Affairs (MHA), Government of India**MHA and South Asia Terrorism Portal (SATP) combined***SATP - Data till November 1, 2009

Nagaland registered 201 fatalities in 307 insurgency-related incidents in 2008, according to combined sources of the MHA and SATP. Year 2009 has seen only 94 such incidents, claiming the lives of 17 persons till November 1, according to the SATP database. These fatalities are due to internecine clashes and the cadres belonged to the National Socialist Council of Nagalim-Khaplang (NSCN-K), National Socialist Council of Nagalim-Isak-Muivah (NSCN-IM) and Naga National Council (NNC). All the internecine clashes were concentrated in three of Nagaland's 11 Districts. While seven such clashes occurred in Dimapur, two clashes were reported from Wokha and one from Kohima.

Suggestions

- The operations in the North East against the rebels should be undertaken by understanding that they are fellow citizens and not enemies. The rebels have to be won over by actions designed to win their hearts and minds. This implies the use of minimum force.

- The solution to any insurgency is always political rather than military. There government should always come up for negotiations.
- North Eastern Council is a very good instrument of Central government by which it can check development and administration. It should be in check that a right and honest person should be the secretary of North East Council, and the subordinate officers should also be chosen carefully.
- The Public Distribution System should be cleaned up and the things of necessity be provided to each and every village at reasonable prices. The emphasis should also be on rural development which should directly be controlled by North East Council, as central agency is more transparent and accountable.
- The most important task which should be undertaken is to revamp the education system.
- Careful, transparent, and fair criminal proceedings aimed at demonstrating the Centre's commitment to supporting rule of law in the North East are likely to win public support. Human rights groups are a tremendous asset in the struggle to re-establish the credibility of the rule of law.[129]
- Ordinary people are to be protected not only from the violence of the rebels, but also from the damage caused by the Security Forces.
- Efficient governance is needed. The administration of the North Eastern states should be improved. A pool of officers on the lines of erstwhile 'Frontier Administration Services' for NEFA, should be created. They should have an adventurous spirit, temperament of service in tribal areas and should not see their tenure in North East as 'hard posting'.
- The economic development should top the priority list. Private investments in North East should be encouraged. There should be tax holiday for budding entrepreneurs. Also, public sector investment in the North East should

continue but the focus should shift to regional rather than on national priorities. Development of down stream industries should be given priority.

- The economic prosperity of the people in the border areas will be greatly improved if border trade with Myanmar, Bangladesh and Tibet is liberalized and made free. Equally important is the development of the road link between the neighbouring countries.
- Border should be fenced thoroughly and the fence should be kept under constant surveillance. More BSF posts should be established to maintain proper check.
- The government should make it clear to Myanmar that narcotics trade is a serious threat to India's security and society. The government should also strengthen the existing narcotics control organization in the country and there should be greater interaction between the Narcotics Control Bureau at Imphal and other security agencies. It should be a national endeavour and not be seen as the responsibility of North Eastern states alone.[130]
- We must also seek cooperation from Bangladesh to close down training camps and bases of insurgent groups located in Bangladesh.
- The security forces have to shift their focus from jungle hideouts to urban centres. Although the destruction of insurgent bases in jungle hideouts will have to be done, they have to develop strategic set of guidelines to fight the militants in crowded urban centres where security forces will be goaded to open fire resulting unavoidably in civilian casualties.[131]
- Effective administration of autonomous council would significantly mitigate the identity consciousness of various ethnic groups.
- Larger ethnic groups have to recognize the spatial demands of the smaller ones and be more accommodative towards them.

- There is a need to differentiate outsiders from foreigners as the economy of the region is dependent upon the former.
- Both the Centre and state have to evolve a bipartisan and non partisan policy vis-a vis foreigners. Even if all these illegal migrants could not be expelled, effective measures are essential to prevent future invasion.[132]
- Because of the inadequate infrastructural development, large projects are not economically viable. Hence, greater emphasis on the development of smaller projects would benefit the region.
- Any investment in biodiversity and its floriculture sector could be highly rewarding and should be a major pre-investment priority.[133]
- Due to the sprinkled settlement in the region, infrastructure facilities could not be provided properly. A new development strategy should be planned which should bring about a spatial planning with a higher level of social infrastructure that stimulates human development.[134]
- Tourism as an industry in North East has a great potential due to scenic beauty. It should be stressed out for growth with the easing of Restricted Area Permit requirements. Development of civil aviation should also be done. Package tours should be offered.

An interview was done with Mr. Amardeep Pegu, who hails from North East, is Asst. Professor, in Political Science Department, Darrang College, Tezpur, Gauhati University. His scholarly insights helped in deeper understanding of the problem of terrorism.

1. In the contemporary world, what are the factors responsible for the rise of violence?

   Ans: In my view, one of the most important reasons for the rise of violence in the contemporary world is the diversity of religions and vast differences and conflicts among the people due to religion. Religions create barriers between people and while every religion has different viewpoints, conflicts are bound to arise. Secondly, I feel that due to the increasing amount of competition to be the best in all aspects of life has lead individuals, societies, communities and states to succumb to violence and dirty politics to survive. Thirdly, I feel that the Media has played a big role in promoting violence in the world rather than solving its issues. Mass Media plays a crucial role in forming and reflecting public opinion, connecting the world to individuals and reproducing the self-image of society. The media can provoke delinquency and violence, cause moral depravity and undermine family life. The media can sometimes reduce educational achievement, destroy children's intellectual and imaginative abilities and brainwash them into racism, sexism and consumerism. Fourthly, the advancement of information and technology has also helped in making terrorism a global phenomena and has made its effect more profound than earlier. With the apprehensions that the weapons of mass destruction, viz., chemical, biological, nuclear weapons and missiles, are being developed and acquired by the terrorists, the scourge of terrorism has assumed catastrophic proportions.

2. How far poverty and unemployment is responsible for increase in terrorist activities?

   Ans: Poverty and hunger definitely plays a very strong role in increasing terrorist activities. In the present day world, the number of unemployed educated persons is increasing. Only a tiny fraction of the many educated people are actually employed. This scenario is particularly and abundantly seen in India. Thus, majority of the unemployed section of people adopt dishonest means to survive. Most of them seek justice against their unemployed situation. Thus, they rebel against the state, terrorizing the people within. Poverty gives similar reasons to people to choose this path of survival.

3. Does religion increase the intensity of violent acts? Will it play more important role in contemporary world?

Ans: Yes... Religion is the most important factor of violence. Different religions and sects have become the most dangerous aspects of the present day terrorism. The religiously motivated terrorists are committing dastardly and heinous crimes in the name of religion. These fanatics are bent upon perpetrating communal violence and hatred at global level and dividing the world on communal lines.

4. Has Iraq and Afghanistan become breeding grounds of terrorism?

   Ans: By the look of it- Yes

5. Is there growing Anti-Americanism in West Asia?

   Ans: Don't have much idea about this.

6. Do you think that terrorism in South Asia is bound to spill beyond its immediate borders?

   Ans: Yes. It seems so. The rate at which Terrorism is altogether spreading, it can spread to each and every corner of the world, not only its immediate borders...

7. Has the death sentence for Ajmal Kasab got any implication for other terrorists?

   Ans: So far, it hasn't shown any sign. I don't think it has succeeded in moving any part of other terrorists. They are always ready to kill and die. They are not going to stop just because one of them has failed.

8. Do you believe that Pakistan is emerging as an epicentre of global terrorism?

   Ans: 100% YES!

9. Is media playing an effective and positive role in countering terrorism?

   Ans: Not much. It has won half the battle. On the other side, it is playing a bigger role in promoting n increasing terrorism.

10. What are your observations about the issue of suicide attacks in relation to secular and religious terrorism?

Ans: These kind of attacks only prove that religious views are of more importance for them instead of moral principles or humanitarian feelings. They are ready to die themselves for the sake of religion. This has become a serious issue since it has now become very difficult to combat terrorism with the people involved having such mindsets. There is no way to stop them.

11. How far do you think security forces have failed in controlling violence?

    Ans: Not a single bit... I think security forces have entirely failed in controlling violence.

TERRORIST ORGANIZATIONS IN INDIA

Many terrorist, insurgent and extremist groups are operating across India. The maximum number 40, operate in Manipur, followed by 36 in Assam, 32 in Jammu and Kashmir, and 30 in Tripura. Punjab is home to 12 terror groups, Meghalaya to four, Nagaland to three, Mizoram to two and Arunachal Pradesh to one.[135] The regions with long term terrorist activities today are Jammu and Kashmir, Central India (Naxalism) and North Eastern States having independence and autonomy movements. In the past, the Punjab insurgency led to militant activities in the Indian state of Punjab as well as in Delhi.

At present, the central India is affected by Maoist activities. The states of West Bengal, Bihar, U.P. are the main centers of Maoist insurgency. This movement started from Naxalbari village in West Bengal in 1967. It was a minor incident of loot of crops. Gradually its intensity grew in size and Naxalism came to be known for upsetting the exploitative state set up. The main target of the Naxalites was landlords, police officers and money lenders. Naxalite movement came into being due to social and economic exploitation of the poor. It has concentrated mainly on targeting the so called 'class enemies.' They differ from the other violent movements in the sense that though they want to get rid of the prevailing exploitative system, they do not advocate secession from the country. Moreover, the population of the area supports these insurgents.[136] Rural terrorism, in the form of naxalite attacks, has been going on for many years. Major incidents of naxalite attacks are becoming increasingly common, taking the lives of large numbers of innocent and poor villagers, and policemen on duty.

Terrorism in North East

India's Northeast has often been referred to as the most terrifying theatre of violent conflicts and insurgency. This extremely diverse region of India has not only become the most conflict ridden area, the scale and intensity of violence overtaking Kashmir, but it is increasingly recognized as South Asia's hottest warring spots. Northeastern India consists of 7 states: Assam, Meghalaya, Tripura, Arunachal Pradesh, Mizoram, Manipur, and Nagaland. Tensions exist between these states and the central government. The states have accused New Delhi of ignoring the issues concerning them. There is a rise of insurgent activities and regional movements in the northeast, especially in the states of Assam, Nagaland, Manipur, Mizoram and Tripura. Most of these organizations demand independent state status or increased regional autonomy and sovereignty.

United National Liberation Front

The United National Liberation Front (UNLF), the oldest Meitei insurgent group in the State was formed under the leadership of Areambam Samrendra Singh on November 24, 1964 to achieve independence and a socialist society. A pan-Manipuri Youth League was formed in December 1968, which functioned as an overground body for the UNLF. Later, differences within the outfit surfaced over the issue of strategies to be adopted. While Samrendra Singh sought to spread ideological consciousness before launching an armed struggle, the more radical leader Oinam Sudhir Kumar established a Revolutionary Government of Manipur (RGM). Samarendra Singh was killed by unidentified terrorists in Imphal on June 10, 2001. In the seventies and eighties, the UNLF concentrated mainly on mobilisation and recruitment. In 1990, it decided to launch an armed struggle for the 'liberation' of Manipur from India.

In the same year, it formed an armed wing called Manipur People's Army (MPA).

The UNLF aims to establish an independent socialist Manipur.[137] The outfit operates in the Jiribam valley and Cachar district of Assam. Soon after its formation, the UNLF leaders established a political relationship with the authority of the then East Pakistan, and underwent military training in that country in 1969. They also supported the Pakistani army during the 1971 Bangladesh liberation war. Later, the group also developed a relationship with China even while continuing its relations with Pakistan. On June 14, 1975, UNLF leader N. Bisheswar Singh and 16 other Meitei rebels proceeded to Lhasa to seek Chinese assistance. The group has links with Naga and Mizo terrorist outfits as well. On May 22, 1990, the UNLF, along with other insurgent groups operating in the Northeast – the National Socialist Council of Nagaland – Khaplang (NSCN-K), the United Liberation Front of Asom (ULFA), and the Kuki National Army (KNA) – floated a pan-Mongoloid coalition called the Indo-Burma Revolutionary Front (IBRF) to wage a "united struggle for the independence of Indo-Burma". The UNLF has training camps in Myanmar and Bangladesh. It also maintains close association with the NSCN-K. On April 30th, two UNLF cadres were arrested by the Police at Patharquwariri at Guwahati in Assam. They were identified as 'vice-president' Kh. Tomba *alias* Vikram Singh and self styled 'lieutenant colonel' Abu *alias* Dilip Singh. Sources said that they were arrested when they were planning to proceed to Myanmar. One lap top, cash in terms of hundreds of thousands and documents were recovered from their possession. Similarly on April 16th, a UNLF cadre, Haobam Dhanachandra alias Tomba (29), was shot dead by the Assam Rifles personnel during an encounter at Thampalok under Tengnoupal Police Station in Chandel District. He joined the UNLF since 2003. One AK series Rifles loaded with one magazine containing 10 live rounds, one Chinese hand grenade and two IEDs were recovered from the possession of the slain militant.

Kamtapur Liberation Organization (KLO)

Kamtapuris, a martial race spread over in plains of Assam and parts of West Bengal and Bangladesh, have emerged as a new entrant into the demand for separation. Operating primarily from Siliguri in West Bengal, their militant outfit Kamtapur Liberation Organization has been demanding a separate state comprising of 12 districts of Assam and West Bengal. The militants move freely into Bangladesh and Bhutan due to the favourable geographic terrain and is also known to have links with ULFA.

National Democratic Front of Bodoland

The National Democratic Front of Bodoland (NDFB) was formed on October 3, 1986. The outfit was originally established as the Bodo Security Force (BdSF) under the leadership of Ranjan Daimary. On November 25, 1994, the BdSF rechristened itself as the NDFB.

The outfit, since May 2005, is under a ceasefire agreement with the Assam and Union Government. The NDFB was formed with the professed objective of securing a 'sovereign Bodoland' in the areas north of the river Brahmaputra. According to the 'constitution' of the outfit, which was adopted on March 10, 1998, nearly twelve years after its formation, the objectives of the outfit are the following:

- Liberate Bodoland from the Indian expansionism and occupation;
- Free the Bodo nation from the colonialist exploitation, oppression and domination;
- Establish a Democratic Socialist Society to promote Liberty, Equality and Fraternity; and uphold the integrity and sovereignty of Bodoland.

During its active days, the areas in the north and north-west of the river Brahmaputra in Assam formed the main expanse of operation of the outfit. The NDFB was active in the Bongaigaon, Kokrajhar, Darrang, Barpeta, Dhubri, Nalbari and Sonitpur districts. It was also known to be active in the Garo hills region of Meghalaya, close to the Assam-Meghalaya border.

Before the outfit announced a unilateral ceasefire with the Security Forces in 2004, its activities were reported from Nalbari, Barpeta, Dhubri, Sonitpur, Kokrajhar, Bongaigaon, Chirang and KarbiAnglong Districts.

The NDFB cadres, during their operations, had access to sophisticated arms and ammunition. They were found to be using AK Series rifles, light machine guns, M-16 rifles, rocket propelled grenades, mortars and Chinese-make grenades. Many of the NDFB cadres are trained in making and planting improvised explosive devices (IEDs).

The NDFB acts in collaboration with the ULFA. Authorities in Assam blamed the outfit to have acted in cooperation with the ULFA to carry out the October 2008 serial explosions in the State. In addition, the NDFB shares a close relationship with the other outfits like the Kamatapur Liberation Organisation (KLO), the Achik National Volunteers Council (ANVC) and the National Socialist Council of Nagaland-Khaplang (NSCN-K). Unconfirmed reports also suggest linkages between the Maoists of Nepal and the NDFB. According to a list submitted by the Indian authorities to their counterparts in Bangladesh, the NDFB maintains at least two camps in the Khagrachari and Tangail districts of that country. Prior to its dislodgment from Bhutan, the outfit was reported to have established working relationship with certain elements in Bhutan.

National Socialist Council of Nagaland (NSCN)

Issac Swu and Muivah, along with S.S. Khaplang formed the National Socialist Council of Nagaland on January 31, 1980. With its creation, the insurgency in Nagaland took a new turn. They set up camps in the North Cachar Hills and committed several bank robberies there. The N.S.C.N. armed and trained many groups. A major share of the extortion by all these groups went to the N.S.C.N. In Tripura, both National Liberation Front of Tripura (NLFT) and the All Tripura Tiger Force (ATTF) were armed and trained by them. In Manipur too, the NSCN has strong links with a Meiti insurgent group, which runs a big extortion network in Imphal valley. NSCN cadets began extorting activities in Imphal valley and there was a steep rise in NSCN's funds. Mostly the share of money extorted for NSCN is 80 per cent. It is a rich organization and maintains offices in Bangkok, Manila and the Netherlands. Its H.Q. are located in Hemi Naga in northern Burma. The main reason behind its establishment of H.Q.s there is because of its link with the Kachin Independent Organisation (KIO). AASU had also requested NSCN for arms and military training of its military wing. Meanwhile inter tribal feelings in the NSCN camp were getting exacerbated and in 1988 it boiled over in a violent clash. Thus, it got split into two factions- NSCN (I.M.) consisting of Issac Swu and Muivah, and NSCN (K) headed by Kaphlang. Khaplang controlled over the Burmese Naga and Konyaks and retained its base in Burma while the other group shifted its H.Q. from Burma to the western Sema region in Nagaland, in addition to retaining a few bases in Naga Burma Hills and Somra tract. The NSCN (IM) leaders soon joined ULFA in Bangladesh and had many arms deals with ISI. It started operating mostly opposite the Ukhrul district of Manipur from December 1987 onwards. It is in Manipur that the NSCN (IM) has played its biggest games. But when it gained strength, the Meithis in Manipur, began to feel insecure.[138]

Terrorism in Jammu & Kashmir

The terrorism in Jammu and Kashmir has also increased in its intensity. The local militants are now supported by cross border terrorists. There has been increase in number of terrorist organizations.

Jammu and Kashmir Liberation Front

There are two distinct outfits, each of which identifies itself by the name Jammu and Kashmir Liberation Front (JKLF). Amanullah Khan heads the first while Yasin Malik, who parted ways with Amanullah Khan and formed another JKLF, heads the other. In May 1994, Yasin Malik who was released from jail (after his arrest in August 1990) declared that his faction would renounce violence as a tool to achieve the goal of 'independence'.

Both the Fronts trace their origin to the Jammu and Kashmir National Liberation Front (JKNLF). The JKNLF was an offshoot of the Plebiscite Front, a forum allegedly launched at the behest of the late Sheikh Abdullah, who was Chief Minister of Jammu and Kashmir and President of the National Conference, at a time when he was at loggerheads with India's Union Government. After the Sheikh-Indira Accord was signed, militant, pro-independence elements within the Plebiscite Front walked out to continue with the movement to secede from India.

The JKLF was set up in the United Kingdom, in May 1977, by one of the co-founders of the JKNLF, Amanullah Khan, after most of his JKNLF colleagues were either killed or captured by Indian security forces. The outfit is reportedly supported by expatriates of the Mirpur community that belongs to Pakistan Occupied Kashmir (PoK). Another JKLF, a splinter group headed by Yasin Malik, was founded in September 1995, after Malik split from Khan over differences on the strategy to be pursued to achieve perceived goals.

While both the JKLFs share a common goal, self-determination for the people of Jammu and Kashmir, the Yasin Malik faction has renounced the use of violence to attain this goal. It lays emphasis on adopting non-violent means and mobilising public opinion in India and Pakistan in favour of its objectives. It is a constituent of the All Party Huriyat Conference.

Jaish-e-Mohammed

The Jaish-e-Mohammed (JeM) is a relatively new terrorist outfit, compared to other major outfits active in Jammu and Kashmir (J&K). Like the Lashkar-e-Toiba (LeT), the JeM too is an outfit formed, controlled and manned by Pakistan. The outfit was launched on January 31, 2000, by Maulana Masood Azhar in Karachi after he was released from an Indian jail during the terrorists for hostage swap of December 31, 1999, following the hijacking of the Indian Airlines Flight IC 814.

The formation of the outfit was endorsed by three religious school chiefs, Mufti Nizamuddin Shamzai of the Majlis-e-Tawan-e-Islami (MT), Maulana Mufti Rashid Ahmed of the Dar-ul Ifta-e-wal-Irshad and Maulana Sher Ali of the Sheikh-ul-Hadith Dar-ul Haqqania. The outfit's creation can be linked to the popularity surrounding Masood Azhar after his release from India. Maulana

Masood Azhar was the general secretary of the newly established Harkat-ul-Ansar (HuA) in 1994 and was on a 'mission' in J&K when he was arrested on February 11. When he was released, the HuA had been included in the US list of Foreign Terrorist Organisations which had compelled the outfit to rename itself as the Harkat-ul-Mujahideen (HuM). However, Masood Azhar decided to float the new outfit JeM rather than rejoin his old outfit. He was also reported to have received assistance in setting up the JeM from Pakistan's Inter-Services Intelligence (ISI), the then Taliban regime in Afghanistan, Osama bin Laden and several Sunni sectarian outfits of Pakistan.

The Jaish-e-Mohammed is part of the Islamist terror network with its base in Pakistan and active in the terrorist violence in J&K. The outfit, like other terrorist outfits in J&K, claims to using violence to force a withdrawal of Indian security forces from J&K. The outfit claims that each of its offices in Pakistan would serve as schools of jihad. Delivering speeches at various cities and towns in Pakistan after his release, Masood Azhar threatened that the outfit would eliminate Indian Prime Minister Atal Behari Vajpayee who he termed as 'Abu Jahl' (Father of Ignorance). In its fight against India, he added that the outfit would not only "liberate" Kashmir, but also would take control of the Babri Masjid in Ayodhya, Amritsar and Delhi.

The Jaish-e-Mohammed has largely confined its operations within J&K. The only recorded instance of its operations outside J&K has been the December 13, 2001, Parliament attack in New Delhi. However, several of its cadre have, on occasions been arrested or killed by security forces in states other than J&K.

The outfit is closely linked, through the Binoria Madrassa in Karachi, with the former Taliban regime of Afghanistan and its protégé, Osama bin Laden and his Al Qaeda. JeM chief, Masood Azhar was released by Indian authorities in Kandahar and has reportedly met Taliban and Al Qaeda leaders in Afghanistan on various occasions.The JeM is also reported to have links with Sunni terrorist outfits operating in Pakistan such as the Sipah-e-Sahaba Pakistan (SSP) and Lashkar-e-Jhangvi (LeJ).

Lashkar-e-Taiba

Lashkar-e-Taiba means the army of Taiba. Taiba is the old name of the holy city of Medina in Saudi Arabia. The group was found in 1990 to fight Indian rule in Kashmir. Its members include thousands of Afghan veterans. It was blamed for the coordinated attacks on Mumbai in November last year. Of all the Pakistani based groups, it is widely believed to be the most closely leashed to the Pakistani ISI.

It's first recorded presence in Kashmir came in 1993 when 12 Pakistani and Afghan terrorists infiltrated across the LoC along with the Islami Inquilabi Mahaz, a now defunct outfit. When it began operations in J&K, it was actively promoted by Pakistan's external intelligence agency, the ISI. Among the LeT's objective is a union of all Muslim majority regions in the countries that surround Pakistan. Majallah al-Dawat, the in-house magazine of the LeT, had as early as December 1998 proclaimed that its campaign in J&K was 'just the beginning,' and described plans to extend the jihad throughout India. LeT literature sharply differentiates it from terror organizations who have represented their involvement in Jammu and Kashmir as one driven by the need to support a legitimate national liberation struggle. Instead, the jihad in Jammu and Kashmir is asserted to be a battle for the defence of Islam, one necessitated by the conditions of Muslims in India and the rest of the world.[139]

Harkat-ul-Jihad- Al-Islami

HuJI is linked to Harkat-ul Ansar or Harkat-ul Mujahideen. It was raised with the objective of nurturing militancy in the Jammu and Kashmir in 1991. The leadership and the cadre of this group was initially raised from the madrasas run by clerics associated with the raising of the Taliban and hence have irrefutable association with Al Qaeda. The terrorists which were being trained for Kashmir were sent to Afghanistan to fight alongside the Taliban both for gaining combat experience and learning strategies to engage a regular army in a mountainous area.[140]

Hijbul Mujahiddin

The HM came into being in the Kashmir Valley in September 1989. It was reportedly formed as the militant wing of the Jamaat-e-Islami (JeI), an Islamist organisation. The Jamaat-e-Islami is reported to have set up the Hizb at the behest of the Inter Services Intelligence (ISI), Pakistan's external intelligence agency, to counter the Jammu and Kashmir Liberation Front, which had advocated complete independence of the State. It soon gained prominence after the Jamat-i-Islami and Islami Jamat-i-Tauba of PoK provided liberal arms, funds and cadre support to the HM. Many of the early Hizb cadres were former JKLF members. Headquartered at Muzaffarabad in Pakistan occupied Kashmir (PoK), the Hizb-ul-Mujahideen with an estimated cadre strength of at least 1500, is presently headed by Syed Salahuddin.

This pan-Islamic group gained exclusive controls over the terrorist operations in Kashmir in 1990 by diluting the influence of JKLF, by eliminating such Kashmiri secessionists considered inimical to the pan-Islamic ideology and interests of Pakistan, by maintaining hegemony through sufficient arms strength and by utilizing the infrastructure and apparatus of Jamat-i-Islami in Kashmir and PoK. Its mercenaries who are specialized in improvised explosive devices, laying machine, ambush, operating heavier vehicles like rockets, are providing training to the local youth of the region. They are using these weapons not in the Kashmir region but also in other parts of India.

Terrorism in Punjab

Though the terrorist-secessionist movement for Khalistan was comprehensively defeated in 1993, there remain a handful of terrorist outfits chiefly supported by Pakistan and some NRI Sikh groups who continue to propagate the ideology of Khalistan.

Babbar Khalsa International

One of the most prominent among them is the Babbar Khalsa International, among the oldest and most organised Khalistan terrorist groups. It is headed by Wadhawa Singh, who is reportedly hiding in

Pakistan. Mehal Singh is the deputy chief of BKI. Wadhwa Singh is making efforts to mobilise volunteers from Punjab as also from the US, who could be made to travel to India via Malaysia or Singapore.[141] Sukhdev Singh Babbar and Talwinder Singh Parmar were the founding members of this organisation. The first unit of the BKI was founded in Canada in 1981 under the leadership of late Talwinder Singh Parmar. The outfit at present is active in the USA Canada, the UK, Germany, France, Belgium, Norway, Switzerland and Pakistan. Talwinder Singh Parmar, a co-founder of the BKI, formed the Babbar Khalsa (Parmar) faction in 1992, when he split from the BKI after serious differences erupted between him and its leadership of. The Parmar faction has a presence in the UK, Germany, Belgium and Switzerland. The BKI wants an independent Sikh state called Khalistan.

Currently, Wadhwa Singh, who is reportedly hiding in Pakistan, heads the outfit. Mehal Singh is the deputy chief of BKI. Both of them are among the 20 terrorists whom India wants Pakistan to extradite. Wadhwa Singh is reported to have personally supervised the assassination of Punjab Chief Minister Beant Singh on August 31, 1995. He is also believed to have masterminded the January 2004 escape of the assassination-accused, Jagtar Singh Hawara, from the Burail jail in Chandigarh.

Available evidence suggests that the Babbar Khalsa is part of a terrorist network sponsored by Germany-based terrorist groups as well as Pakistan's external intelligence agency—the Inter Services Intelligence (ISI)—to revive terrorism in the Indian Punjab. Media reports in August 2001 said a joint committee was formed in Germany to coordinate the activities of major terrorist organisatoins abroad. Media reports in April 2002 said the ISI has entrusted the Lashkar-e-Toiba (LeT) with the task of reviving terrorism in Punjab. The LeT will impart arms training to groups like the BKI, the ISYF and the Khalistan Zindabad Force (KZF). Reports also said the LeT has opened at least eight camps in Pakistan to train the Khalistanis. These are at Kot Lakhpat, Chakwal, Gujranwala, Mianwali, Peshawar, Attock, Shahidan Da Banga and Gulbarg in Lahore. Available evidence also suggests that the BKI has established a nexus with Dawood Ibrahim, the fugitive Indian underworld kingpin residing now in Karachi.

A few recent incidents exhibit that still the organization is active in many areas of Punjab.[142]

- April 17: A suspected Babbar Khalsa International BKI militant, identified as Avtar Singh, was arrested by Zirakpur Police from Materi village in Ambala on April 17. He was produced in the Derabassi court on April 18 from where he was sent in Police remand till April 22. Station House Officer Yogi Raj stated that they raided the accused's hideout on a tip-off and arrested him from Materi village bus stand. He is said to be brother of another BKI cadre Purshotam Singh, who is living in France. According to Police sources, Purshotam was regularly sending money to BKI cadres in India to sustain their criminal activities.
- March 30: A special court sentenced BKI militant Paramjit Singh Bheora to life imprisonment, after convicting him of involvement in the 1995 assassination of the then Punjab Chief Minister Beant Singh. A fine of INR 65000 was also slapped on Bheora, who was on March 29 convicted of criminal conspiracy for his involvement in the assassination of Beant Singh by a suicide bomber, Dilawar Singh, August 31, 1995, at the high-security Punjab Civil Secretariat complex in Chandigarh. Jagtar Singh Hawara, an accomplice of Bheora, was earlier sentenced to death in 2007 in the same case.
- March 29: A BKI militant, identified as Piara Singh, a resident of Gattikatar village in Ferozepur, was arrested with 3.5 kilograms of RDX, which he had reportedly smuggled from Pakistan for supplying to BKI militants in Punjab, Mohali SSP Gurpreet Singh Bhullar said at a press conference. With the arrest of the explosives supplier to BKI, the Mohali District Police claimed to have foiled another

> bid of the Pakistan's Inter-Services Intelligence (ISI) backed BKI to revive militancy in Punjab, Delhi and across country. The SSP added that Piara Singh was a known smuggler of heroin and other contrabands and had walked out of jail a fortnight ago after serving a term in a drug smuggling case. During his stay in jail, he allegedly came in contact with some BKI militants, who asked him to smuggle and supply explosives after his release from jail, Bhullar claimed, while adding that Piara was arrested from the clues extracted during interrogation of suspected BKI militants, Gurpreet Singh and Balveer Singh Bhootna, who were taken into custody from Nabha jail last week on production warrants.

CONCLUSION

Much of the tension and conflict in the North East are driven by ethnic and tribal consciousness. The political demands of various groups have often manifested into violence. Very often military option has become inevitable to either bring about a negotiated settlement or create the necessary conditions for peace. This has thus given rise to hostility between civilians and armed forces.

The nature of insurgency in North East is quite distinct. All most every scholar believes that secessionism in North East is virtually impossible. The tiny insurgencies are unlikely to succeed as they are badly organized and have lost their ideological stand and popular support. But still violence has persisted there. The intensity of insurgency in this region is much less than that of Kashmir. Much of the fighting in the region is inter-communal, aimed at hitting a rival militant group territory or ethnic cleansing. Many insurgent groups in the region are also difficult to distinguish from the criminal organizations because they are heavily involved in extortion, kidnapping and cross border drug trade.[143]

In spite of the numerous peace accords, the region still suffers from militancy and low intensity conflict in various forms. The reorganization of the region to satisfy the needs of the varied ethnic groups has resulted in a new problem. Expansionist tendencies of the dominant ethnic group contribute to regional tension and conflict. The demand for greater Nagaland places the state at odds with its neighbours including Manipur, Mizoram and Tripura.

The insurgency situation in the North East India, is beginning to witness a new phenomenon. Islamic militant activities have begun to breed in the region. Earlier religious insurgency had not erupted in the North East. But in the recent years, Islamic fundamentalism has grown in North East. This has been linked to the rise of religious extremism in Bangladesh. The ISI of Pakistan has also been aiming at promoting new militant groups based on communal and ethnic lines, supplying arms and explosives to militants and promoting communal tension.[144] These movements have a communal flavor and are trying to take over the agenda from ethnic agenda. This has been seen particularly after the 'detalibanization of Afghanistan', when the active remnants of al- Qaeda and the Taliban reportedly entered Bangladesh which borders North East India. The growing Islamisation of Bangladesh has direct consequences for the secular space of North East and characterizes an atmosphere which is ripe for the growth of Islamic militant activities in the region. The Islamic militant movements in the region are also finding an organized parish in the illegal migrant population whose ideology and socio-religious commitments continue to be informed by experiences from across the border.[145]

Another phenomenon which is on rise is the ties between the insurgents and the politicians. The bureaucrats and politicians depend upon these insurgents for their political and career gains. More specifically, in the North East, there frequently is a tacit association between political organizations and insurgent groups. In some cases, there are historical origins in common between the organization and the rebel group. Local politicians receive sufficient benefits from conditions of ongoing insurgency and are hence unlikely to disturb the equilibrium. Low levels of insurgency help in receiving sufficient development money from the centre.[146]

The conflict in the region has been that of 'proxy war'. A phenomenon is emerging in which enemy country is helping the insurgents with safe havens, arms, training etc. To stop this, a change of policy is needed to divert the aspirations of the North Eastern communities from the path of armed struggle into democratic and peaceful channels.

REFERENCES

1. According to various media reports.
2. Praveen Swami, "In the midst of Kashmir crisis, some islands of peace", *The Hindu*, August 21, 2010, New Delhi.
3. Praveen Swami, "The making of Srinagar's teenage martyrs", *The Hindu*, July 10, 2010, New Delhi.
4. "Kashmir's missing government", *The Hindu*, August 17, 2010, New Delhi.
5. An interview with Omar Abdullah by Praveen Swami, *The Hindu*, July 11, 2010. New Delhi.
6. Shujaat Bukhari, "Valley on fire", *Frontline*, August 27, 2010, pp. 130-131.
7. Barkha Dutt, "Don't look away again", *Hindustan Times*, August 7, 2010, Chandigarh.
8. Lt-Gen Harwant Singh, "The unrest in Kashmir", *The Tribune*, August 23, 2010, Chandigarh.
9. Shujaat Bukhari, "Valley on fire", *Frontline*, August 27, 2010, p. 134.
10. *Ibid.* p. 133.
11. Praveen Swami, "The autumn of Kashmir's Islamist patriarch?", *The Hindu*, August 20, 2010, New Delhi.
12. Suhasini Haidar, "Kashmir: finding the face of the protester", *The Hindu*, August 25, 2010, New Delhi.
13. Shujaat Bukhari, "Valley on fire", *Frontline*, August 27, 2010, p. 134.
14. Kaveree Bamzai, "Lost in the valley", *India Today*, August 25, 2010, p. 29.
15. Kaveree Bamzai, "Lost in the valley", *India Today*, August 25, 2010, p. 26.
16. Sudipto Mundle, "Conversations in Kashmir", *The Times of India*, July 8, 2010.

17. Shujaat Bukhari, "Valley on fire", *Frontline,* August 27, 2010, p. 132.
18. Kaveree Bamzai, "Lost in the valley", *India Today,* August 25, 2010, p. 27.
19. *Ibid.*
20. Shujaat Bukhari, "Valley on fire", *Frontline,* August 27, 2010, p. 133.
21. Suhasini Haidar, "Kashmir: finding the face of the protester", *The Hindu,* August 25, 2010, New Delhi.
22. Malini Parthasarathy, "Reviving true kashmiriyat", *The Hindu,* August 19, 2010, New Delhi.
23. Suhasini Haidar, "Kashmir: finding the face of the protester", *The Hindu,* August 25, 2010, New Delhi.
24. Happymon Jacob, "Kashmir and the poverty of politics", *The Hindu,* July 22, 2010, New Delhi.
25. "Kashmir's politicians must act", *The Hindu,* July 10, 2010, New Delhi.
26. Praveen Swami, "Inside kashmir's New Islamist movement", *The Hindu,* August 19, 2010, New Delhi.
27. *Ibid.*
28. Suhasini Haidar, "Kashmir: finding the face of the protester", *The Hindu,* August 25, 2010, New Delhi.
29. Meredith Weiss, 'The Jammu & Kashmir Conflict'. 25 June 2002. *www.yale.edu/macmillan/globalization/kashmir.pdf*
30. *Ibid.*
31. Schofield, Victoria, Kashmir in Conflict: India, Pakistan and the Unfinished War, Tauras, NY, 2000.
32. Sumit Ganguly, "Explaining the Kashmir Insurgency: Political Mobilization and Institutional Decay, *International Security,* Vol. 21, no. 2, (Fall 1996).
33. South Asia Terrorism Portal.
34. According to various media reports.
35. Deepak Lal, 'KASHMIR', Paper for Carnegie project on Globalization, National self-determination, and Terrorism, UCLA, December, 2000, p. 3.

36. *Ibid*

37. Ved Marwah, *Uncivil Wars: Pathology of Terrorism in India,* Indus Publishers, New Delhi, 1995, p. 39.

38. Schofield, Victoria, Kashmir in Conflict: India, Pakistan and the Unfinished War, Tauras, NY, 2000, p. xv.

39. Sumit Ganguly, "Explaining the Kashmir Insurgency: Political Mobilization and Institutional Decay, *International Security,* Vol. 21, no. 2, (Fall 1996).

40. Rathnam Indurthy, 'Kashmir between India and Pakistan: An Intractable Conflict', 2000. *www1.appstate.edu/.../Kashmir%20Between%20India%20and%20Pakistan.pdf*

41. Sumit Ganguly, "Explaining the Kashmir Insurgency: Political Mobilization and Institutional Decay, *International Security,* Vol. 21, no. 2, (Fall 1996).

42. *Ibid.*

43. Riyaz Punjabi, "The concept of an Islamic Caliphate: The Religious and Ethnic pulls of Kashmir Militant Movement", *Journal of Peace Studies,* Vol. 1, No. 1, Nov.-Dec. 1993, p. 42.

44. K. Warikoo, "Religious Extremism and Terrorism in Kashmir", in Mahavir Singh (ed.), 2004, *International Terrorism and Religious Extremism,* Anamika Publishers, New Delhi, pp. 253-254.

45. *Ibid.,* p. 256.

46. K. Warikoo, "Islamist Extremism and Terrorism in Kashmir", in V.D. Chopra (ed.), *Rise of Terrorism and Secessionism in Eurasia,* Gyan Publishimg House, New Delhi. 2001, p. 126.

47. K. Warikoo, "Religious Extremism and Terrorism in Kashmir", in Mahavir Singh (ed.), *International Terrorism and Religious Extremism,* Anamika Publishers, New Delhi, 2004. p. 259.

48. K. Warikoo, "Islamist Extremism and Terrorism in Kashmir", in V.D. Chopra (ed.), *Rise of Terrorism and Secessionism in Eurasia,* Gyan Publishimg House, New Delhi, 2001. p. 128.

49. K. Alan Kronstadt & Bruce Vaughn, "Terrorism in South Asia", CRS Report for Congress, 8 March, 2004.

50. Deepak Lal, 'KASHMIR', Paper for Carnegie project on Globalization, National self-determination, and Terrorism, UCLA, December, 2000. p. 6.
51. Sumit Ganguly, "Explaining the Kashmir Insurgency: Political Mobilization and Institutional Decay", *International Security,* Vol. 21, no. 2, (Fall 1996).
52. Bir Good Gill, "India and the Problem of Cross Border Terrorism: Challenges in Kashmir", in Mahavir Singh (ed.), *International Terrorism and Religious Extremism,* Anamika Publishers, New Delhi, 2004, p. 276.
53. Brig. Chandra B. Khanduri, "The face of the proxy war in J&K", in V.D. Chopra (ed.), *Rise of Terrorism and Secessionism in Eurasia,* Gyan Publishing House, New Delhi, 2001, p. 121.
54. K. Warikoo, "Religious Extremism and Terrorism in Kashmir", in Mahavir Singh (ed.), *International Terrorism and Religious Extremism,* Anamika Publishers, New Delhi, 2004, p. 260.
55. Rajen Harshe, "Cross-Border Terrorism: Road Block to Peace Initiatives", *Economic and Political Weekly,* Vol. 38, No.35, p. 3624.
56. K. Warikoo, "Religious Extremism and Terrorism in Kashmir", in Mahavir Singh (ed.), *International Terrorism and Religious Extremism,* Anamika Publishers, New Delhi, 2004, p. 261.
57. K.P.S. Gill, 'Tackling Terrorism in Kashmir: Some Lessons from Recent History' in M.L. Sondhi (ed.), *Terrorism and Political Violence: A Sourcebook,* Har-Anand Publishers, New Delhi, 2000, p. 72.
58. Shaheen Akhtar, 'War on Terrorism and Kashmir Issue', *www.pu.edu.pk/polsc/jops/...pdf/SHAHEEN%20AKHTAR.pdf*
59. P.R. Kumaraswami, "Terrorism in South Asia: The Changing Trends", in P.R. Kumaraswami & Ian Copland (ed.), *South Asia: The Spectre of Terrorism,* Routledge, New Delhi, 2009. p. 19.
60. Wilson John, "Harkat-ul Jihad al- Islami" in Wilson John & Swati Parashar (ed.), *Terrorism in South East Asia: Implications for South Asia,* Pearson, New Delhi, 2005. p. 85.
61. www.satp.org
62. K. Warikoo, "Islamist Extremism and Terrorism in Kashmir", in V.D. Chopra (ed.), 2001, *Rise of Terrorism and Secessionism in Eurasia,* Gyan Publishimg House, New Delhi. p. 133.

63. Izzat Zaarudi, "The people of Kashmir", *Murj,* Vol. 6, 2002.
64. 'Yasin Malik, supporter held', *The Hindu,* June 19, 2010, New Delhi.
65. Sunil Sondhi, "Terrorism and Governance in Kashmir", *Journal of conflict Studies,* Vol. XXIV, No.2, Winter 2004.
66. S.P. Sinha, *Lost Opportunities,* Lancer Publications, New Delhi, 2007. p. xxiv.
67. Bethany Lacina, "The Problem of Political Stability in North East India", *Asian Survey,* Vol. XLIX, No. 6, Nov/Dec. 2009, pp. 1000-1001.
68. Quoted in Bethany Lacina, "Rethinking Delhi's North East India policy", Sanjib Baruah, ed. *Beyond Counter insurgency: Breaking the impasse in North East India,* Oxford, New Delhi, 2009, p. 331.
69. Bhagat Oinam, "Preparing for a cohesive North East: Problems of Discourse", Sanjib Baruah, ed., *Beyond Counter Insurgency: Breaking the impasse in North East India,* Oxford, New Delhi, 2009. p. 179.
70. S.K. Sinha, Violence and Hope in India's North East, *Faultline,* Jan 2002, p. 21.
71. Jaideep Saika, "Circle of design: Proxy wars in North East India", Jaideep Saika & Ekaterina Stepanova, eds. *Terrorism: Patterns of Internationalization,* Sage, New Delhi, 2009, pp. 142-143.
72. Wasbir Hussain, "Ethno-Nationalism and the Politics of Terror in India's Northeast", *South Asia: Journal of South Asian Studies,* Routledge, Vol.XXX, no. 1, April 2007, p. 94.
73. Sreeradha Dutta, *North East Complexities and it's Determinants,* Institute for Defence Studies and Analysis, New Delhi, 2004, p. 23.
74. Rajesh Rajagopalan, "Force and Compromise: India's Counter-Insurgency Grand Strategy", P.R. Kumaraswami and Ian Copland, ed., *South Asia: The Spectre of Terrorism,* Routledge, New Delhi, 2009, p. 88.
75. Sreeradha Dutta, *North East Complexities and it's Determinants,* Institute for Defence Studies and Analysis, New Delhi, 2004, p. 28.
76. *Ibid.* p. 33.
77. Jaideep Saika, "Circle of design: Proxy wars in North East India", Jaideep Saika & Ekaterina Stepanova, eds. *Terrorism: Patterns of Internationalization,* Sage, New Delhi, 2009, p. 143.

78. Sreeradha Dutta, *North East Complexities and it's Determinants,* Institute for Defence Studies and Analysis, New Delhi, 2004. p. 14.
79. Sreeradha Dutta, *North East Complexities and it's Determinants,* Institute for Defence Studies and Analysis, New Delhi, 2004. p. 27.
80. As quoted in *Ibid.*, p. 61.
81. Wasbir Hussain, Ethno-Nationalism and the Politics of Terror in India's Northeast, *South Asia: Journal of South Asian Studies,* Routledge, Vol.XXX, no. 1, April 2007, p. 96.
82. Ved Marwah, *Uncivil wars: pathology of terrorism in India,* Centre for Policy Resesarch, New Delhi, 1997, p. 270.
83. S.P. Sinha, *Lost Opportunities,* Lancer Publications, New Delhi, 2007, p. 72.
84. Ved Marwah, *Uncivil wars: pathology of terrorism in India,* Centre for Policy Resesarch, New Delhi, 1997, pp. 274-280.
85. Sreeradha Dutta, *North East Complexities and it's Determinants,* Institute for Defence Studies and Analysis, New Delhi, 2004, p. 121.
86. Wasbir Hussain, Ethno-Nationalism and the Politics of Terror in India's Northeast, *South Asia: Journal of South Asian Studies,* Routledge, Vol.XXX, no. 1, April 2007. p. 97.
87. Sanjib Baruah, *Durable Disorder: Understanding Politics of North East India,* Oxford, New Delhi, 2005, p. 102.
88. Sreeradha Dutta, *North East Complexities and it's Determinants,* Institute for Defence Studies and Analysis, New Delhi, 2004, pp. 42-43.
89. "Manipur, Assam continue to be hotbed of insurgency", *The Times of India,* April 3, 2010.
90. Sushanta Talukdar, "Victims of Crossfire", *Frontline,* vol. 21, 2004.
91. M.S. Prabhakara, "Insurgencies in Manipur: politics and Ideology", *The Hindu,* January 28, 2010.
92. "India: Army killings fuel emergency in Manipur", www.humanrightswatch.com
93. Praveen Swami, "Army and the Special powers", *Frontline,* vol. 21, 2004.
94. Sushanta Talukdar, "Victims of Crossfire", *Frontline,* vol. 21, 2004.
95. "Manipur, still a part of India", *Hindustan Times,* October 6, 2009.

96. "India: Army killings fuel emergency in Manipur", www.humanrightswatch.com
97. Sushant Talukdar, "Manipur on fire", *Frontline,* vol. 21, 2004.
98. Siddharth Vardhrajan, "Insult upon injury", *Frontline,* vol. 21, 2004.
99. Ved Marwah, *Uncivil wars: pathology of terrorism in India,* Centre for Policy Resesarch, New Delhi, 1997, p. 299.
100. H.N. Rafiabadi, *Assam: From Agitation to Accord*, Genuine Publications, New Delhi, 1988.
101. S.P. Sinha, *Lost Opportunities,* Lancer Publications, New Delhi, 2007, p. 164.
102. *Ibid.*, p. 159.
103. Ved Marwah, *Uncivil wars: pathology of terrorism in India,* Centre for Policy Resesarch, New Delhi, 1997, p. 312.
104. Sreeradha Dutta, *North East Complexities and it's Determinants,* Institute for Defence Studies and Analysis, New Delhi, 2004, p. 44.
105. Ved Marwah, *Uncivil wars: pathology of terrorism in India,* Centre for Policy Resesarch, New Delhi, 1997, p.314.
106. *Ibid.* pp. 233-237.
107. Sreeradha Dutta, *North East Complexities and it's Determinants,* Institute for Defence Studies and Analysis, New Delhi, 2004, p. 122.
108. M. Sajjad Hassan, "The Mizo Exception: State- Society Cohesion and Institutional Capability", Sanjib Baruah, ed., *Beyond Counter Insurgency: Breaking the impasse in North East India,* Oxford, New Delhi, 2009, p. 207.
109. Ajai Sahni, *Survey of conflicts and resolution in India's North East.* Accessed on 10.05.2010.http://www.satp.org/satporgtp/publication/faultlines/volume12/Article3.html.
110. Kunal Ghosh, *Terrorists in North-East India get support from America.* Accessed on 07.05.2010. www.mainstreamweekly.com.
111. S.P. Sinha, *Lost Opportunities,* Lancer Publications, New Delhi, 2007, p. 169.
112. *Ibid.*
113. As reported by different newspapers.

114. Ashima Jahangir, *States of Violence: Nature of Terrorism and Guerilla Warfare,* Dominant Publishers, New Delhi, 2000, pp. 139-140.
115. Rahul Karmakar, "Manipur's Boxer Army", *Hindustan Times,* August 22, 2004.
116. Quoted in Jaideep Saika, 'Circle of design: Proxy wars in North East India, Jaideep Saika & Ekaterina Stepanova, eds. *Terrorism: Patterns of Internationalization,* Sage, New Delhi, 2009.
117. S.P. Sinha, *Lost Opportunities,* Lancer Publications, New Delhi, 2007, p. 211.
118. Jaideep Saika, "Circle of design: Proxy wars in North East India", Jaideep Saika & Ekaterina Stepanova, eds. *Terrorism: Patterns of Internationalization,* Sage, New Delhi, 2009. p. 148.
119. *Ibid.*, pp. 146-147.
120. *Ibid.*, p. 149.
121. Jaideep Saika, "Circle of design: Proxy wars in North East India", Jaideep Saika & Ekaterina Stepanova, eds. *Terrorism: Patterns of Internationalization,* Sage, New Delhi, 2009. p. 154.
122. Jaideep Saika, *Terror Sans Frontiers,* Vision Publishers, New Delhi, 2004, p. 76.
123. Tara Kartha, *Tools of Terror: Light weapons and India's security,* Knowledge World, New Delhi, 1999, p. 254.
124. S.P. Sinha, *Lost Opportunities,* Lancer Publications, New Delhi, 2007, p. 238.
125. *Ibid.* p. 239.
126. *Ibid.* p. 241.
127. Ranjit K. Prachanda, *Terrorism and Response to Terrorist Threat,* UBS Publishers, New Delhi, 2002, p. 135.
128. www.satp.org.
129. Bethany Lacina, "Rethinking Delhi's North East India policy", Sanjib Baruah, ed. *Beyond Counter insurgency: Breaking the impasse in North East India,* Oxford, New Delhi, 2009, pp. 340-341.
130. S.P. Sinha, *Lost Opportunities,* Lancer Publications, New Delhi, 2007, p. 317.

131. *Ibid.* p.320.
132. Sreeradha Dutta, *North East Complexities and it's Determinants,* Institute for Defence Studies and Analysis, New Delhi, 2004, p. 142.
133. B.G. Verghese, *India's North East Resurgent,* Konark Publishers, New Delhi, 1996, p. 343.
134. *Ibid.* 343.
135. These figures are compiled by the South Asia Terrorism Portal .
136. Ved Marwah, *Uncivil wars: pathology of terrorism in India,* Centre for Policy Resesarch, New Delhi, 1997, p. 318.
137. Rahul Karmakar, "Manipur's Boxer Army", *Hindustan Times,* August 22, 2004.
138. E.N. Rammohan, *Insurgent Frontiers: essays from the troubled North East,* India Research Press, New Delhi, 2005. p. 140.
139. Praveen Swami, "Lashker-e-Taiba", in Wilson John & Swati Parashar (ed.), *Terrorism in South East Asia: Implications for South Asia,* Pearson, New Delhi, 2005, pp. 62-63.
140. *Ibid.* p. 78.
141. www.thaindia.com.
142. www.satp.org.
143. Bethany Lacina, "Rethinking Delhi's North East India policy", Sanjib Baruah, ed. *Beyond Counter insurgency: Breaking the impasse in North East India,* Oxford, New Delhi, 2009, p. 332.
144. S.P. Sinha, *Lost Opportunities,* Lancer Publications, New Delhi, 2007, p. 175.
145. Jaideep Saika, *Terror Sans Frontiers,* Vision Publishers, New Delhi, 2004, p. 16-17.
146. Bethany Lacina, "Rethinking Delhi's North East India policy", Sanjib Baruah, ed. *Beyond Counter insurgency: Breaking the impasse in North East India,* Oxford, New Delhi, 2009, pp. 336-337.

5

Combating Strategies

MAJOR EXISTING RULES AND REGULATIONS FOR ERADICATION OF TERRORISM IN INTERNATIONAL ARENA

The fight against terrorism is not new. The laws for checking terrorist acts date back to the times of League of Nations. In the 1960s and 1970s, the first UN treaties were made in connection with the then prevalent phenomenon of hijacking and hostage-taking.

In the domestic field, the countries have taken resort to several measures, by implementing special anti-terrorism legislation in an attempt to solve the problem. Various regional groups have also taken anti terrorism measures to strengthen their security.

The 1937 Convention on the Prevention and Punishment of Terrorism and an associated Convention on the establishment of an International Criminal Court were first major efforts in this direction but it never came into force.[1] The provisions of this convention broadly enclosed five major areas. They were:

i. The principle of non use of territory for terrorist activities against another state.

ii. Definition of terrorism

iii. Recognition of acts of terrorism committed within one state against another state, which are to be regarded as criminal offences.

iv. An extradition regime

v. International cooperative measures to prevent acts of terrorism.

The capacity of the convention was limited to enclose only acts of terrorism of 'an international character.'[2]

Legislation in United Nations Organisation

The issue of terrorism was first introduced in the United Nations in the early 1970s at a time when Europe had become the epicentre of terrorist activity. On December 18, 1972, the United Nations General Assembly at its 27th Session adopted resolution 3034 on international terrorism. This resolution had a twofold approach of emphasizing on effective cooperative measures among states to combat terrorism and focusing on the need to study and eradicate terrorism.[3]

Resolution 1373 and the Counter-Terrorism Committee

After the September 2001 attacks terrified the world, the Security Council adopted Resolution 1373. This resolution allowed the Council to take measures for international peace and security. The Member states also need to give their obedience. The resolution does not define "terrorism" and leaves each state to define the term by itself. Resolution 1373, which was an idea of the United States, represents exercise of an "unparalleled" scheme that reacts to the actions of September 2001 and call for observance with existing international laws dealing with terrorism. It also makes new, obligatory set of laws of international character that are not restricted in time. This Resolution requires member states to check the financing for terrorist acts and to freeze assets or resources of persons who are involved in the charge of terrorist acts. It also asks to make illegal the making of any assets, resources, or services available to persons who commit or are involved in the commission of terrorist acts, and to make separate, "serious criminal offenses" proscribing "terrorist acts" under domestic law. The Resolution established the Counter-Terrorism Committee, which composed of all fifteen Council members. It called upon states to inform about their progress of implementation to the CTC within 90 days and thereafter from time to time. The resolution did not give any further details about the CTC's mandate, leaving the CTC itself to describe its agenda and approach. States have taken the resolution more seriously and have been implementing the measures. Observance with the resolution's requirements has been higher than with previous Security Council mandates with the states having responded positively to the CTC's effort to support sanction of existing international antiterrorism conventions and protocols.[4] Thus the resolution calls on states to take action rapidly to the CTC's requirements for information, remarks and questions, and instructs the CTC to report to the Council of the development, or any difficulty it encounters.[5]

Legislation in USA

In the efforts for eradication of the menace of terrorism, nations of the world have come forward to fight against terrorism. The US is leading this war on terrorism. The legislation in U.S.A. was modified to effectively curtail the crimes of terrorism, the most noticeable of which was the introduction of the Patriot Act. Earlier during President Clinton's administration, an extension was undertaken in 1995 by issuing a presidential decree within the structure of the implementation of the International Emergency Economic Powers Act (IEEPA).

Patriot Act

Providing Appropriate Tools Required to Intercept and Obstruct Terrorism Act, known as the USA PATRIOT Act 2001, is the domestic legislation of the USA to curb the terrorist act. Since its passage after the September 11, 2001 attacks, the Patriot Act has played a key role in controlling the violence through a number of successful operations. In passing The Patriot Act, Congress did very humble and incremental alterations in the law. It took already existing legal doctrines and retrofitted them to safeguard the lives and liberty of the American people from the global terrorist network. The USA PATRIOT Act gives the officials larger authority to track and capture communications for law enforcement and foreign intelligence gathering purposes. It vests the Secretary of the Treasury with regulatory powers to combat corruption of U.S. financial institutions for foreign money laundering purposes.

This Act defines "terrorism" as activities that:

- Involve violent acts or acts dangerous to human life that are a violation of the criminal laws of the United States or of any State, or that would be criminal violation if committed within the jurisdiction of the United State or of any State;
- Appear to be intended to intimidate or coerce a civilian population; to influence the policy of a government by intimidation or coercion; or to affect the conduct of a government by mass destruction, assassination, or kidnapping.[6]

These activities can be termed as international or domestic terrorism according to their occurrences, whether outside or within the territorial jurisdiction of the US.

The Act defines "terrorist organisation" as a group designated under the Immigration and Nationality Act or by the Secretary of State as a group of two or more individuals, whether related or not, which engages in terrorist-related activities (this includes providing material support to terrorists or soliciting funds for terrorist organisations).[7] The US has several mechanisms whereby it can designate terrorists or terrorist organisations. All have severe legal implications in terms of blocking property, restricting access to support or funds, or providing grounds for blocking entry to the US or in some circumstances for deportation. Designating Foreign Terrorist Organisations (FTO) under Section 219 of the Immigration and Nationality Act (as amended by the 1996 Anti-Terrorism and Effective Death Penalty Act) makes it unlawful for a person in the United States or subject to the jurisdiction of the United States to knowingly provide material support or resources to a designated FTO. Representatives and members of a designated FTO, if they are not US citizens, are inadmissible to and, in certain circumstances, removable from the United States. Any U.S. financial institution that becomes aware that it has possession of or control over funds in which a designated FTO or its agent has an interest must retain possession of or control over the funds and report this to the Federal government.

Section 411 of the USA PATRIOT Act allows for the insertion of organisations on the Terrorism Exclusion List (TEL). Non-US citizens linked with TEL-designated organisations cannot be allowed to visit the U.S. This can be the consequence of association with a TEL-designated organisation; enjoying such position of reputation within any country to influence others to support an organisation on the TEL list; solicitation of funds, or providing material support to an organisation on the TEL list.[8]

Executive Order 13224, signed by President George W Bush on September 23 2001, declared a state of national emergency. All property and interests in property of designated individuals were blocked. Through this order, any transaction by US persons or within the US, in property or interests is prohibited. Any deal by any US person or within the US that seeks to abuse any of the prohibitions in the Order is barred. Any conspiracy formed to violate any of the prohibitions is also outlawed. Also, under the Intelligence Reform and Terrorism Prevention Act of 2004, aliens involved in or inciting genocide, torture or extrajudicial killing are inadmissible and deportable.

The USA PATRIOT Act was noteworthy in widening the scope of existing surveillance powers on the terrorist crimes like chemical-weapons offences, the use of weapons of mass destruction and terrorism financing. The Act also provides federal agents with more powers to investigate suspected terrorists.

The USA PATRIOT Act restructured the US Penal Code relating to terrorism and set new penalties on those who commit and support terrorist operations, both at home and abroad.

The USA PATRIOT Act gives the Attorney General the power to detain foreigners suspected of terrorism and delineates the process by which detentions are to be reviewed. Where the Attorney General exercises his power to detain foreigners suspected of terrorism, the

USA PATRIOT Act requires him to have reasonable grounds to believe that the individual has or will commit espionage or sabotage; attempt to overthrow the government; has or will commit terrorist acts; or is otherwise engaged in activities that threaten national security. Following detention the Attorney General must place the individual in removal proceedings or level criminal charges within 7 days of commencement of detention. In situations where deportation within the reasonably foreseeable future is unlikely, the individuals may be detained for additional periods of up to six months only if their release will threaten the national security of the US or the safety of the community or any other person. The Attorney General is required to review the initial certification every six months. Each individual has the right to request a review every six months and is permitted to present evidence in support of the request. If the individual in question is finally determined not to be removable, on the above grounds, they must be released.[9]

Federal Communications Privacy Law

This law has a three tiered system for the dual purpose of protecting the privacy of private telephone and computer communications while enabling authorities to recognize and capture criminal communications. The Crime Control and Safe Streets Act of 1968 s give authorities right to electronic surveillance, which is to be used as a last resort in serious criminal cases. Law enforcement officers may seek a court order authorizing them to secretly intercept conversations concerning any of the offenses.

The Act eases some of the limitations on foreign intelligence gathering within the United States and gives the U.S. intelligence greater access to information revealed during a criminal investigation. But at the same time, it also establishes and expands safeguards against official abuse. More specifically, it permits roving surveillance (court orders omitting the identification of the particular instrument, facilities, or place where the surveillance is to occur when the court finds the target is likely to thwart identification with particularity). The Act contains a number of provisions to prevent alien terrorists from entering the United States.

The Act creates new crimes for attacks on mass transportation facilities, for biological weapons offenses, for harboring terrorists, for giving terrorists material support, for money laundering, for conducting the affairs of an enterprise which affects interstate or foreign commerce through the commission of terrorist offenses and for fake charity.

The Act increases the penalties for acts of terrorism and for crimes, which terrorists might commit. It creates maximum penalty for acts of terrorism, raises the penalties for plotting to commit certain terrorist offenses, envisions sentencing some terrorists to life-long imprisonment, and increases the penalties for counterfeiting, cyber-crime, and charity fraud.

Legislation in France

France has a civil law legal system under which the French Constitution of 4 October 1958 is the founding text. France is a dualist system, requiring domestic legislation to give effect to international treaties. Acts of terrorism are a criminal offence and are set out in Articles 421-1 et seq. of the Penal Code (as amended in Law 96-647 of 22 July 1996). The offences which constitute acts of terrorism are those which are committed intentionally and undertaken with the intention of troubling the public order through terror by various means like determined attacks on life, on the physical integrity of persons, abduction, hijacking, theft, extortion, destruction, and damage. It also includes the production or keeping or sale or transport of machines, dangerous or explosive devices or substances and the detention, carrying and transport of weapons and ammunition. The offences related to the prohibition of the designing, production, keeping, stocking, purchase or sale of biological or toxin-based weapons also comes under the purview.

The financing of a terrorist organization directly or indirectly is also known to constitute the act of terrorism. The law also mentions the introduction into the environment of any substance likely to endanger human or animal health or the natural environment with the aim of seriously disturbing public order through fear or terror. Money laundering or trading relating to terrorist activities and close contacts with a person or persons who engage in terrorist activities, also constitute the terrorist offences.

In 1986 a section within the Trial Court of Paris of prosecutors and examining magistrates was created, which has proficiency in cases of terrorism. A local prosecutor decides whether a crime committed in his area of responsibility is related to terrorism and if so, refers the case to the special section of the Paris Court. There the examining magistrate conducts an investigation to determine whether there is a case to send to trial. The examining magistrate is empowered to carry out a wide range of acts. These may be delegated to the police authorities where appropriate. The prosecution, suspect and victim/civil parties can request that the examining magistrate carry out particular investigative acts, and can appeal against a refusal to do so. Once the investigation and examination are complete, the examining magistrate decides whether there is enough evidence to send the case for trial. The prosecutor and civil parties can appeal against a decision not to send the case for trial. In practice, the creation of the special counter-terrorism section of the Paris court has resulted in the establishment of specific and expert counterterrorism magistrates. This system also supports close working between investigating magistrates and the domestic French intelligence agency.

France has introduced a number of laws like laws on interception of electronic communications, use of video surveillance, biometric checks and the introduction of a computerised database holding data files on individuals. Another law determines conspiracy to commit terrorist acts to also be a terrorist act. Together they make a strong case for investigating possible terrorist activity through the targeting of logistics networks that support terrorists.

After the attacks of 11 September 2001, the statutory provisions seeking to prevent money laundering were extended to the fight against financing of terrorism. There exist a number of national agencies intended to counter money laundering as it relates to terrorist finance. These include the Cell for the repression of serious financial delinquency (OCRGDF), the Cell for treating information and action against clandestine financial networks (TRACFIN) and the Cell for the fight against financing of terrorism (FINATER). The Monetary and Financial Code provides that a Declaration of suspicion must be made whenever funds "may be used for the financing of terrorism". This obligation lies upon credit establishments, financial institutions, insurers, notaries, real estate agents, advocates, auditors, official auctioneers, sellers of works of art, of antiques, and of precious stones, the legal representatives and managers of casinos, and welfare insurance institutions.

Exceptions for terrorist offences are made under the Code of Criminal Procedure in relation to initial custody, pre-trial detention for certain conspiracy cases, searches and the limitation period. The initial custody time limits to those being questioned in relation to a terrorist act can be extended. The normal custody period of 48 hours can be extended by two further periods of 24 hours. The extensions must be necessary for the purposes of the enquiries and must be authorised by a judge. The person held in custody may only speak with a lawyer after 72 hours. The lawyer may not make known that such a meeting took place to any third party throughout the duration of the custody. This obligation is not limited to the derogation relating to matters of terrorism and has already given rise to criminal sanctions for lawyers who have breached this provision. Under Law *Perben II*, certain types of secret investigative methods in the investigation of organised crime and terrorism are permitted. This law broke new ground in the fight against organized crime. As part of the new procedure that defines organized crime by means of an offense catalog, special judicial panels have been established and special investigative measures allowed. Existing investigative measures have been expanded and new measures introduced.[10]

Legislation in Pakistan

IN 1997, Pakistan adopted the Anti-Terrorism Act, 1997. It was intended to provide for the prevention of terrorism and sectarian violence. The 1997 Anti-Terrorism Act also prevents people convicted and sentenced from using their right to appeal. Section 31 prohibits the appellate process in the judiciary. It says: 'A judgment or order passed, or sentence awarded, by a special court, subject to the result of an appeal under this act shall be final and shall not be called in question in any court.' This excludes the possibility of appealing to the regular high courts and the Supreme Court of Pakistan.

The right to shoot to kill 1997 Anti-Terrorism Act Under Section 5(2)(1): an officer of the police, armed forces and civil armed forces may: (i) after giving prior warning use such force as may be deemed necessary or appropriate, bearing in mind all the facts and circumstances of the situation, against any person who is committing, or in all probability is likely to commit a terrorist act or a scheduled offence, and it shall be lawful for any such officer, or any superior officer, to fire, or order the firing upon any person or persons against whom he is authorized to use force in terms hereof.

This act was amended in 1999 by the 1999 Anti- Terrorism Ordinance. As amended by it, a terrorist act is defined as follows, Terrorist Act – A person is said to commit a terrorist act if he, (*a*) in order to, or if the effect of his actions will be to, strike terror or create a sense of fear and insecurity in the people, or any section of the people, does any act or thing by using bombs, dynamite or other explosive or inflammable substances, or such fire-arms or other lethal weapons as may be notified, or poisons or noxious gases or chemicals, in such a manner as to cause, or be likely to cause, the death of, or injury to, any person or persons, of the people; or damage to, or destruction of, property on a large scale, or a widespread disruption of supplies of services essential to the life of the community, or threatens with the use of force public servants in order to prevent them from discharging their lawful duties; or (*b*) commits a scheduled offence, the effect of which will be, or be likely to be, to strike terror, or create a sense of fear and insecurity in the people, or any section of the people, or to adversely affect harmony among different sections of the people; or (*c*) commits an act of gang rape, child molestation, or robbery coupled with rape as specified in the Schedule to this Act; or (*d*) commits an act of civil commotion as specified in section 7A.'[11]

As a result, the adoption of these anti-terrorism laws has included a large number of criminal acts covered under the Pakistan Penal Code as terrorist offences. In 2002, ordinance was issued for the inclusion of military officers in the panel of judges to try terrorist offences. This not only undermined the independence of the judiciary but made the anti-terror law in the country even more draconian. These anti-terrorism laws opened the door to grave violations of human rights including the right to life, the prohibition of torture, the right to liberty and security and the right to fair trial. They provide for the establishment of anti-terrorist courts and give wide powers of arrest and interrogation to the police and army. This provision violates the principle of equality before law laid down in the Constitution of Pakistan.

Legislation in Britain

Though the British government passed permanent counter-terrorism legislation only a year earlier, in the shape of the Terrorism Act 2000, however in the wake of September 11, 2001 attacks, it instantly rushed to legislate to enlarge powers to deal with persons suspected of planning or assisting terrorist attacks within the UK. Thus Anti-terrorism, Crime and Security Act 2001 was passed. A key feature of this bill is that resident foreigners suspected of terrorism could be interned without trial, if they could not be deported to another country without breaching British human rights.

The Counter-Terrorism Act 2008[12]

It is an Act of the Parliament of Britain which widened the police powers for the purpose of countering terrorism.

Provisions of the Act:

- Removal of the prohibition on post-charge questioning.
- Longer terrorism sentences.
- A register and monitoring for those convicted of terrorism related offences.
- Changes to some of the rules surrounding the use of "intercept evidence".

- Powers to seize the assets of convicted terrorists.
- Police will be able to remove documents from a property search to decide whether or not they need to be legally seized as part of an investigation.
- Greater use of DNA samples, and powers to allow the police to take fingerprints or DNA from those subject to a control order (these orders are civil restraints, not criminal offences).
- Any person found guilty faces 10 years imprisonment and an unlimited fine. It is a defence for a person charged with this offence to prove that they had a reasonable excuse for their action. There are exemptions for communications service providers, web caches and web hosting services.

Major Anti –Terrorism Laws in India

India's anti-terrorism laws have been shaped by domestic political background which has evolved over many decades. In the aftermath of the September 2001 terrorist attacks, the debate in India has been influenced significantly by the anti-terrorism initiatives of other countries, including the United States, and the U.N. Security Council. The laws have become much more rigorous to curb such activities. The Indian outlook changed specifically after the 13 December attack on the Indian parliament.

India is facing diverse challenges in the management of its internal security. There is an expansion of terrorist activities, growth of cross border terrorist activities and insurgent groups in different parts of the country. In view of this situation it was felt necessary to enact legislation for the prevention of and for dealing with terrorist activities.

History of anti-terrorism laws in India

The legal and institutional framework that independent India inherited from the British to govern criminal law largely remains in place today. Police matters are governed primarily by the Police Act of 1861. Enduring the same model established by the British, India's anti-terrorism and other security laws have periodically been enacted, repealed, and re-enacted in the years since independence.[13]

The first law made in independent India to deal with terrorism and terrorist activities that came into force on 30 Dec 1967 was the Unlawful Activities (Prevention) Act 1967. The UAPA was planned to deal with associations and activities that questioned the territorial integrity of India. The National Integration Council appointed a Committee on National Integration and Regionalization to look into the aspect of putting reasonable restrictions in the interests of the sovereignty and integrity of India. With the acceptance of recommendations of the Committee, the Constitution (Sixteenth Amendment) Act, 1963 was enacted to impose reasonable restrictions in the interests of the sovereignty and integrity of India; on the Freedom of Speech and Expression; Right to assemble peaceably and without arms; and Right to Form Associations or Unions. The purpose of this Bill was to widen the powers for dealing with actions intended against the integrity and sovereignty of India. *The Bill was passed by both the Houses of Parliament and received the assent of the President on 30 December 1967.*

The sphere of the Act was strictly limited in dealing with the challenge to the territorial integrity of India. The Act contained various laws which declared secessionist associations as unlawful, and imposed penalties on their members etc. The Act is completely within the purview of the central list in the 7th Schedule of the Constitution.

The Armed Forces (Special Powers) Act

The Armed Forces (Special Powers) Act of 1958 (AFSPA) is one of the most draconian legislations that the Indian Parliament has made. Under this Act, all security forces are given unrestricted power to carry out their operations, once an area is declared disturbed. Even a non-commissioned officer is granted the right to shoot to kill based on mere suspicion that it is necessary to do so in order to "maintain the public order".

It was later extended to Jammu and Kashmir as the The Armed Forces (Jammu and Kashmir) Special Powers Act, 1990 in July 1990.

According to the Armed Forces Special Powers Act (AFSPA), in an area that is proclaimed as "disturbed", an officer of the armed forces has powers to:

- "Fire upon or otherwise use force, even to the causing of death, against any person who is acting in contravention of any law" against "assembly of five or more persons" or possession of deadly weapons.
- To arrest without a warrant and with the use of "necessary" force anyone who has committed certain offenses or is suspected of having done so.
- To enter and search any premise in order to make such arrests.

It gives Army officers legal immunity for their actions. There can be no prosecution, suit or any other legal proceeding against anyone acting under that law. Nor is the government's judgment on why an area is found to be "disturbed", subject to judicial review.[14]

The Act And Its Provisions[15]

Section 1: This section states the name of the Act and the areas to which it extends.

Section 2: This section sets out the definition of the Act, but leaves much un-defined. Under part (a) in the 1972 version, the armed forces were defined as "the military and Air Force of the Union so operating". In the 1958 version of the Act, the definition was of the "military forces and the air forces operating as land forces". Section 2(b) defines a "disturbed area" as any area declared as such under Clause 3. Section 2(c) states that all other words not defined in the AFSPA have the meanings assigned to them in the Army Act of 1950.

Section 3: This section defines "disturbed area" by stating how an area can be declared disturbed. It grants the power to declare an area disturbed to the Central Government and the Governor of the State, but does not describe the circumstances under which the authority would be justified in making such a declaration. Rather, the AFSPA only requires that such authority be "of the opinion that whole or parts of the area are in a dangerous or disturbed condition such that the use of the Armed Forces in aid of civil powers is necessary." However, since the declaration depends on the satisfaction of the Government official, the declaration that an area is disturbed is not subject to judicial review. So in practice, it is only the government's understanding which classifies an area as disturbed. There is no mechanism for the people to challenge this opinion.

The 1972 amendments to the / FSPA extended the power to declare an area disturbed to the Central Government. In the 1958 version of the AFSPA only the state governments had this power.

Section 4: This section sets out the powers granted to the military stationed in a disturbed area. These powers are granted to the commissioned officer, warrant officer, or non-commissioned officer, only a jawan (private) does not have these powers. The Section allows the armed forces personnel to use force for a variety of reasons.

The army can shoot to kill, under the powers of section 4(a), for the commission or suspicion of the commission of the following offenses: acting in contravention of any law or order for the time being in force in the disturbed area prohibiting the assembly of five or more persons, carrying weapons, or carrying anything which is capable of being used as a fire-arm or ammunition. To justify the invocation of this provision, the officer need only be "of the opinion that it is necessary to do so for the maintenance of public order" and only give "such due warning as he may consider necessary".

The army can destroy property under section 4(b) if it is an arms dump, a fortified position or shelter from where armed attacks are made or are suspected of being made, if the structure is used as a training camp or as a hide-out by armed gangs or absconders.

The army can arrest anyone without a warrant under section 4(c), who has committed, is suspected of having committed or of being about to commit, a cognizable offense and use any amount of force "necessary to effect the arrest".

Under section 4(d), the army can enter and search without a warrant to make an arrest or to recover any property, arms, ammunition or explosives which are believed to be unlawfully kept on the premises. This section also allows the use of force necessary for the search.

Section 5: This section states that after the military has arrested someone under the AFSPA, they must hand that person over to the nearest police station with the "least possible delay". There is no definition in the act of what constitutes the least possible delay.

Section 6: This section establishes that no legal proceeding can be brought against any member of the armed forces acting under the AFSPA, without the permission of the Central Government. This section leaves the victims of the armed forces abuses without a remedy.

The use of the AFSPA pushes the demand for more autonomy, giving the peoples of the particular area more reason to want to secede. Under section 4(a) of the AFSPA, which grants armed forces personnel the power to shoot to kill, the constitutional right to life is violated. This law is not reasonable because it allows the armed forces to use an undue amount of force. This contradicts Article 14 of the Indian Constitution which guarantees equality before the law. This article guarantees that "the State shall not deny to any person equality before the law or the equal protection of the laws within the territory of India." The AFSPA is in place in limited parts of India. Since the people residing in areas declared "disturbed" are denied the protection of the right to life and prohibited from seeking judicial redress, they are also denied equality before the law. The AFSPA has allowed the security forces to imprison people for months. In its application, the AFSPA does lead to arbitrary detention. If the AFSPA were defended on the grounds that it is a preventive detention law, it would still violate Article 22 of the Constitution. Preventive detention laws can allow the detention of the arrested person for up to three months. Under AFSPA a person can be arrested by the armed forces without a warrant and on the mere suspicion that they are going to commit an offence. The armed forces are not obliged to communicate the grounds for the arrest. There is also no advisory board in place to review arrests made under the AFSPA. Since the arrest is without a warrant it violates the preventive detention sections of article 22.

Terrorist and Disruptive Activities (Prevention) Act, 1987 (TADA)

This act came into force on 3 September 1987. This act had much more harsh provisions than the UAPA and it was purposely designed to deal with terrorist activities in India. When TADA was enacted it came to be challenged before the Apex Court of the country as being unconstitutional. The Supreme Court of India upheld its constitutional validity on the grounds that those entrusted with such draconic statutory powers would act for the public good. However, there were many instances of misuse of power for security purposes. The rigorous provisions contained in the statute came to be abused in the hands of law enforcement officials. TADA lapsed in 1995.

Maharashtra Control of Organized Crime Act, 1999 (MCOCA)

Other major Anti-terrorist law in India is The Maharashtra Control of Organized Crime Act, 1999 which was enforced on 24th April 1999. This law was specifically made to deal with rising organized crime in Maharashtra. The definition of a terrorist act can be widely interpreted in MCOCA. MCOCA not only mentions organized crime, but also includes 'promotion of insurgency' as a terrorist act. Under the Maharashtra law, a person is presumed guilty unless he is able to prove his innocence. MCOCA does not stipulate prosecution of police officers found guilty of its misuse.

Prevention of Terrorist Activities Act (POTA)

In 2002, the Prevention of Terrorist Activities Act was introduced in the Indian parliament and it was greeted with resistance throughout India as the Act violated most of the fundamental rights provided in the Indian constitution. The makers of the Act have, argued that it has been effective in ensuring the speedy trial of those accused of indulging in terrorism.

The Act replaced the Prevention of Terrorism Ordinance (POTO) of 2001 and the Terrorist and Disruptive Activities (Prevention) Act. The Act provided the legal structure to strengthen executive rights to fight terrorism within the country of India and was to be applied against any individual. The Act defined a terrorist act and a terrorist and grants special powers to the investigating authorities described under the Act. To ensure the misuse of power and violation of human rights specific safeguards were made in the act. Under the law, detention of a suspect for up to 180 days without the filing of charges in court was permitted. It also allowed law enforcement agencies to withhold the identities of witnesses and treat a confession made to the police as an admission of guilt. Under regular Indian law, a person can deny such confessions in court, but not under POTA.

Once the Act became law there emerged many reports of the law being misused. POTA legislation contributed to corruption within the Indian administration system. Human rights groups protested against it. On September 17, 2004 the Union Cabinet in keeping with the UPA government's Common Minimum Programme, repealed the controversial Prevention of Terrorism Act, 2002 and amended the Unlawful Activities (Prevention) Act, 1967.

Repealation of Pota and Amendments to UAPA

By the promulgation of Ordinance No.1 of 2004, it repealed POTA, a law specially designed to deal with the peril of terrorism.[16]

By Ordinance No 2 almost all the penal provisions of POTA concerning terrorist organisations and activities were transferred to the already existing soft Unlawful Activities (Prevention) Act, 1967 (UAPA). By Ordinance No 2, the definition of unlawful association has been expanded to also include any association which has for its object any activity which is punishable under Section 153A of the Indian Penal Code, or which encourages or aids persons to undertake any such activity, or of which the members undertake any such activity. Section 153A is about promoting enmity between different groups on grounds of religion, race, place of birth, residence, language, etc. There would be no arrests made after the ordinance is promulgated. Among the special provisions dropped are those restricting release on bail and allowing longer periods of police remand for the accused. Now suspected terrorists may roam free under the bail.

All terrorist organizations banned under POTA remain banned, under the Unlawful Activities Act, after the repeal of the Act.

Some of the clauses contained in POTA, which were left out in the amended Unlawful Activities Act, are: the obligation on the accused to prove his innocence, necessary denial of bail to accused and admission as evidence in the court of law, the confession made by the accused before the police officer.

Another difference from POTA is that government has removed all traces of strict accountability. The responsibility of proof has transferred from the accused to the police. There is no presupposition of guilt under UAPA. The police will have to prove that the accused person had a criminal objective for committing the said offence.

Unlawful Activities (Prevention) Amendment Act, 2004

The Act does not define the word terrorist but defines a terrorist act. Terrorist act is defined in the Act as – "Whoever, with intent to threaten the unity, integrity, security or sovereignty of India or to strike terror in the people or any section of the people in India or in any foreign country, does any act by using bombs, dynamite or other explosive substances or inflammable substances or firearms or other lethal weapons or poisons or noxious gases or other chemicals or by any other substances (whether biological or otherwise) of a hazardous nature, in such a manner as to cause, or likely to cause, death of, or injuries to any person or persons or loss of, or damage to, or destruction of, property or disruption of any supplies or services essential to the life of the community in India or in any foreign country or causes damage or destruction of any property or equipment used or intended to be used for the defense of India or in connection with any other purposes of the Government of India, any State Government or any of their agencies, or detains any person and threatens to kill or injure such person in order to compel the Government in India or the Government of a foreign country or any other person to do or abstain from doing any act, commits a terrorist act.". The above definition was absent in the 1967 Act. The previous Act only defined and dealt with unlawful activity. An unlawful activity includes an activity which intends to bring about cession of a part of the territory of India or the secession of a part of the territory of India from the Union, or which incites any individual or group of individuals to bring about such cession or secession; or which disclaims, questions, disrupts or is intended to disrupt the sovereignty and territorial integrity of India, or which causes or is intended to cause disaffection against India Section 2(o).[17]

Pretrial imprisonment extended up to 180 days giving unlimited powers to investigating agencies to detain people without a fair trial, in which the possibility of false evidence increases. For taking cognizance of any offence under this Act prior sanction of the Central or the State government is necessary. Criminal Procedure Code, 1973, is made applicable in matters of arrest, bail, confessions and burden of proof. Those arrested are to be brought before a magistrate within 24 hours, confessions are no longer admissible before police officers and bail need not be denied for the first three months. The presumption of innocence leaving the burden of proof on the prosecution has also been restored. Search can be conducted at any time of a house of any person on the basis of any document, article or any other thing which may furnish evidence of the omission of such an offence. This overrides the basic fundamental right of due process of law as laid down under the Constitution and the Criminal P.C. This amendment overrides the provisions of Cr PC (section 43 C). All offences mentioned in the Act allow arrest without warrant, and searches without orders of the Court.[18]

Chapter VI of the amended Act gives power to the Central government under section 35 to add or remove an organization in the schedule as a terrorist organization. Under section 36, an application can also be made to remove an organization from the schedule. Such an application can be made by an organization or any affected person.

Voices have been raised by Human Right activists in the name of constitution, constitutional provisions, and equality before law and civil rights. The law has also provided for the prevention of the misuse of the law by ensuring numerous safeguards against the unscrupulous investigating officers. This law is softer than the previous anti-terrorism laws in India and has no discretionary authority to deal with a various kinds of terrorist activity. UAPA is more draconian than POTA when it comes to cyber evidences like e-communication. The police can now produce these evidences in the court without resorting to the safeguards provided by the repealed law. Thus, if the police cannot produce confession in custody, they have been given more possibility than before to make evidence in the form of interceptions. There is also contradiction in the provision for banning terrorist organisations and unlawful organisations. UAPA originally banned unlawful organisations. Now, it has included terrorist organisations also. Thus, the dealings agreed upon by the same law for the two kinds of bans are different. But the problem lies in the procedure for banning a group on the charge of terrorism which is easier than to ban it on the milder charge of unlawful activities. The government cannot ban any group for unlawful activities without having its decision ratified within six months by a judicial tribunal headed by a sitting high court judge. There is no such requirement if the ban is on the charge of terrorism. This variance has arisen because of the strategy adopted by the UPA government to hide special provisions in an ordinary law.

The National Investigation Agency Bill, 2008 (NIA)

It seeks to set up Special Courts to investigate and prosecute offences affecting "the sovereignty, security and integrity of India" clearly for quick trials. The NIA can investigate an offense in response to a request from a State Government or on a suo motu direction of the Central Government. Prior to this bill, since law and order is a state subject, the Centre could intervene only upon a request being made from State Governments. It could not suo motu take up offences for investigation. The NIA Bill now permits the Centre to take over the prosecution or investigation of an offense.

Thus, though prior to this Act offences could be investigated only upon (1) orders from Court or (2) consent of the State, this is no longer true and the CBI has now been entrusted with enormous powers.[19]

The NIA Act provides for a Schedule of Central acts covering offences against the State, namely terrorism, atomic energy, anti-hijacking, weapons of mass destruction etc., all of which fall within the domain of the Centre, empowering the agency to act on these offences.

The phrase "affecting the sovereignty, security and integrity of India" is not clear and the vagueness of the terms has made the scope open for the arrest of any individual. Thus, a mere criticism of the State could bring a citizen under the purview of both the NIA Act and the UAPA. These two Acts seek to undermine and strip the fundamental right to free expression.

Preventive Detention Laws

The Indian Constitution unambiguously authorizes preventive detention during non-emergency periods. There are limited procedural safeguards. The Constitution grants both the central and state governments power to legislate on preventive detention. Preventive detention does not extend beyond three months without approval of an "Advisory Board." The detainee must be told the basis for detention and have an opportunity to challenge the detention order. Parliament may specify circumstances justifying extended detention without Advisory Board review, and the detaining authority may withhold any information if it deems disclosure against the "public interest." Preventive detention laws also are explicitly excused from complying with other constitutional protections, such as the right to counsel, to be produced before a magistrate within 24 hours of being taken into custody, or to be informed promptly of the grounds for arrest. Parliament had enacted the Preventive Detention Act of 1950, which authorized detention for up to 12 months by both the central and state governments if necessary to prevent an individual from acting in a manner prejudicial to the defence or security of India, India's relations with foreign powers, state security or maintenance of public order, or maintenance of essential supplies and services.[20]

Initially, the PDA was to expire after one year. The bill was a temporary expedient, proposed only to address difficult circumstances after independence and partition. However, this "temporary expedient" was routinely re-enacted each year for almost 20 years. While it finally lapsed in 1969, preventive detention authority returned less than two years later under the Maintenance of Internal Security Act, which largely restored the provisions of the PDA. [21]

ROLE OF INTELLIGENCE

Intelligence is a key to success in the fight against terrorism. Without adequate intelligence it is not possible to counter it. We are at such a war which has an enemy that has no infrastructure to attack, and no geographic boundaries. As Robert Baer observes, "The only way to defeat such an enemy is by intelligence, by knowing that what they plan to do next, and where they might launch their next attack from." [22] The U.S. National Commission on Terrorism stated that no other single policy effort is more important for preventing, pre-empting and responding to such attack than intelligence.[23] Thus, intelligence is a vital pre-requisite for a successful outcome of counter measures against a movement. Prior knowledge of the plans and lines of action to be followed by one side can give a tremendous advantage to the other in the outcome of the conflict. The US Congress Report of the National Commission on Terrorism stressed that "good intelligence is the best weapon against international terrorism." It should be remarked that intelligence in the field of counter-terrorism is different, and in many aspects a more arduous task, than the classical intelligence, military and political, against enemy or rival states as the lives of many people are in continuous danger.[24] Operations to counter terrorism and insurgency depend largely on timely accurate intelligence. So, in order to defeat any political terrorists campaign, it is imperative that high quality intelligence be developed.

Intelligence is a product, process and organization. Intelligence, as a process, offers the law enforcement a coherent, rational, and consistent methodology in dealing with terrorism. Intelligence is also the end product of the information, which has been subject to the intelligence process. The meaning of development of intelligence is wide apart from traditional investigative work. Although the two are interrelated, the investigative reporting is evidentiary in nature and the intelligence reporting should be viewed as an early warning system. Intelligence provides foreknowledge and warning and it is intended to be an integral part of government decision making process. Generally, there are the three key stages recognized in generating intelligence: collection of raw data, carrying out analysis and generating intelligence. The criminal intelligence process consists of nine stages: planning, collection of information, assessment of information validity, and collation of information, analysis of information, assessment of analytical rigour and value, dissemination of intelligence, application of intelligence and review and assessment of criminal intelligence project. The fight against terrorism calls for locating and measuring terrorist risks, analyzing information and using intelligence to guide operations. Law enforcement organizations collect data and stores information. This raw data needs to be analyzed so that it produces intelligence.[25]

It becomes more effective to counter crime and terrorism if intelligence is applied in policing. The intelligence led-policing means that there is a need for gathering intelligence and that intelligence is used to lead policing. This is achieved through an atmosphere that makes intelligence a precondition to effective policing. Although there are several methods and models of using intelligence to lead policing, all intelligence-led policing models exhibit key common features, as the following: [26]

1. Production of the accurate and timely analytic products and intelligence relevant to the operational goals, which describe the nature and extent of problems affecting jurisdiction of the organization.

2. The use of these analytic and intelligence products to develop and guide strategy, operational planning or any action that addresses these problems.
3. Monitoring and assessment to establish the impact of action upon the problems and ongoing development to encompass change and/or improvement as necessary.

Tasks of Intelligence

Containment is one of the major tasks of the intelligence. The major intelligence prerequisite to contain the enemy is to checking movements of terrorists with special consideration given to the periphery of the region, preventing their strikes, and restricting their interaction with the population. The intelligence agencies would need to recognize the sensitive groups or pockets located outside the region which may give backing to the movement. Familiarity of routes, mode of movement and identity of the terrorists and couriers, who operate beyond the region, prove to be beneficial.[27]

The function of the intelligence is to find out the level and degree of contact and interaction between terrorists and the people. The information requires details regarding various issues being raised by the terrorists to win their support, the modes of their propaganda and the channels through which such propaganda is carried out. This information would provide the basis for adopting suitable measures to ensure that the efforts of terrorists for mass contact are checked and contained.

Intelligence agencies also have to find out details of the foreign support given to the movement by harnessing information from outside the country. It checks the active supporters in the related countries. Another aspect of the intelligence in the foreign countries is the willpower of public opinion and prominent lobbies which may have taken pro-terrorist standpoint. Isolation calls for acquirement of such information as is necessary to segregate a movement from the sources of its material support and shield the population against the influence of the terrorists. It also requires to taking internal and external sources of supplies, means of acquirement and dispatch, channels through which these are actually moved and the collection arrangement and the receiving end.[28]

An important intelligence task would be to discover the places where weapons, explosives and other equipments are kept. In addition, location of hideouts used by the terrorists would also need to be found out. Precise information about pro-terrorist elements existing among the population as also places and timings of contact between the terrorists and their sympathizers would be necessary. The channels of taking new members for their organization, too, would have to be determined by the intelligence set up.

Another important task of intelligence is to find out the effect of various anti-terrorist dealings on the course of movement. There should be a regular analysis of the effect of every measure on its activities, reaction to every action of the government. This feedback is important to the planners on the apex body to review, monitor, modify and regulate future planning and execution of the operations.[29]

An all important function of the intelligence is that of counter-intelligence. There is easy access of terrorists to the information held by government departments. The efforts of the terrorists to penetrate into the governmental departments have asked for the need of counter intelligence. Counter intelligence is as important as the acquisition of intelligence.[30]

Intelligence has to be obtained through informers. Informers will have to be developed in large numbers and maintained by providing appropriate incentives and motivation. It is a very slow process which requires patience. The informers are the top targets on the hit list of terrorists. Even a suspicion of being an informer would be enough for the eradication of an insider. This emphasizes the requirement of keeping the informers protected from disclosure. Within the intelligence organization itself, few should be allowed to know about the informer's identity. Personal safety of the informers has to be a major concern in intelligence operations.[31]

An important source of information is the interrogation of the arrested terrorists. Interrogation provides highly valuable information, keeping in view the status of the terrorist in the movement and the expertise with which interrogation is conducted. Intelligence collected from interrogation has remarkable scope for intelligence.[32]

Another method of gathering information about terrorist plot is by penetration. Penetration can be achieved either by infiltrating agents in the terrorist organizations or by creating informers.

But intelligence is difficult to acquire and analyze. Three separate processes are involved in intelligence gathering:[33]

- First, establishing detailed background dossiers on active and potential terrorists and those who might lend them support and compiling organizations' chart to show the command structure of underground organizations.
- Second, creating an efficient retrieval system so that the information can be passed on quickly to the men in the field as they need it.
- Third, developing strategic and tactical intelligence through local contacts that will make it possible to lay hands on the right man at the right time.

Role and function of intelligence at strategic level and tactical level:

Strategic Intelligence is intelligence concerned with the policies, cultural tendencies, thinking processes, intentions, capabilities, limitations and possible courses of action of foreign or enemy nations or international terrorist's organizations. It is used in carrying out national security measures in determining its foreign and anti-terror policies or in conducting journal security and military operations. The strategic roles of intelligence are further explained as those mission objectives relating to intelligence efforts to predict, penetrate and pre-empt threats to a country's security and protect its laws. Tactical intelligence can be defined as an awareness of the target timing and type of attack being planned by an enemy. It can also be described as intelligence pertaining to capabilities, limitations, vulnerabilities or reactions of a hostile force which is used in carrying out tactical operations. The special investigations techniques which are employed at tactical level are:[34]

- Undercover operations which included covert investigations.
- Front store operations.
- The use of informants.
- Observation activities to include cross border observations.
- Electronic surveillance.
- Interception of communications which include telephone, fax, email and monitoring of public and private networks.
- Searches of cars, premises and computers.
- Agents provocateurs.

In various texts, writers have discussed intelligence assisting in combating terrorism. Collection plans, trend analysis, telephone record analysis, bank record analysis and strategic intelligence assessments as analytical techniques and event-flow charts and association chart as products can be utilized when dealing with terrorism.[35]

Operations to counter terrorism and insurgency depend largely on timely accurate intelligence. In order to gain such intelligence it is essential that the various intelligence agencies co-operate effectively. One of the major reasons for intelligence failure is the difficulty in achieving intelligence co-operation.[36] The growing intensity of terrorism has once again asked for the importance of good inside intelligence on all levels. They have also brought forth the absolute necessity of close international co-operation in the fight against terrorism. Countering terrorism can best be done by effective law enforcement and Intelligence Co-operation. This implies intelligence co-operation between key counter terrorism allies and between intelligence agencies such as civilian intelligence, military intelligence and crime intelligence. But, cooperation in the form of intelligence sharing between security and crime intelligence is challenging. Interlinking their networks will be achieved with difficulty. Intelligence sharing between states is highly restricted.[37]

The security and intelligence agencies have taken various measures to advance their potentials. The FBI has tripled its counter-terrorism force since the World Trade Center attack and the CIA has created its Counter-Terrorism Center (CTC) to deal with the threat at the highest civilian and military levels. The German authorities have greatly enhanced the police and security units. Russia has formed new elite units in order to cope with the threat of terrorist attacks against its nuclear facilities.

International cooperation has improved, mainly on the bilateral level. Even the Israeli security services have been cooperating with Palestine. The Arab League countries have arrived at an agreement to coordinate their intelligence and security activities against the radical Islamist movements. Even Russia and China have come forward together with their efforts to fight Islamic radicals in Central Asia. Russia has widened its intelligence cooperation with the United States, Great Britain, Turkey, and Israel. The European body, Europol, is also a step in the improvement of cooperation at the regional level. But it must be clear that the activity of the intelligence agencies and international cooperation will be affected and influenced by the international environment and new international laws.[38]

Role of police and paramilitary forces

The security forces, particularly the police and the paramilitary, have a vital role to play in dealing with terrorism. Police agencies are in burning need for more sophisticated intelligence gathering and analysis, as well as better dissemination of terrorism intelligence among local, state and federal agencies. There is also the need for more sophisticated operational policies, greater cooperation and sharing of resources among different agencies, and more comprehensive training that educates police officers to the realities of contemporary terrorist methods and activities. Finally, the need for effective investigation and prosecution of terrorist acts demands that agencies ignore or overcome the traditional organizational boundaries and rivalries that impede the achievement of these and other goals.

Agencies responsible for fighting terrorism in India

A number of organizations in the India contribute to counterterrorism efforts. These comprise of police forces, special security forces and paramilitary forces that patrol the borders and help the police in the time of need. India has several intelligence agencies that monitor terrorist activities. The Research and Analysis Wing (RAW) is the external intelligence agency and the Intelligence Bureau (IB), a division of the Home Affairs Ministry, collects intelligence inside India. A Joint Intelligence Committee analyzes intelligence data from RAW and IB. The IB oversees an inter-agency counterterrorism center similar to the CIA. The Ministry of External Affairs oversees its own counterterrorism body, which oversees diplomatic counterterrorism functions such as briefing other nations on suspected Pakistani sponsorship of terrorism in India. The Indian State has not succeeded in developing a consistent plan. The ARC suggests that "intelligence network and policing capacity at both Union and State levels need to be significantly improved to meet the challenges posed by terrorism."[39]

The sharing of intelligence needs a lot of improvement. There is generally overabundance of intelligence agencies. The Intelligence Bureau, Research & Analysis Wing, Military Intelligence, BSF G-branch, Revenue Intelligence, etc., operate in India. But in the event of a catastrophe there is always a failure of intelligence.[40]

The causes of intelligence failure against terrorism are not faulty analysis because there are normally few tactical intelligence indicators available to analyze anyway. The fault lies primarily in the defective collection of information. Technical sources of intelligence are less useful in counter insurgency than they are unconventional operations. The only significant type of intelligence encountering terrorism is gained from human sources. The right tactic to defeat post Cold War terrorism is not conventional warfare but tedious intelligence work done by monitoring telephone calls, tracking financial transactions, shadowing suspects and infiltrating terrorists cells. A clear conclusion from the many investigations into intelligence failures is that intelligence agencies of all disciplines must cooperate and share intelligence. It remains difficult to formalize systems to ensure the needed cooperation but it is essential. In the war of terror cooperation between the intelligence agencies of different countries has also proved essential.[41]

Efforts for improvement

Efforts to develop and restructure the intelligence community have been recurrent and have tried to refocus the intelligence community on managerial improvements, or on efforts to prevent the recurrence of abuses of authority or illegal acts.[42] Vital involvement of intelligence in every part and aspect of anti terrorist operations dictates an extensive intelligence network. The existing organizations would need to be resistant and more resources to be included to make the overall network capable of undertaking the enhanced workload. Any organization or an agency that can assist in the intelligence work in any matter and to any extent, should be co-opted with.[43] Best results are possible only if all agencies operate in a mutually coordinated manner and with due interaction.

For maximum efficiency, the functional frictions need to be lessened. There is also the need for centralizing the intelligence operations. Best results are only possible if all agencies operate in a mutually coordinated manner and with due interaction.

Intelligence comes through technical and human sources. But technical intelligence is nothing compared to human intelligence. Moreover, expansion of the intelligence network requires an atmosphere of public confidence at two levels: confidence that the government will, at the end prevail, and confidence that the individuals who cooperate with the government will have their identities protected and, therefore, they and their families will not be targeted by the terrorists.[44]

Creation of an effective intelligence network takes time and resources. But it can achieve tremendous growth in fighting terrorism. It is concluded that the role of intelligence in countering terrorism and insurgency is absolutely critical. Intelligence can make use of special investigations techniques to find the terrorists or to capture or destroy them.

To sum up, the work of intelligence against terrorism in the 21st century will be difficult task, which will ask for new social and technological developments and an objective scrutiny of the new trends and threats. Intelligence is essential in countering terrorism, in thinning its tactical effects and strategic importance. But without a comprehensive and firm policy of the government, terrorism will continue to pose a threat to future generations.

SUGGESTIONS

Terrorism has become a buzzword now and it is a herculean task to overcome this evil. However, the strategies should be made keeping in view the nature of terrorism. Different measures have been suggested in the past but the need of the hour is to properly implement them. Thus, combating terrorism requires a focussed vision. We should learn the lessons from past mistakes and should invest in preventive measures and ensure human security for all.

Need for a Clear-cut Policy: First and foremost, a clear cut policy is needed. It is essential to formulate a clear-cut policy against terrorism through effective enforcement measures. A body of laws is urgently required to deal with the menace of terrorism that would cover essential problems like the provision of asylum, financing of terrorist organizations, money laundering, and allied issues.[45] Devising a tough policy in place of ad hoc approaches to this problem when the need arises is necessary. A national strategy can be based on four broad areas of response. These are:

1. Prevention: Initiatives to discourage the support of terrorism.
2. Deterrence: Protection and security efforts or measures to discourage the terrorist. This involves internal security efforts.
3. Prediction: The intelligence and counter-intelligence effort.
4. Reaction: Action or operations in response to specific acts or incidents of terrorism.

Checking Socio-economic Disparities and Unemployment: Steps to reduce socio-economic inequalities, disparities in employment and educational opportunities should be taken and an effective machinery should be there for redressal of grievances. By taking effective steps to reduce ethnic and social inequalities, disparity in educational and employment opportunities, and by creating an effective machinery for redressing public grievances, the environment can be considerably improved. At the same time steps to reduce economic deprivation must also be taken. Improving economic and social status could solve the problem. The satisfaction with the functioning of the government is any way to win the support of the marginalized population.[46]

Political Rights: Denial of political rights lead to violent contention than only economic deprivation. It is the political environment in which terrorist violence flourishes, which has to be altered. The problem is to find out how this can be done without giving in to their secessionist demands.[47] Thus, not only economic issues, but political issues also need to be settled down. People should not be devoid of their political rights.

Establishment of an Early Warning System: A very important tool in the prevention of conflicts is the establishment of early warning systems. Studies have also revealed that early warning systems, together with preventive capacity building, can help to diminish conflict.

Early warning can be defined as an information system which can provide timely information to decision makers. An effective early warning system is essentially an information system with a well-developed database, which can predict and forecast future conflict scenarios.

Intelligence: Intelligence should play an important role in combating terrorism by detecting the terrorist threat, defining its nature, supplying the "alert bearing" information to prevent acts of terror and in waging psychological warfare.[48] It is the indefinable, conspiring and secretive nature of the terrorist organizations that gives the intelligence an important role to play. Intelligence should be crafted to create the discord within terrorists. Intelligence requires perseverance and adequate intelligence is very important. Not only can the intelligence mechanism provide advance information, enabling the authorities to take timely steps to avert an incident or minimize the intensity of the damage, it also aids them in tracking down suspected terrorists and identifying support from the patron states.[49] A pool of trained and experienced interrogators should be constituted to interrogate the suspects. Interrogators must be well-acquainted with the ideology and organisation of the terrorist group.

Cooperation with other Governments: In view of the transnational character of terrorism, collaboration amongst nations is vital to any successful endeavor to control and repress terrorism. The need for cooperation between nations to meet the challenge of international terrorism successfully also needs to be reiterated, since a holistic approach is needed to deal with terrorism and its allied threats to international security, like arms and drugs trafficking, money laundering, and so on. International understanding is lacking. The excessive secrecy between different intelligence agencies and the authorities need to be dismantled. Cooperation between regional anti-terrorist organizations, for intelligence sharing and checking terrorists from crossing national borders is indispensable.[50]

There also exists a relationship between terrorism and cooperative security, because without taking collective measures at the governmental and non-governmental level, it becomes quite difficult to either prevent or combat terrorism. Some of the measures which could be taken at the governmental and non-governmental level to prevent and combat terrorism are as follows.[51]

i. Bilateral consultation to effectively deal with terrorism. This would require periodic interaction between the officials of the countries to explore the causes which breed terrorism and formulate strategies for effectively dealing with that issue. Regular meetings between the officials and intelligence agencies may help in finding the terrorist.

ii. Looking for close coordination between the concerned institutions responsible for curbing terrorism. It means institutions established at the non-governmental level should provide with the policy suggestions to deal with that issue. Full cooperation should be given by different agencies to each another.

Setting up of Database: A skillfully networked database should be available about terrorists, their associates, modus operandi, sources of finance, hideouts in other states, their relatives and harbourers. It should be possible to send descriptive rolls, finger prints and photographs through computer. There is an all important need for building a comprehensive data bank for systematic collection, collation and easy retrieval of information about terrorist groups all over the world. It is suggested that Interpol set up a separate and permanent 'coordination cell', with a separate staff, to exclusively deal with the problem of terrorism all over the world, build up a computerized data bank of all terrorist groups in the world, all major terrorist occurrences, all major wanted terrorists, etc. Systems can be created in this cell by which all concerned nation-states keep the cell supplied with vital information and also avail of its services in updating their own information.

Increased role of Police: Tackling extremist violence should be entirely in the domain of the police. As far as possible, the army should not be involved in dealing with internal security problems.

Training of the civilians: Better training will lead to higher morale and more efficiency. Even the civil population should be given courses in paramilitary training, anti-terrorism measures and handling of firearms in case of an emergency. This will infuse discipline in the citizens and give them a sense of experience, responsibility, honour and patriotism. Thus, it is important to adopt policies of self-help and self-defence, particularly against the changing dimensions of the threat.

Systematic Propaganda: Terrorism has to be blocked on the psychological policy. A systematic propaganda campaign has to be launched to win the hearts of the people as so to delineate them from the terrorists.[52] Security forces frequently make the mistake of treating the militants and their sympathizers alike. This often leads to the development of hostile relation between the people and the security forces, which in turn leads to many practical problems in fighting terrorism. The cost of ruling reluctant people can be very high indeed. It could strengthen the secessionist forces by polarizing inter-communal relations and generating strong anti-government sentiments.[53] Therefore, the alienation of the people must be reduced to the minimum.

If the means used to capture the terrorists lead to greater alienation of the entire people, then those means need to be eschewed. The terrorists purposely provoke security forces to react in anger and panic. This is where the leadership can play a crucial role. Only the leaders, who have the physical and moral courage, to lead their men from the front, and the imagination and tact to calm them down when angry, can succeed in this "dirty" war. They should not succumb to their provocative acts and, at times, soil their own hands with the same methods as employed by the terrorists.

Mutual respect for all: A clash of cultures is occurring between the Western and Islamic civilizations, which should be mitigated through a dialogue between them. The roots of this cultural clash lie in an observation of injustice and humiliation having been inflicted upon the Islamic civilization by the West which is encouraging for the growth of isolation and terrorism in Muslim countries. It is important that minorities be treated humanely and fairly, and that majority communities not mistreat them. There is a need to look for new allies in the Islamic world.[54]

Checking misuse of law: The examination of captured terrorists must be done keeping in view the trustworthiness of the judicial process and the effectiveness of anti-terrorist operations. In the absence of an efficient criminal justice system the security forces and the people could be tempted to resort to extra-legal measures. The executive, legislator, judiciary, or the media should not tolerate any extra-legal measure. There should be no misuse of any law. The special laws should not remain on the statute book when not needed. The situation in different parts of the country facing terrorism should be kept under constant review and the laws should be suitably amended modified or even repealed depending on the ground situation. Those guilty of misusing these laws should be punished and suitable safeguards ensure that they are not misused. The violence has to be dealt with, within the framework of law.

Government should take all possible steps to ensure that no innocent person is harassed, but let it also be ensured that guilty terrorists do not manage to get out of the clutches of law.[55]

Criminal Justice System: Trials should be swift and special courts should be set up. The judiciary should appreciate that if the terrorists have human rights so also do the common citizens who are butchered by the terrorist. Proper remand should be given to the police to effectively interrogate the terrorist and lead to recoveries.

Blocking of Funding : All measures should be taken to block the finance at the disposal of the terrorists. For this the cooperation of different police and enforcement agencies is a must. Immediate steps needs to be taken to freeze the assets of terrorist groups and individuals associating with them.

Respect for Human Rights: Terrorism buds in a setting when the protectors are seen as violators of human rights. The more brutal the security forces become, the more blunders they are likely to make. For pursuing anti-terrorism operations, the degree of torture given to suspects make them fill with hatred towards the state agents. Such illicit activities would only result in further marginalization and alienation of the concerned population and increased support to terrorist organizations.[56]

Checking states that sponsor terrorism: States that sponsor terrorism and escape their responsibility by either denying this fact or explaining it away as their support to a freedom struggle have to be deterred. The need for the international community to evolve a policy for disciplining the states that provide protection, encouragement and support to terrorist groups stands accentuated. States should give up their short-sighted national policies of shifting convenience and endeavour to adopt a crime-free world policy. For example, if all countries refuse to grant safe haven to a terrorist, there will be no place where terrorists can take refuge.

Role of United Nations: An enlarged role for the UN and the Security Council is required to make a fair determination in this regard. Since the 1990s, many conflicts have been brought to an end either through UN mediation or the action of third parties acting with UN support. The list includes El Salvador, Gua-temala, Namibia, Cambodia, Mozambique, Afghanistan, Sierra Leone, Burundi etc. UN peacemaking, peacekeeping and conflict prevention activities have been credited as a major factor behind a 40 per cent decline in conflict around the world since the 1990s. UN preventive diplomacy and other forms of preventive action have defused many potential conflicts. The United Nations should promote and strengthen democratic institutions and practices around the world, by helping people in many countries to participate in free and fair elections. It should also help in alleviating rural poverty in developing countries.[57]

Systematic Planning: The key to a successful anti-terrorism strategy lies in the creation of conditions in which the cost of waging such violent movements is made too high, and the possibility of terrorists achieving their goal too remote. The will of the extremist groups to continue terrorist activities has to be systematically exhausted. The strategy should aim at exhausting their supporters physically as well as mentally. The strategy will have to include both physical and psychological measures to combat the terrorists. The physical measures would include military, administrative, legal, economic, and political measures. But physical measures alone will not be adequate. The fight against terrorism has also to be waged on the psychological front. A systematic propaganda campaign has to be launched to win over the minds, as well as the hearts, of the people. The strategy should not concentrate only on the hard-core militants, their many sympathizers and supporters are just as important. It should systematically aim at loosening the link between the hardcore elements and their sympathizers and supporters.

Role of special agencies: Special units should be constituted which could hit terrorists hard and flush them out of their hideouts- a force which can move swiftly and surely with special skill, mental alertness and sophisticated weapons. These units should be better trained and conditioned; unit which has experts on explosives, rescuing of hostages that the local police is not trained to do. The U.S. Statute makes specific provision for funding of terrorist related cases with various agencies like the FBI; Customs services, Drug Enforcement etc. Such provision for additional funding for creation of additional infrastructure for investigation and trial of terrorist cases does not pose an unplanned additional burden on the overburdened judiciary and other related agencies which have to deal with the problem of terrorism. The comprehensive provision for assistance and compensation to the victims' of terrorism should be made and funds for the purpose should be allocated. Such a provision can standardize and streamline machinery for compensation of victims of terrorist crimes.

Role of Media: Media plays an important role both in spreading and containing terrorism. It is in the very nature of terrorism that it must be noticed. Media can achieve two of its important objectives: building the morale of its cadres and bringing the instrument of government into dispute. Media can be a double-edged weapon and must be handled by a person who is well-trained to handle it, and not by a senior officer looking for personal glorification.

Curbing the link between Arms, Drugs and Terrorism: No strategy of controlling terrorism can be successful which does not take into consideration the narco-link. The cultivation, processing, transport and distribution of narcotics are perhaps the greatest single generator of political violence and crime in the world. Profits from this business are used to finance and arm terrorists and insurgents. Thus it should be checked effectively.

It is always better to declare war against the terrorists than to succumb to their designs. Terrorists must be defeated on their own ground, with their own weapons of surprise mobility, flexibility and firepower. Giving in to the demands of the terrorists inevitably means that the demands would be stiffer the next time. For effective deterrence it is important to convince the terrorists that the authorities have the capability to punish and prevent terrorist actions, and have the determination to do so.

We should be careful in judging the intensity of terrorism — whether the theatre of this proxy war has shifted from small sporadic attacks to a form of low intensity warfare. This is important because, accordingly, the counter measures and law enforcement shall also have to change.

Setting up of a Committee at international level: An International Coordination Committee on Terrorism can also be established by the nations of the world. This committee can meet once in three months to exchange, update information about terrorist groups, illegal trafficking in firearms and to generate actionable information by different states. The Coordination Committee Secretariat, which should work on a permanent basis, could have the following functions:

i. Ensuring coordination among and despatch of information to the member states in their day-to--day anti-terrorist functioning, as and when such requests are received.

ii. Pursuing with members enquiries received from different sources like members and foreign agencies.

iii. Preparing lists of terrorists and their associates on the basis of interrogations carried out, and circulating them among the members and other authorities.

iv. Preparing lists of hideouts, which were used by terrorists from time to time, lists of relations of terrorists, smugglers and sympathizers helping terrorists, foreign-based persons helping terrorists/vehicles used by terrorists, telephones used by terrorists, modus operandi used by terrorists, descriptive rolls and miscellaneous data based on interrogation of terrorists.

v. Rendering technical help in certain cases.

vi. Compiling and circulating of lists of terrorist group and gangs, and the latest information about them.

vii. Preparing and disseminating comprehensive notes and data on various terrorists and terrorist-related subjects.

viii. Holding training sessions on sensitizing member representatives and providing video-graphed demonstrations about the mental set up, morale and ideology of terrorists, apart from their motives to join terrorist outfits and commit crimes.[58]

This will also help generate a united will amongst all countries of the world to fight the terrorist.

Efforts may be made to organize an international symposium on terrorism and exchange information, once in a year, where all countries participate, while the subcommittee can meet more often.

Increased Aviation Security: To tackle the growing problem of airplane hijacking and aviation insecurity, the security procedure should be uniform at every airport and any inbound passenger should be considered as a potential security risk. Screening of checked baggage is now a recommended practice. Screening implies the application of technical means to detect arms, etc. in baggage, because physical checking is impractical. New facilities need to be planned to improve security. Security measures must be proportionate and appropriate to the threat.

The following major steps must be taken to improve the aviation threat:[59]

(i) It must be ensured that the threat assessment is correct.

(ii) What is of importance is the ability to pass information, *i.e.* the communication between the government, law enforcement agencies and airports must be effective and timely.

(iii) Attention must be given to be given to loading of mail, freight, etc.

(iv) Level of baggage screening must be increased.

(v) Badges for identification are a must for all employees, restricting them to their required area of operation.

(vi) There should be an increase in security training and awareness programmes.

(vii) Security measures must be introduced by the concerned government since it is they who have the direct responsibility.

India will have to develop a comprehensive long-term anti-terrorism strategy to neutralize the serious threat posed by it to its national security, which simultaneously deals with both the internal and external dimensions of the threat. It would be short sighted to ignore it by pursuing a passive policy whose only objective is to wear down the terrorists. Foreign sponsored terrorism cannot make much headway, if the internal situation in the country does not favour it. A successful policy will concentrate more on tackling the internal problems. But that does not mean that the country should completely rule out the options of "hot pursuit" of the terrorists in the border region, or of escalating the low-intensity conflicts into a conventional war.

Former President Dr. APJ Abdul Kalam argues that a single intelligence system is needed to curb the menace of terrorism as the cooperation among different agencies will prove to be beneficial. The fast trial of the terrorism related cases and economic growth are needed for an effective check. The public participation is also the most effective way to curb the menace. The eradication of poverty will also help in checking terrorism. He has suggested an action oriented solution for evolving a happy, prosperous and peaceful society. This action plan has three components - education with a value system, transforming religion into spirituality, and economic development for societal transformation.[60]

CONCLUSION

As terrorism continues to be one of the gravest threats to the security of nations and to the safety of innocent citizens in all affected countries, a systematic and rational approach to terrorism becomes extremely important. We have to personally identify the real factors for the mushrooming growth of each terrorist movement. There should be more international conferences and seminars on international cooperation, which should be effectuated with the right large-hearted zeal and not by visionless, perverted and narrow-minded forces to subvert peace. All these require leadership of a high order and the need to back the police agencies which are assigned the task of eliminating terrorism.

All nation states should join hands to advance the cause of peace and international brotherhood, for their own good, in the world. We must realize that terrorism threatens every country and all people, and not live under any illusion that terrorism affects only certain countries. Let us all understand that terrorism is the common enemy of us all and we have to fight it unitedly. Using terrorism as a political tool by any nation-state is a crime against mankind and we must relentlessly educate ourselves about it.

REFERENCES

1. A.S. Narang & Pramila Srivastava, eds. *Terrorism: The Global Perspective,* Kanishka, New Delhi, 2001, p.220.
2. Amrith Rohan Parera, *International Terrorism,* Vikas, New Delhi, 1997, p. 22.
3. *Ibid.,* p. 47.
4. Anil Kalhan, et al. "Colonial Continuities: Human Rights, Terrorism, and Security Laws in India", *Columbia Journal of Asian Law,* vol. 20, 2006, pp. 214-215.
5. V.P. Srivastav, *Terrorism: A Global Dimensions,* Indian, New Delhi, 2004, p. 4.
6. *The U.S.A. Patriot Act, 2001.*
7. *Ibid.*
8. Bill Scheppler, *The U.S.A. Patriot Act,* The Rosen Publishing Group, New York, 2006.
9. Howard Ball, *The U.S.A. Patriot Act,* Abc-clio, Santa Barbara, 2004.
10. "Counter-Terrorism Legislation and Practice: A survey of Selected Countries", http://www.privacyinternational.org/issues/terrorism/library/ukforeignofficedetentionstudy.pdf.
11. Kellie Ortega, "Anti-terrorist Laws in Pakistan", *Seminar,* April, 2002.
12. http://en.wikipedia.org/wiki/Counter-Terrorism_Act_2008
13. Anil Kalhan., et al. "Colonial Continuities: Human Rights, Terrorism, and Security Laws in India", *Columbia Journal of Asian Law,* vol. 20, 2006, P. 110.
14. http://www.hrdc.net/sahrdc/resources/armed_forces.htm
15. http://youngsocialworker.wordpress.com/social-issues/

16. "Parliament passes POTA repeal bill", *The Hindu,* Dec. 10, 2004.
17. www.satp.org
18. *Ibid.*
19. http://en.wikipedia.org/wiki/National_Investigation_Agency_(India)
20. Anil Kalhan., et al. "Colonial Continuities: Human Rights, Terrorism, and Security Laws in India", *Columbia Journal of Asian Law,* vol. 20, 2006, pp. 135-136.
21. *Ibid.*
22. Thomas Johnson, *The War on Terrorism: A Collision of Values, Strategies and Societies,* Cic Press, 2008. p. 96.
23. GPH Kruys, "The role of intelligence in countering terrorism and insurgency", *Strategic Review for Southern Africa,* vol. 29, no. 1. p. 84.
24. Ely Karmon, "The role of intelligence in counter terrorism", *The Korean Journal of Defense Analysis*, Vol. XIV, No. 1, Spring 2002. p. 120.
25. Robert Kopal, "The role of criminal intelligence analysis in anti-terrorism", http://webzoom.freewebs.com/swnmia/The%20Role%20of%20Criminal%20 Intelligence%20Analysis% 20On%20Terrorism.pdf
26. *Ibid.*
27. Virinder Uberoy, *Combating Terrorism,* Intellectual Publishing House, New Delhi, 1992. p. 127.
28. *Ibid.* p. 128.
29. *Ibid.* p. 129.
30. *Ibid.* p. 130.
31. Ranjit Kumar Pachnanda, *Terrorism and Response to Terrorist Threat,* UBS Publishers, New Delhi, 2002. pp. 164-165.
32. *Ibid.* p. 165.
33. *Ibid.* p. 168.
34. GPH Kruys, "The role of intelligence in countering terrorism and insurgency", *Strategic Review for Southern Africa,* vol. 29, no. 1. pp. 92-93.

35. Robert Kopal, "The role of criminal intelligence analysis in anti-terrorism", http://webzoom.freewebs.com/swnmia/The%20Role%20of %20Criminal %20Intelligence%20Analysis% 20On%20Terrorism.pdf

36. "The Role of intelligence in countering terrorism and insurgency", *Strategic Review for Southern Africa,* 2007.

37. GPH Kruys, "The role of intelligence in countering terrorism and insurgency", *Strategic Review for Southern Africa,* vol. 29, no. 1. pp. 86-88.

38. Ely Karmon, "The role of intelligence in counter terrorism", *The Korean Journal of Defense Analysis*, Vol. XIV, No. 1, Spring 2002. pp. 125-126.

39. Kamala Kanta Dash, "Counter-Terrorism and Police Community Engagement in India", http://monash.academia.edu/KamalaKantaDash/Papers/197757/COUNTER-TERRORISM-AND-POLICE-COMMUNITY-ENGAGEMENT-IN-INDIA

40. Tara Kartha, *Tools of Terror,* Knowledge World, 1999. p. 325.

41. GPH Kruys, "The role of intelligence in countering terrorism and insurgency", *Strategic Review for Southern Africa,* vol. 29, no. 1. p. 100.

42. Thomas Johnson, *The War on Terrorism: A Collision of Values, Strategies and Societies,* Crc Press, 2008. p. 139.

43. Virinder Uberoy, *Combating Terrorism,* Intellectual Publishing House, New Delhi, 1992. p. 130.

44. Ved Marwah, *Uncivil wars: pathology of terrorism in India,* HarperCollins, 1998. p. 347.

45. Sridhar Khatri, *Terrorism in South Asia,* Shipra Publications, 2009. p. 444.

46. Ved Marwah, *Uncivil wars: pathology of terrorism in India,* Centre for Policy Resesarch, New Delhi, 1997. p. 340.

47. *Ibid.* p. 339.

48. *Ibid.* p. 347.

49. Ranjit K. Prachanda, *Terrorism and Response to Terrorist Threat,* UBS Publishers, New Delhi, 2002, p. 188.

50. Sridhar Khatri, *Terrorism in South Asia,* Shipra Publications, 2009, p. 444.

51. *Ibid.*, p. 465.
52. Ranjit K. Prachanda, *Terrorism and Response to Terrorist Threat,* UBS Publishers, New Delhi, 2002, p. 188.
53. Ved Marwah, *Uncivil wars: pathology of terrorism in India,* Centre for Policy Resesarch, New Delhi, 1997, pp. 341-342.
54. Jason Burke, "Seven ways to stop the terror", *The Observer,* 7 August, 2005.
55. Ved Marwah, *Uncivil wars: pathology of terrorism in India,* Centre for Policy Resesarch, New Delhi, 1997, p. 361.
56. Sridhar Khatri, *Terrorism in South Asia,* Shipra Publications, 2009, p. 446.
57. *www.un.org/un60/60ways_book.pdf* -
58. Ranjit K. Prachanda, *Terrorism and Response to Terrorist Threat,* UBS Publishers, New Delhi, 2002, pp. 211-212.
59. Ranjit K. Prachanda, *Terrorism and Response to Terrorist Threat,* UBS Publishers, New Delhi, 2002, p. 217.
60. *www.un.org/un60/60ways_book.pdf*

Bibliography

PRIMARY SOURCES

Bowman, Steve (2002). Weapons of Mass Destruction: The Terrorist Threat, *CRS Report for Congress,* MARCH.

Council of Europe (2002). *Guidelines on Human Rights and the Fight against Terrorism.* Strasbourg.

Craign, K., P. Chalk, S.A. Daly and B.A. Jackson (2007). *Sharing the Dragon's teeth- Terrorist Groups and the Exchange of New Technologies.* Report prepared for the Department of Homeland Security, Santa Monica, California: RAND.

Crime in India, (1998 & 1999). National Crime Records Bureau, M.H.A.

Department of State (2007). CRS Report for Congress. *Combating Terrorism: The Challenge of Measuring Effectiveness,* March 12.

Draft Report dated 29 June 2000 of the U.N. Convention against Transnational Organized Crime.

Europol (2007). *EU Terrorism Situation and Trend Report 2007.* Europol. The Hague.

Govt. of India (2002). Press Information Bureau, *Prevention of Terrorism* Act.

Govt. of India (2004). Press Information Bureau, *Unlawful Activities* (Prevention) Amendment Act.

Govt. of India (2008). Press Information Bureau, National Investigation Act.

Home Office (2004). Counter Terrorism Powers. Cm. 6147, London.

Hudson, R. (1999). *The Sociology and Psychology of Terrorism: Who Becomes a Terrorist and Why?* Report prepared by the Federal Research Division of the Library of Congress.

Jane's Terrorism and Insurgency Centre Reports (2007). *Changing Meanings of Jihad,* May 1.

Lal, Deepak (2000). KASHMIR. *Paper for Carnegie project on Globalization, National self- determination, and Terrorism,* UCLA, December.

Law Commission of India (2000). *173rd Report on Prevention of Terrorism Bill.*

London Assembly (2006). *Report of the 7 July Review Committee.* London: Greater London Authority.

Medalia, Jonathan (2004). *Nuclear Terrorism: A brief review of Threats and Responses.* Washington, DC: Congressional Research Service.

National Strategy for Combating Terrorism, Washington, DC: Government Printing Office, 2003.

National Strategy for Homeland Security, Washington, DC: Government Printing Office, 2002.

Office of the Coordinator for Counterterrorism. *Patterns of global terrorism 2002.* (2003, April 30). Washington, DC: U.S. Department of State.

Sageman, M. (2007). '*Radicalization of global Islamist terrorists',* Testimony before the U.S. Senate Committee on Homeland Security and Governmental Affairs, 27 June.

Special Report of the Special Advisor to the DCI on Iraq's Weapons of Mass Destruction, Washington, DC: Government Printing Office, 2004, Vol. 3.

Summary of USA Patriotic Act, H.R. 3162, October 24, 2001, Library of Congress.

The 9/11 Commission Report (2004). Washington, DC: Government Printing Office.

Threats and Protection, Department of Homeland Security, Press Release.

U.N. Security Council Resolution 1368 (2001), U.N. document S/RES/ 1368 (2001), adopted September 12, 2001.

U.S. Department of State (2005). Office of Counterterrorism, 'Foreign Terrorist Organizations (FTOS), Factsheet, Washington, DC: 11 October.

USAID Position Paper (2005). National Strategy for Combating Terrorism. March 15.

BOOKS

Alexander, Yonah and Seymour Maxwell Finger eds. (1977). *Terrorism: Interdisciplinary Perspectives,* The John Jay Press, New York.

Al-Khattar, Aref M. (2003). *Religion and Terrorism: An Interfaith Perspective,* Praeger, New York.

Anthony, Cordesman (2001). *Terrorism, Asymmetric Warfare, and Weapons of Mass Destruction: Defending the U.S. Homeland.* CT: Praeger.

Baruah, Sanjib ed. (2005). *Durable Disorder: Understanding Politics of North East India,* Oxford, New Delhi.

Baruah, Sanjib ed. (2009). *Beyond Counter Insurgency: Breaking the impasse in North East India,* Oxford, New Delhi.

Bjorgo, Tore (2005). *Root Causes of Terrorism: Myths, reality and ways forward,* Routledge, Oxon.

Borum, Randy (2004). *Psychology of Terrorism,* University of South Florida.

Byman, Daniel (2005). *Deadly Connections,* Cambridge University Press.

Chari, P.R. & D. Suba Chandran (2005). *Bio-terrorism and Bio-defence,* Manohar Publishers.

Chitkara, M.G. (2003). *Combating Terrorism,* APH, New Delhi.

Chopra, V.D. ed. (2001). *Rise of Terrorism and Secessionism in Eurasia,* Gyan Publishimg House, New Delhi.

Cole, Leonard (2007). *Terror: How Israel Has Coped and What America Can Learn.* Bloomington: Indiana University Press.

Durmaz, Huseyin ed. (2007). *Understanding and responding to Terrorism,* IOS Press, Amsterdam.

Dutta, Sreeradha (2004). *North East Complexities and it's Determinants,* Institute for Defence Studies and Analysis, New Delhi.

Emerson, Steven (2002). *American Jihad: The Terrorists Among Us.* Simon and Schuster, N.Y.

Falk, Avner (2009). *Islamic Terror: Conscious and Unconscious Motives,* Pentagon Press, New Delhi.

Gill, K.P.S. and Ajai Sahni, eds. (2002). *The Global Threat of Terror,* New Delhi.

Goswami, Arnab (2002). *Combating Terrorism: The Legal Challenge,* Har-Anand Publications, New Delhi.

Hoffman, Bruce (1993). *Holy Terror: The Implications of Terrorism motivated by a religious imperative*, Rand, C.A.

Hoffman, Bruce (2006). *Inside Terrorism*, Columbia University Press.

Jahangir, Ashima (2000). *States of Violence: Nature of Terrorism and Guerilla Warfare*, Dominant Publishers, New Delhi.

Janczewski, Lech, Andrew M. Colarik., eds. (2008). *Cyber Warfare and Cyber Terrorism*, IGI Global.

JennifernL, Hesterman (2004). Transnational Crime and Criminal Terrorist Nexus: Synergies and Corporate Trends.

John, Wilson and Swati Parashar, eds. (2001). *Terrorism in Southeast Asia: Implications for South Asia*, Pearson Longman, New Delhi.

Jones, James William (2008). *Blood that cries out from the earth: the psychology of religious terrorism*, Oxford University Press, New York.

Kartha, Tara (1999). *Tools of Terror: Light weapons and India's security*, Knowledge World, New Delhi.

Kumaraswami, P.R. & Ian Copland, eds. (2009). *South Asia: The Spectre of Terrorism*, Routledge, New Delhi.

Lal, Bhure (2002). *TERRORISM INC. The Lethal Cocktail of ISI, TALIBAN & AL-QAIDA*, Siddharth Pub., New Delhi.

Laqueur, Walter (1998). *The Age of Terrorism*. NJ: Transaction Publishers.

— (1999). *The new terrorism: fanaticism and the arms of mass destruction, OUP*, New York.

— (2004). *No End to War*, Continuum International Publishing Group Inc, New York.

Lesser, Ian O. ed. (1999). *Combating the New Terrorism*, RAND, Santa Monica.

Lutz, James M. and Brenda J. Lutz (2004). *Global Terrorism*, Routledge.

Marwah, Ved (1995). *Uncivil wars: Pathology of Terrorism in India*, Indus Harper Collins Pub., New Delhi.

Pachnanda, Ranjit K. (2002). *Terrorism and Response to Terrorist Threat*, UBS Pub.

Pandey, Satish Chandra (2006). *International Terrorism and the Contemporary World, Sarup &Sons Publishers*, New Delhi.

Parera, Amrith Rohan, *International Terrorism*, Vikas Pub. House, New Delhi.

Pedahzur, Ami ed. (2006). *Root Causes of Suicide Terrorism: The globalization of martyrdom,* Routledge, New York.

Pettiford, Lloyd and David Harding (2003). *Terrorism and the New World War,* Areturus Pub, London.

Rafiabadi, H.N. (1988). *Assam: From Agitation to Accord,* Genuine Publications, New Delhi.

Rammohan, E.N. (2005). *Insurgent Frontiers: essays from the troubled North East,* India Research Press, New Delhi.

Saika, Jaideep & Ekaterina Stepanova, eds. (2009). *Terrorism: Patterns of Internationalization,* Sage, New Delhi.

Saika, Jaideep (2004). *Terror Sans Frontiers,* Vision Publishers, New Delhi.

Schmid, Alex P. and Ronald D. Crelinsten, eds. (1993). *Western Responses to Terrorism,* Frank Cass Publishers, Oxon.

Schofield, Victoria (2000). *Kashmir in Conflict: India, Pakistan and the Unfinished War,* Tauras, NY.

Schweitzer, Yoram and Shaul Shay (2004). *The Globalization of Terror,* Viva Books.

Singh, Mahavir ed. (2004). *International Terrorism and Religious Extremism,* Anamika Publishers, New Delhi.

Singh, Naunihal (2002). *World Terrorism and New Age Movement,* Authors Press.

Sinha, S.P. (2007). *Lost Opportunities,* Lancer Publications, New Delhi.

Smelser, Neil J. (2000). *Terrorism: Perspectives from the Behavioural and Social Sciences,* The National Academies Press, Washington DC.

Sodhi, M.L. (2000). *Terrorism and Political Violence: A Sourcebook,* Har-Anand Pub.

Sterba, J.P. (2003). *Terrorism and International Justice,* Oxford University Press, New York.

Tuman, Joseph S. (2010). *Communicating terror: The Rhetorical Dimensions of Terrorism*, Sage Publications.

Uberoy, Gen Virender (1992). *Combating Terrorism,* Intellectual Book Corner Publishers, New Delhi.

Verghese, B.G. (1996). *India's North East Resurgent,* Konark Publishers, New Delhi.

Wilkinson, Paul (1977). *Terrorism and the liberal state*, London: Macmillan Press.

ARTICLES

Arif, Kamran (2009). The establishment of a Taliban Emirate. *Himal*, Vol. 22.

Bamzai, Kaveree (2010). Lost in the valley. *India Today,* August 25.

Bukhari, Shujaat (2010). Valley on fire. *Frontline,* August 27.

Chalk, Peter (2001). Southeast Asia and the Golden Triangle's Heroin Trade: Threat and Response. *Studies in Conflict and Terrorism,* 23:2.

Cherian, John (2009). Axis of terror. *Frontline*, Dec. 19.

— (2009). Sparks of Seperatism. *Frontline*, July 31.

Chouvy, Pierra A. (2004). Narco Terrorism in Afghanistan. *Terrorism Monitor,* Vol. 2.

Council of Europe (2007). *Cyberterrorism: the use of the internet for terrorist purposes*, Council of Europe Publishing.

Crenshaw, Martha (1981). The causes of terrorism. *Comparative politics.*

Cronin, Audrey Kurth (2003). Behind the Curve: Globalization and International Terrorism. *International Security*, Vol. 27, No. 3.

Drug Intelligence Report (1994). *Insurgent Involvement in the Columbian Drug Trade*. Drug Enforcement Administration.

Fair, C. Cristine (2004). Militant Recruitment in Pakistan: Implications for Al Qaeda and Other Organizations. *Studies in Conflict & Terrorism,* 27, Taylor & Francis Inc.

Fine, Jonathan (2008). Contrasting Secular and Religious Terrorism. *Middle East Quarterly*.

Ganguly, Sumit (1996). Explaining the Kashmir Insurgency: Political Mobilization and Institutional Decay. *International Security,* Vol. 21, no. 2, (Fall).

Gause III, F. Gregory (2005). Can Democracy Stop Terrorism? Foreign Affairs. Sep/Oct.

Harshe, Rajen (*n.d.*). Cross-Border Terrorism: Road Block to Peace Initiatives. *Economic and Political Weekly,* Vol. 38, No. 35.

Hindwan, Sudhir (2003). Challenges of Trans-National Terrorism. *Man & Development,* Vol. XXXV, No. 3.

Hussain, Wasbir (2007). Ethno-Nationalism and the Politics of Terror in India's Northeast. *South Asia: Journal of South Asian Studies,* Routledge, Vol.XXX, no. 1, April.

Kalhan, Anil et al. (2006). Colonial Continuities: Human Rights, Terrorism, and Security Laws in India. *Columbia Journal of Asian Law,* vol. 20.

Krueger, Alan and Jitka Maleèková (2003). Education, Poverty, and Terrorism: Is There a Causal Connection? *Journal of Economic Perspectives.* Vol. 17, fall.

Lacina, Bethany (2009). The Problem of Political Stability in North East India. *Asian Survey,* Vol. XLIX, No. 6, Nov/Dec.

Levitt, Matthew and Michael Jacobson (2009). Drug Wars. *New Republic,* January 27.

Lieven, Anatol (2002). The Pressures on Pakistan. *Foreign Affairs,* Vol. 81, No. 1, Jan. - Feb.

Madrid, Club de (2005). International Summit on Democracy, Terrorism and Security. *Addressing the Causes of Terrorism, Volume I.* Spain.

McCauley, C. (2002). Psychological issues in understanding terrorism and the response to terrorism. In C. E. Stout (Ed.)., *The psychology of terrorism* (vol. 3, pp. 3-29). Westport, CT: Praeger.

Mohapatra, Nalin Kumar (2007). Political and Security Changes in Central Asia: The Drug Trafficking Dimension. *International Studies,* Vol. 44.

Moran, Michael (2008). Pakistan's Frankenstein. *Newsweek,* Dec 4.

Nayyar, A.H. and Zia Mian (2009). Enemies within. *Frontline*, January 30.

Ortega, Kellie (2002). Anti-terrorist Laws in Pakistan. *Seminar*, April.

Punjabi, Riyaz (1993). The concept of an Islamic Caliphate: The Religious and Ethnic pulls of Kashmir Militant Movement. *Journal of Peace Studies,* Vol. 1, No. 1, Nov.-Dec.

Shah , Manzoor Ali (2009). Mullah Radio. *Himal,* Vol. 22.

Sinai, Joshua (2008). How to Define Terrorism. *Perspectives on Terrorism,* Volume II, Issue 4.

Sinha, S.K. (2002). Violence and Hope in India's North East. *Faultline,* Jan.

Sondhi, Sunil (2004). Terrorism and Governance in Kashmir. *Journal of conflict Studies,* Vol. XXIV, No.2, Winter.

Steinitz, Mark S. (2002). The Terrorism and Drug Connection in Latin America's Andean Region. *Policy Papers on the Americas,* Vol. XIII.

Stern, Jessica (2000). Pakistan's Jihad Culture. *Foreign Affairs,* Vol. 79, No. 6, Nov. - Dec.

Swami, Praveen (2004). Army and the Special powers. *Frontline,* vol. 21.

Talukdar, Sushanta (2004). Victims of Crossfire. *Frontline,* vol. 21.

Unnithan, Sandeep (2010). The Karachi Project. *India today,* March 1.

Vardhrajan, Siddharth (*n.d.*). Insult upon injury. *Frontline,* vol. 21.

Victoroff, Jeff (2005). The Mind of the Terrorist: A Review and Critique of Psychological Approaches. *Journal of Conflict Resolution,* February.

Williams, Robin M. (1994). The Sociology of Ethnic Conflicts: Comparative International Perspectives. *Annual Review of Sociology.*

Winer, Jonathan M. (2008). Countering Terrorist Finance: A work, Mostly in Progress. *The ANNALS of the American Academy of Political and Social Science.*

Zaarudi, Izzat (2002). The people of Kashmir. *Murj,* Vol. 6.

NEWSPAPERS AND PERIODICALS:

Hindustan Times.

The Asian Age.

The Hindu.

The Indian Express.

The Times of India.

The Tribune.

Frontline.

India Today.

Newsweek.

Index

A

B

C

I

J

K

L

M

N

O

P

R

U

V

W

Z